A Note from the Author

This book has been designed for you to use in preparation for the Advanced Placement English Literature and Composition Exam. In it you will find information about the AP Exam, important test-preparation advice, strategies on approaching multiple-choice questions with poetry and prose passages, advice and examples for dealing with the essay questions, and a comprehensive list of terminology typically used on the test. Finally, three practice exams are included for you to hone your skills. Responses are discussed, so that you can better understand why some responses are wrong, some are almost right, and others are the only possible correct responses.

Those of you who have completed an Advanced Placement course in English Literature and Composition are to be congratulated. Not only have you conquered a challenging curriculum as well as completed many impressive reading and writing assignments, you have learned how to manage your time and assume demanding responsibility and self-discipline. Now you have only to prepare for the AP Exam. I hope that this book will help you with this last step in an arduous but rewarding adventure.

Best wishes,

Denise Pivarnik-Nova

KAPLAN
Test Prep and Admissions

RELATED TITLES FOR COLLEGE-BOUND STUDENTS

Test Prep and Admissions

AP® English Literature & Composition

2005 Edition

By Denise Pivarnik-Nova, M.S.

Simon & Schuster

NEW YORK · LONDON · SYDNEY · TORONTO

Kaplan Publishing
Published by Simon & Schuster
1230 Avenue of the Americas
New York, New York 10020

Kaplan® is a registered trademark of Kaplan, Inc.

"Ambush", from THE THINGS THEY CARRIED by Tim O'Brien. Copyright © 1990 by Tim O'Brien. Reprinted by permission of Houghton Mifflin Company. All rights reserved.

"To be of use," from CIRCLES ON THE WATER by Marge Piercy, copyright © 1982 by Marge Piercy. Used by permission of Alfred A. Knopf, a division of Random House, Inc.

For all references in this book, AP is a registered trademark of the College Entrance Examination Board, which is not affiliated with this book.

For bulk sales to schools, colleges, and universities, please contact: Order Department, Simon and Schuster, 100 Front Street, Riverside, NJ 08075. Phone: (800) 223-2336. Fax: (800) 943-9831.

Contributing Editors: Jon Zeitlin and Seppy Basili
Executive Editor: Jennifer Farthing
Production Manager: Michael Shevlin
Project Editor: Larissa Shmailo
Cover Design: Cheung Tai
Interior Page Layout: Hugh Haggerty

Manufactured in the United States of America.
Published simultaneously in Canada.

January 2005
10 9 8 7 6 5 4 3 2 1

ISBN: 0-7432-6056-2

Table of Contents

Available Online

FOR ANY TEST CHANGES OR LATE-BREAKING DEVELOPMENTS

kaptest.com/publishing

The material in this book is up-to-date at the time of publication. However, the Educational Testing Service may have instituted changes in the test after this book was published. Be sure to carefully read the materials you receive when you register for the test. If there are any important late-breaking developments—or any changes or corrections to the Kaplan test preparation materials in this book—we will post that information online at **kaptest.com/publishing**.

FEEDBACK AND COMMENTS

kaplansurveys.com/books

We'd love to hear your comments and suggestions about this book. We invite you to fill out our online survey form at **kaplansurveys.com/books**. Your feedback is extremely helpful as we continue to develop high-quality resources to meet your needs.

About the Author

Denise Pivarnik-Nova, M.S., is an Advanced Placement English teacher and an independent consultant for the Midwest Office College Board in AP English and English Vertical Teams (pre-AP). She has been scoring English AP Exams for sixteen years. She has also taught freshman literature and composition at the college level. In addition to working on College Board publications and other AP prep materials, Denise is the Advanced Placement Coordinator and AP English teacher at Columbia Heights High School in Columbia Heights, Minnesota. Every summer she facilitates AP teacher workshops throughout the Midwest.

| SECTION ONE: |
The Basics

Chapter One: **Inside the AP English Literature & Composition Exam**

- An Overview of the Test Structure
- How the Exam is Scored
- Getting Your Grades
- Registration and Fees
- Additional Resources
- For More Information

Congratulations! You should be proud of yourself for deciding to take the Advanced Placement English Literature and Composition Exam. If you have taken Advanced Placement English Literature and Composition in high school or have a good foundation in literary analysis, a broad reading background, and strong composition skills, taking the AP exam can help you earn college credit and/or placement into advanced coursework. Think of the money you can save! In addition to getting a head start on your college coursework, you can improve your chances of acceptance to competitive schools since colleges know that AP students are better prepared for the demands of college courses.

This book is designed to help you prepare for the AP exam in English Literature and Composition. We've included information about the format of the exam, test-taking strategies, and an extensive review of essential topics. Each chapter includes review questions, which will help you identify your strengths and weaknesses and help you to establish a plan for preparing for the exam. Also included are three practice tests with answers and explanations. With Kaplan's proven test-taking strategies, dozens of practice questions, a review of literary terms, and guidelines for writing your essay responses, you will be able to take the exam with confidence.

AN OVERVIEW OF THE TEST STRUCTURE

The Advanced Placement English Literature and Composition exam is a three-hour exam, designed yearly by the AP Test Development Committee in English. The exam is an opportunity for you to demonstrate that you have mastered skills equivalent to those typically found in introductory college composition classes. The exam is comprised of two sections:

Section I:	54–60 multiple-choice questions	60 minutes
Section II:	3 essay responses	120 minutes
Total Length:		3 hours

Section I consists of 54–60 multiple-choice questions. You will be presented with four or five passages—from poetry, drama, fiction, or even nonfiction (occasionally). Each piece will be followed by 12–15 questions. The multiple-choice questions are skills questions. These questions will not require you to recall facts from a particular play or novel, but rather they are questions that test your ability to analyze passages critically and/or analytically. The very few fact questions are based upon only the specific selection that is given. Generally, the difficulty of these questions ranges from easy to harder as you progress through each passage.

Section II consists of three essay questions, two on a specific passage or work of poetry, and one "open-ended" question that permits you to select the work you will write on. A prompt will direct your focus as to the themes, aspects, and literary elements to be included in your essay.

HOW THE EXAM IS SCORED

Your final score will be based on your performance on both multiple-choice section (45 percent of the final score) and the scores on your three essays (55 percent of the final grade). The essays are scored on a 9-point evaluation system. Your three essay scores and your total of correct responses on the multiple-choice section are then converted to the 1–5 point final grade. The formula for conversion approximates the following:

Multiple-choice:	Number correct
Minus:	$\frac{1}{4} \times$ Number wrong (does not include questions left blank)
Total:	

Take that total number and multiply it by 1.2272.

For multiple-choice questions, there is a penalty for answering incorrectly, as opposed to simply leaving an item blank—one fourth of the questions you answer incorrectly are subtracted from your score as a correction for guessing. Some people refer to this as a *guessing penalty*, but it is really a *wrong answer penalty*. If you guess correctly, you don't lose anything.

The multiple-choice total is then added to the total of the three essay scores times 3.0556. This final total is then applied to a Conversion Chart. This conversion chart may vary a bit every year. The Chief Faculty Consultant for each year's test makes the final determination for converting students' composite scores to the 5-point AP scale. A sample conversion chart is provided with each of the three Practice Tests in this book.

All Advanced Placement exams are rated on a final scale of 1 to 5, with 5 being the highest grade. The scores are defined as follows:

5	Extremely well qualified
4	Well qualified
3	Qualified
2	Possibly qualified
1	No recommendation

GETTING YOUR GRADES

The Advanced Placement exams are given in May. The multiple-choice sections are scored electronically, soon after they are returned to Princeton, New Jersey. The essay sections of all the exams, however, must be humanly read and scored. This reading of the exams does not take place until June, when the high school and college teachers who read the essays are available.

AP Grade Reports are sent in July to home, high school, and to any colleges designated by you. You may designate the colleges you would like to receive your grade on the answer sheet at the time of the test. You may also contact AP Services to forward your grade to other colleges after the exam or to cancel or withhold a grade. Each report is cumulative and includes grades for all the AP Exams you have ever taken, unless you have requested that one or more grades be withheld from a college or cancelled.

AP grades by phone are available for $15 per call beginning in early July. A touch-tone phone is needed. The toll-free number is (888) 308-0013

REGISTRATION AND FEES

To register for the AP English Literature and Composition Exam, contact your school guidance counselor or your school's AP Coordinator. If your school does not administer the exam, contact AP Services no later than March 1 for a listing of schools in your area that do. Contact the AP Coordinators at these schools by March 15.

The fee for each AP Exam is $82. The College Board offers a $22 credit to qualified students with financial need. Only a portion of the exam fee will be refunded if a student does not take the test. Also, if there is an unavoidable conflict with the scheduled exam date, you may be able to take the alternative exam. If a student has a certified learning disability, special circumstance testing is available. Check with AP Services for further information about any of these circumstances.

KAPLAN
Test Prep and Admissions

ADDITIONAL RESOURCES

The College Board offers a number of publications about the Advanced Placement Program including *Advanced Placement Course Description—English, Teacher's Guide AP Literature and Composition,* and the *AP Bulletin for Students and Parents;* in addition, past essay exams with students responses and discussion are released, and every five years the multiple-choice questions are also released.

FOR MORE INFORMATION

For more information about the AP Program and/or the AP Services contact:

AP Services
PO Box 6671
Princeton, NJ 08541-6671
Phone: (609) 771-7300; (888) 225-5427
TTY: (609) 882-4118
Fax: (609) 530-0482
E-mail: apexams@info.collegeboard.org
Website: www.collegeboard.com/studenttesting/ap/about.html

Chapter Two: **Strategies for Success: It's Not Always How Much You Know**

- How to Use This Book
- Know the Test
- Strategies for the Multiple-Choice Questions
- Strategies for the Essay Questions
- Take Control: Ten Strategies for Success
- Stress Management
- Countdown to the Test

HOW TO USE THIS BOOK

As you work your way through the chapters, we'll show you precisely what knowledge and skills you'll need in order to do your very best on the AP English Literature and Composition Exam. You'll discover the most effective way to tackle each type of question, and you'll reinforce your studies with lots of practice questions. At the back of the book you'll find three full-length, formatted tests with answer keys, scoring instructions, sample student essays, and detailed explanations. In addition, the Stress Management section in this chapter contains helpful tips on beating stress while you prepare for the test and on pulling off a victory on Test Day.

The Classic Plan

If possible, work your way through this book bit by bit over the course of a few weeks. Cramming the week before the test is not a good idea; you probably won't absorb much information, and it's sure to make you more anxious.

If you find that your anxiety about the test is interfering with your ability to study, start off by reading the Stress Management section later in this chapter. It provides many practical tips to help you stay calm and centered. Use these tips before, during, and after the test.

Learn the Basics

The first thing you need to do is find out what's on the AP English Literature and Composition Exam. In the first chapter of this book, Inside the AP English Literature & Composition Exam, which you may have already read, we've provided you with background information about the test. We'll also give you the lowdown on the most effective test strategies to help you score your best.

Do the Review

Once you have the big picture, it's time to focus on literature and composition. Section II gives you a succinct overview of key terminology, essay writing, and how to approach both poetry and prose on the exam. When you feel you have mastered the material in the chapter, try your hand at the multiple-choice and essay practice questions.

Take the Practice Tests

At the back of the book are three full-length practice tests. These include detailed explanations for each question. There are sample student responses for each essay question, and a commentary from a "grader" who'll tell you exactly why they got the score they did. Use the scoring guides provided and these commentaries to get a sense of your own essay strengths and weaknesses.

The best way to use these tests is to take them under testlike conditions. Don't just drop in and do a random question here and there. Use these tests to gain experience with the complete testing experience, including pacing and endurance. You can do these tests at any time. You don't have to save them all until after you've read this whole book. Just be sure to save one test for a dress rehearsal some time in the last week before Test Day.

Take a Break Before Test Day

A day or two before the test, be sure to review the Countdown to the Test section of this chapter. It includes essential "how-to" tips that will help you get the upper hand on test day. Then, relax! Read a book or watch a movie. And most important, get a good night's sleep. How you approach the days leading up to the test really does matter!

On the morning of the test, eat a light breakfast (nothing too heavy to make you sleepy!) and quickly review a few questions if you feel like it (just enough to get you focused). Walk into the test center with confidence—you're ready for the challenge!

The Emergency Plan

What if you have only two or three weeks until the test—or even less time than that—and you haven't started prepping yet? Don't worry! *AP English Literature & Composition* has been designed to work for students in your situation, too. If you go through a chapter of section II every day, you can finish this book in four days.

Be sure to read Section One, The Basics, to find out what to expect on Test Day and how to deal with it. Then take as many of the practice tests as you can—under timed conditions. Review your results, with special attention to the questions you missed.

AP English Lit Emergency FAQs

Q: It's two days before the test and I'm clueless. What should I do?

A: First of all, don't panic. If you have only a day or two to prepare for the test, then you don't have time to prepare thoroughly. But that doesn't mean you should just give up. There's still a lot you can do to improve your potential score. First and foremost, you should become familiar with the test by reading chapters one and two. And if you don't do anything else, take one of the full-length practice tests in this book under reasonably testlike conditions. When you finish the practice test, check your answers and look at the explanations to the questions you didn't get right.

Q: My parents are upset with me for waiting till the last minute to study, and now I can't concentrate. Help!

A: Take a deep breath! Anxiety and stress are the enemies of all test takers—no matter how much time they have to prepare. Turn to section III of this book and read through Kaplan's suggestions for managing stress. Do the suggested exercises. And don't forget to think positively!

Q: The exam is tomorrow. Should I stay up all night reading?

A: The best thing to do right now is to try to stay calm. Read chapter eight, Countdown to the Test, to find out the best way to survive, and thrive, on Test Day. If you haven't yet taken a practice test, do it now, just to familiarize yourself with the exam. And get a good night's sleep.

Q: I don't feel confident. Should I just guess?

A: You should always guess if you can do so intelligently. The AP English Literature and Composition Exam does have a wrong-answer penalty, but that doesn't mean you should never guess. If you can rule out two answer choices, you should consider guessing, because you have significantly increased your chances of guessing correctly. Also, on questions that appear early in a section, more obvious answers will tend to be correct, so you can guess more confidently on those questions.

Q: So it's a good idea to panic, right? *Right?*

A: No! No matter how prepared you are for the exam, stress will hurt your performance, and it's really no fun. Stay confident, and don't cram. So . . . breathe. Stay calm, and remember, it's just a test.

WHAT THE TEST REQUIRES

This chapter will help you tackle the Advanced Placement English Literature and Composition examination. Although it is not a test that one passes or fails, generally a 3 or higher on the 5-point scale is necessary to receive advanced placement, credit, or both in the college of your choice. Many states such as Minnesota, Texas, and Wisconsin post online or offer in hard copy these AP test score requirements for the various colleges and universities within their state. This will vary from state to state, just as score requirements vary from college to college.

The AP English Literature and Composition exam is a unique test: It does not expect you to have memorized specific authors and/or their works. Instead, it tests your critical and analytical thinking skills; it asks you to understand the ways writers use language to provide both meaning and pleasure for their readers; it requires you to apply concepts and terms to most any piece of writing presented, and, most important, it necessitates your translating some of this information into multiple-choice selections and written responses. These multiple-choice questions and written responses ask you to make careful observations of textual detail, establish connections among their observation, and draw from your observations a series of associations and inferences that lead to a meaningful and interpretive conclusion about a piece of literature.

The more familiar you become with the test as a whole, the better (and more relaxed) you will perform. Your teacher has probably given you bits and pieces of the exam, but due to the usual constraints of a school day's schedule, often students do not have the opportunity to sit down and take an entire exam. Use the three exams in this book; go to the College Board website; ask your teacher for samples of old exams.

Having the experience of taking the entire exam in one sitting (10–15 minutes only between multiple-choice and essay responses) will give you a better handle on the test. Use this book not only to study what types of questions may be on the exam, but also spend time studying the directions and format of the exam. Be sure you know exactly what you are expected to do in the Multiple-Choice Section I and the Essay Section II of the AP English Literature and Composition Exam.

HOW TO APPROACH THE MULTIPLE-CHOICE QUESTIONS

The following are some must-know tips for the multiple-choice section. We'll be returning to some of these ideas throughout the book. Here they are in a nutshell.

The Critical Words

Read the instructions carefully, paying particular attention to critical words such as **ONLY, EXCEPT, ALWAYS, NOT, NEVER, BEST.** Students often find the most difficult of this type of multiple-choice question to be the one that asks for "all of the following **EXCEPT**." This is understandable. You are used to looking for one correct response among other wrong answers. In **EXCEPT** questions, however, all but one of the responses is correct. Pay particular attention to these when you take the practice exam.

The Answer Grid Has No Heart

Frequently check to make sure that the number of the question on your answer sheet corresponds to the number of the question in your exam booklet. It is easy to get out of sequence if you skip a question. Put a large, easy-to-see mark in your test booklet (not on your answer sheet) when you skip a question.

To Guess, or Not to Guess

Guess intelligently and with caution. Random guessing will not help your score and it may very well hurt it. You lose .25 point for each wrong answer, but no deduction for a blank answer. It is best to be able to eliminate at least one wrong answer before you make an educated guess. If you can narrow it down to two, definitely take a chance and pick one of the two, regardless of any uncertainty you might have. You have a 50-50 chance of being right.

Think Ahead

Before you look at the possible responses, try to think of the answer on your own. That will usually help you narrow down your choice. It will also help you avoid the seductions of wrong answers that "seem" right at first glance, a favorite trap of the testmaker.

Use Process of Elimination (POE)

As you read through the possible responses, cross off the ones you know are wrong, being sure to read every possible answer before you make your selection. Once again, look out for words like **EXCEPT** or **NEVER** in the question stem.

Put Your Pride Aside

Easy questions are worth just as much as more difficult ones. To maximize your score, you need to answer as many questions correctly as possible. Generally speaking, the easier questions are at the beginning of a series of questions following a passage.

How Many Passages?

Remember that the 60-minute time limit includes reading and understanding four or five passages as well as answering the questions that follow. When you open the multiple-choice section, check to see if the test has four or five passages to deal with. If it is four, estimate about 15 minutes for each section. If it contains five passages, estimate about 12 minutes. Remember than if the test has only four passages, then it will have more questions following each passage.

Don't be too rigid about these timing rules. Remember, some passages will be harder than others. Skip hard passages and work first on the ones you find easier and can do faster, coming back to the tougher passages later. Keeping your time remaining in mind.

Use Your Test Booklet

Do not hesitate to write in your test booklet. It is wise to circle limiting words such as **ALWAYS**, **NEVER**, etc. Also, it may be helpful to you to underline or circle words, or briefly annotate the passages.

Don't Sweat It

Never agonize for too long over any one multiple-choice question. If you are not sure, circle the question clearly in the test booklet so that you can find it readily after you have completed all the other questions. Be sure to leave that number unmarked on the answer sheet. You may have time to return to the question before the 60 minutes are up.

Grid Carefully and Cleanly

You will need a No. 2 pencil to fill in the answer sheet for the multiple-choice section of the exam. Bring several on Test Day. Be sure to erase changes thoroughly and do not allow any stray marks to appear on your answer sheet.

HOW TO APPROACH THE ESSAY QUESTIONS

Here's what you need to know and do to succeed on the essay portion of the test.

What is the Question Asking?

Before you begin writing, read and decode the essay prompt carefully. What is it asking? Is there more than one part to the question? Then read the passage and be sure to reread the prompt to assure that you respond to all tasks accurately. In a 40-minute situation, you should study the problem (identify the focus of the question), read the selection, and start writing within seven to ten minutes. If you are confused about how to start, restate the topic as it is addressed in the question.

Most AP essay questions ask you to analyze on a two-level system: what did the author do (in terms of main idea, central attitude, or basic emotion evoked from the reader) and how did he or she do it (examining such elements as imagery, figurative language, diction, syntax, structure, style)? Brainstorm and plan quickly by jotting notes in the test booklet.

Choose the Easiest Question First

You do *not* have to answer the essays in the order in which they appear. When you open your essay test packet, quickly scan the three choices and begin responding to the question for which you seem to have the most ready response. Beginning with the "easiest" question will help give you confidence and reduce your stress. You are asked to identify which question you are answering by putting a 1, 2, or 3 in a box at the top of each page. However, if the reader cannot readily identify what question you are answering by your answer, then you have a real problem.

Organize Your Essay

In responding to the prose and poetry selections, it is good to write one body paragraph for each major section of the passage. Determine sections by noting shifts in setting, action, or time. Avoid organizing around techniques or devices on which the questions ask you to focus (items such as diction, figurative language, etc.). Organize around factors in the piece of literature itself: how the speaker's thoughts change and move.

Keep Your Quotes Short

Quote words and phrases so they are integrated within your piece. A quote of more than one line from the text is too much. You need not always write out actual quotes. Sometimes you can simply make a reference to a particular section by giving the line numbers.

Be Prepared to Discuss and Explain, Not Retell or List

When writing about poetry, direct your attention to the elements addressed in the prompt. You should be prepared to discuss tone, point of view, imagery, figurative language, structure, syntax, narrator/persona, and the poem's impact upon the reader. In writing about prose, you are often asked to deal with some of the same items as with poetry. Sometimes, contrasting passages (as well as poems) are presented. Avoid the trap of just rephrasing or retelling the passage with quotes. Avoid listing, but not explaining. Show your thinking. Also, refrain from preaching. Freudian and religious interpretations usually don't "work" well as responses.

How Long?

The length of your answer is no guarantee of quality; however, it takes more than a paragraph or two to merit an upper-half score (remember essays are scored on a scale of 1–9). As a rule, five paragraphs—an introduction, three body paragraphs, and a good conclusion—make an adequate essay, but this can vary depending on the length of your paragraphs, your writing style, etc. See the student responses to the essay questions in the Answers and Explanations for the Practice Tests for some guidelines.

The Open-Ended Question

On question three (the open-ended question), be sure to follow explicit directions. A novel or full play of literary merit is acceptable; never write about a short story or a movie. Remember, you will be writing to someone who is already familiar with what you have chosen. There is no need to "fill in" with nonessential plot information.

What If I Make Mistakes?

Those who read and score AP essays are trained to reward students for what they do well, rather than look for the little "missing pieces." They recognize that essays are barely revised first drafts. They also realize students are under great pressure. For example, a student might mix character names in an otherwise solid essay and not be graded down.

Legibility Counts

Be sure to write your essays in blue or black ink. If you make an error, cross it out neatly and go on. Cross outs will not count against you. Pencil-written responses are often difficult for readers to decipher. Avoid using pens that may bleed through the paper; it's best to use a ballpoint pen. Bring at least two pens just to be prepared. The test booklet has many pages. Consider writing on only one side of the page.

Work for good penmanship. If your writing is indecipherable, then print. Remember, human eyes will be trying to read your response. Mechanical difficulties will reduce your score if they hamper communication. If a response is *very* badly written, it can only be awarded a lower-half score.

Reminders

- Food and drinks are not allowed during the exam. Remember, however, that this is a 3-hour test. You may want to eat a piece of fruit or have a juice drink during the short break between the multiple-choice and essay sections. Be sure to have a good breakfast before the test—nothing unusual or too greasy. And watch your caffeine intake. Test Day isn't the best time to give it up, or to ingest large quantities your body is not used to.

- Never count on there being clock in your testing room. Even if one is available, it may not work, or it may be too difficult for you to easily see it. Bring your own watch, but you will not be permitted to use alarm or timer settings.

- You may write and underline in your test booklet, but you may not use a highlighter.

TAKE CONTROL: HOW TO APPROACH THE TEST AS A WHOLE

The AP English Lit exam requires a creative mindset, not only in the subject matter you'll be approaching, but in your overall attitude towards the test. Remember these basic strategies as you prep and on Test Day.

1. Do Question Triage

In a hospital emergency room, the triage nurse is the person who evaluates each patient and decides which ones get attention first and which ones should be treated later. You should do the same thing on the AP English Lit Exam.

Practicing triage is one of the most important ways of controlling your test-taking experience. It's a fact that there are some multiple-choice questions on the test that most students could never answer correctly, no matter how much time or effort they spent on them.

The first time you look at a multiple-choice question, make a quick decision about how hard and time-consuming it looks. Then decide whether to answer it now or skip it and do it later.

- If the question looks comprehensible and reasonably doable, do it right away.
- If the question looks tough and time-consuming, but ultimately doable, skip it, circle the question number in your test booklet, and come back to it later.
- If the question looks impossible, forget about it. Make a guess if you can narrow down the choices; leave it blank if you have no clue. Then move on, never to return.

This triage method will ensure you spend the time needed to do all the easy questions before getting bogged down with a tough one. Remember, every question on a subject test is worth the same number of points. You get no extra credit for test bravado.

2. Develop a Plan of Attack

The best plan of attack is to do each passage as a block. Make a longish first pass through the questions (call it the "triage" pass), doing the easy ones, guessing on the impossible ones, and skipping any that look like they might cause trouble. Then, make a second pass (call it the "cleanup pass") and do those questions you think you can answer with some thought.

3. Put the Material Into a Form You Can Understand

AP English Lit questions are not always presented in the simplest, most helpful way. If the material is presented in an intimidating way, one of your best strategies for taking control is to recast (reword) the material into a form you can handle better.

4. Mark Up Your Test Booklet

This strategy should be employed on both the multiple-choice and essay sections. The secret is to put the passages into a form you can understand and use. Circle or underline the main idea, for one thing. And make yourself a road map of the passage, labeling each paragraph so you understand how it all fits together. That way, you'll also know—later, when you're doing the questions or writing your essay—where in the passage to find certain types of information you need. (We'll show you how to do all of these things in the subsequent chapters.)

5. Check Back

Don't be afraid to refer to the passages. Much of the information is too complex to remember accurately. Often, the wrong answers on the multiple-choice section will be "misplaced details"— details taken from different parts of the passage. They are things that don't answer the question properly but that might sound good to you if you aren't careful. By checking back with the passage, you can avoid choosing such devilishly clever wrong choices.

There's another important lesson here: Don't pick a choice just because it contains "key words" you remember from the passage. Many wrong choices are distortions: They use the right words but say the wrong things about them. Look for answer choices that contain the same ideas you find in the passage. One of the best ways to avoid choosing misplaced details and distortions is to check back with the passage.

6. Answer the Right Question

This strategy is a natural extension of the last. The test makers often include among the wrong choices for a question the correct answer to a different question. Keep an eye out for those key words **NOT** and **EXCEPT**. Under time pressure, it's easy to fall for one of these red herrings, thinking that you know what's being asked for when really you don't.

Always check the question again before choosing your answer. Doing all the right work but then getting the wrong answer can be seriously depressing. So make sure you're answering the right question.

7. Guess Intelligently

As we've told you before, wild guessing won't help you on the AP English Literature exam, and can hurt your score. But smart guessing can make a big difference in your score. If you can eliminate two answer choices, definitely make your best guess.

8. Be Careful with the Answer Grid

We can't stress this enough: A big part of your AP score is based on the multiple-choice answers you select on your answer grid. Even if you answer each question correctly, you'll get a low score if you misgrid your answers. So be careful! Don't disdain the process of filling in those little "bubbles" on the grid. Sure, it's mindless, but under time pressure it's easy to lose control and make mistakes.

It's important to develop a disciplined strategy for filling in the answer grid. Some students find that it's smart to grid the answers in groups rather than one question at a time. What this means is this: As you figure out each question in the test booklet, circle the answer choice you come up with. Then transfer those answers to the answer grid in groups of five or more (until you get close to the end of the section, when you start gridding answers one by one).

Gridding in groups like this cuts down on errors because you can focus on this one task and do it right. It also saves time you'd otherwise spend moving papers around, finding your place, and redirecting your mind. Answering AP questions takes deep, hard thinking. Filling out answer grids is easy, but you have to be careful, especially if you do a lot of skipping around. Shifting between "hard thinking" and "careful bookkeeping" takes time and effort.

For most students, it makes sense to circle your answers in your test booklet as you work them out. Then, when you're finished with each passage and its questions, grid the answers as a group.

9. Keep Track of Time

Pace yourself. Multiple-choice passages should take about 12 to 15 minutes each. Check to see if there or four of five passages in the multiple-choice section, and work accordingly (remember to do the easiest passages first). Essay questions should take about 40 minutes each—again, do the easiest question first.

10. Take Control

You are the master of the test-taking experience. A common thread in all the strategies above is: Take control. Do the questions in the order you want and in the way you want. Don't get bogged down or agonize. Remember, you don't earn points for suffering, but you do earn points for moving on to the essay question you can shine on and to the next multiple-choice question and getting it right.

STRESS MANAGEMENT

The countdown has begun. Your date with THE TEST is looming on the horizon. Anxiety is on the rise. The butterflies in your stomach have gone ballistic. Perhaps you feel as if the last thing you ate has turned into a lead ball. Your thinking is getting cloudy. Maybe you think you won't be ready. Maybe you already know your stuff, but you're going into panic mode anyway. Worst of all, you're not sure of what to do about it.

Don't freak! It is possible to tame that anxiety and stress—before and during the test. We'll show you how. You won't believe how quickly and easily you can deal with that killer anxiety.

Lack of control is one of the prime causes of stress. A ton of research shows that if you don't have a sense of control over what's happening in your life, you can easily end up feeling helpless and hopeless. So, just having concrete things to do and to think about—taking control—will help reduce your stress. This section shows you how to take control during the days leading up to taking the test.

Identify the Sources of Stress

In the space provided, jot down anything you identify as a source of your test-related stress. The idea is to pin down that free-floating anxiety so that you can take control of it. Here are some common examples to get you started:

- I always freeze up on tests.
- I'm nervous about the essays (or the poetry passages, or defining *synechdoche*.)
- I need a good/great score to go to Acme College.
- My older brother/sister/best friend/girl- or boyfriend did really well. I must match their scores or do better.
- My parents, who are paying for school, will be really disappointed if I don't test well.
- I'm afraid of losing my focus and concentration.
- I'm afraid I'm not spending enough time preparing.
- I study like crazy, but nothing seems to stick in my mind.
- I always run out of time and get panicky.
- I feel as though thinking is becoming like wading through thick mud.

Now add your own:

Sources of Stress

_____   _____

_____   _____

_____   _____

_____   _____

Take a few minutes to think about the things you've just written down. Then rewrite them. List the statements you most associate with your stress and anxiety first, and put the least disturbing items last. Chances are, the top of the list is a fairly accurate description of exactly how you react to test anxiety, both physically and mentally. The later items usually describe your fears (disappointing Mom and Dad, looking bad, etc.). As you write the list, you're forming a hierarchy of items so you can deal first with the anxiety provokers that bug you most. Very often, taking care of the major items from the top of the list goes a long way toward relieving overall testing anxiety. You probably won't have to bother with the things you placed last.

TAKE STOCK OF YOUR STRENGTHS AND WEAKNESSES

Take one minute to list the areas in AP Literature & Composition where you have the most skill. They can be general ("poetry") or specific ("poetic devices and figures"). Write down as many as you can think of, and if possible, time yourself. Write for the entire time; don't stop writing until you've reached the one-minute stopping point.

Strong AP Literature & Composition Skills

_____   _____

_____   _____

_____   _____

_____   _____

Next, take one minute to list areas of AP Literature & Composition where you are weakest, just plain bad at, have failed at, or keep failing at. Again, keep it to one minute, and continue writing until you reach the cutoff. Don't be afraid to identify and write down your weak spots! In all probability, as you do both lists, you'll find you are strong in some areas and not so strong in others. Taking stock of your assets and liabilities lets you know the areas you don't have to worry about, and the ones that will demand extra attention and effort.

Weak AP Literature & Composition Skills

_____   _____

_____   _____

_____   _____

_____   _____

Facing your weak spots gives you some distinct advantages. It helps a lot to find out where you need to spend extra effort. Increased exposure to tough material makes it more familiar and less intimidating. (After all, we mostly fear what we don't know and are probably afraid to face.) You'll feel better about yourself because you're dealing directly with areas of the test that bring on your anxiety. You can't help feeling more confident when you know you're actively strengthening your chances of earning a higher overall test score.

Now, go back to the "good" list, and expand it for two minutes. Take the general items on that first list and make them more specific; take the specific items and expand them into more general conclusions. Naturally, if anything new comes to mind, jot it down. Focus all of your attention and effort on your strengths. Don't underestimate yourself or your abilities. Give yourself full credit. At the same time, don't list strengths you don't really have; you'll only be fooling yourself.

Expanding from general to specific might go as follows. If you listed "poetry" as a broad topic you feel strong in, you would then narrow your focus to include areas of this subject about which you are particularly knowledgeable. Your areas of strength might include Shakespearean sonnets, metrical scansion, modern free verse, etc.

Whatever you know comfortably goes on your "good" list. Okay. You've got the picture. Now, get ready, check your starting time, and start writing down items on your expanded "good" list.

Strong AP Literature & Composition Skills: An Expanded List

_____   _____

_____   _____

_____   _____

_____   _____

After you've stopped, check your time. Did you find yourself going beyond the two minutes allotted? Did you write down more things than you thought you knew? Is it possible you know more than you've given yourself credit for? Could that mean you've found a number of areas in which you feel strong?

You just took an active step toward helping yourself. Notice any increased feelings of confidence? Enjoy them.

Here's another way to think about your writing exercise. Every area of strength and confidence you can identify is much like having a reserve of solid gold at Fort Knox. You'll be able to draw on your reserves as you need them. You can use your reserves to solve difficult questions, maintain confidence, and keep test stress and anxiety at a distance. The encouraging thing is that every time you recognize another area of strength, succeed at coming up with a solution, or get a good score on a test, you increase your reserves. And, there is absolutely no limit to how much self-confidence you can have or how good you can feel about yourself.

Imagine Yourself Succeeding

This next little group of exercises is both physical and mental. It's a natural follow-up to what you've just accomplished with your lists.

First, get yourself into a comfortable sitting position in a quiet setting. Wear loose clothes. If you wear glasses, take them off. Then, close your eyes and breathe in a deep, satisfying breath of air. Really fill your lungs until your rib cage is fully expanded and you can't take in any more. Then, exhale the air completely. Imagine you're blowing out a candle with your last little puff of air. Do this two or three more times, filling your lungs to their maximum and emptying them totally. Keep your eyes closed, comfortably but not tightly. Let your body sink deeper into the chair as you become even more comfortable.

With your eyes shut you can notice something very interesting. You're no longer dealing with the worrisome stuff going on in the world outside of you. Now you can concentrate on what happens inside you. The more you recognize your own physical reactions to stress and anxiety, the more you can do about them. You might not realize it, but you've begun to regain a sense of being in control.

Let images begin to form on the "viewing screens" on the back of your eyelids. You're experiencing visualizations from the place in your mind that makes pictures. Allow the images to come easily and naturally; don't force them. Imagine yourself in a relaxing situation. It might be in a special place you've visited before or one you've read about. It can be a fictional location that you create in your imagination, but a real-life memory of a place or situation you know is usually better. Make it as detailed as possible, and notice as much as you can.

Stay focused on the images as you sink farther back into your chair. Breathe easily and naturally. You might have the sensations of any stress or tension draining from your muscles and flowing downward, out your feet and away from you.

Take a moment to check how you're feeling. Notice how comfortable you've become. Imagine how much easier it would be if you could take the test feeling this relaxed and in this state of ease. You've coupled the images of your special place with sensations of comfort and relaxation. You've also found a way to become relaxed simply by visualizing your own safe, special place.

Now, close your eyes and start remembering a real-life situation in which you did well on a test. If you can't come up with one, remember a situation in which you did something (academic or otherwise) that you were really proud of—a genuine accomplishment. Make the memory as detailed as possible. Think about the sights, the sounds, the smells, even the tastes associated with this remembered experience. Remember how confident you felt as you accomplished your goal. Now start thinking about the upcoming test. Keep your thoughts and feelings in line with that successful experience. Don't make comparisons between them. Just imagine taking the upcoming test with the same feelings of confidence and relaxed control.

This exercise is a great way to bring the test down to Earth. You should practice this exercise often, especially when the prospect of taking the exam starts to bum you out. The more you practice it, the more effective the exercise will be for you.

Exercise Your Frustrations Away

Whether it is jogging, walking, biking, mild aerobics, pushups, or a pickup basketball game, physical exercise is a very effective way to stimulate both your mind and body and to improve your ability to think and concentrate. A surprising number of students get out of the habit of regular exercise, ironically because they're spending so much time prepping for exams. Also, sedentary people—this is a medical fact—get less oxygen to the blood and hence to the head than active people. You can live fine with a little less oxygen; you just can't think as well.

Any big test is a bit like a race. Thinking clearly at the end is just as important as having a quick mind early on. If you can't sustain your energy level in the last sections of the exam, there's too good a chance you could blow it. You need a fit body that can weather the demands any big exam puts on you. Along with a good diet and adequate sleep, exercise is an important part of keeping yourself in fighting shape and thinking clearly for the long haul.

There's another thing that happens when students don't make exercise an integral part of their test preparation. Like any organism in nature, you operate best if all your "energy systems" are in balance. Studying uses a lot of energy, but it's all mental. When you take a study break, do something active instead of raiding the fridge or vegging out in front of the TV. Take a 5- to 10-minute activity break for every 50 or 60 minutes that you study. The physical exertion gets your body into the act, which helps to keep your mind and body in sync. Then, when you finish studying for the night and hit the sack, you won't lie there, tense and unable to sleep because your head is overtired and your body wants to pump iron or run a marathon.

One warning about exercise, however: It's not a good idea to exercise vigorously right before you go to bed. This could easily cause sleep onset problems. For the same reason, it's also not a good idea to study right up to bedtime. Make time for a "buffer period" before you go to bed: For 30 to 60 minutes, just take a hot shower, meditate, simply veg out.

Take a Deep Breath . . .

Here's another natural route to relaxation and invigoration. It's a classic isometric exercise that you can do whenever you get stressed out—just before the test begins, even during the test. It's very simple and takes just a few minutes.

Close your eyes. Starting with your eyes and—without holding your breath—gradually tighten every muscle in your body (but not to the point of pain) in the following sequence:

1. Close your eyes tightly.
2. Squeeze your nose and mouth together so that your whole face is scrunched up. (If it makes you self-conscious to do this in the test room, skip the face-scrunching part.)
3. Pull your chin into your chest, and pull your shoulders together.
4. Tighten your arms to your body, then clench your hands into tight fists.
5. Pull in your stomach.
6. Squeeze your thighs and buttocks together, and tighten your calves.
7. Stretch your feet, then curl your toes (watch out for cramping in this part).

At this point, every muscle should be tightened. Now, relax your body, one part at a time, in reverse order, starting with your toes. Let the tension drop out of each muscle. The entire process might take five minutes from start to finish (maybe a couple of minutes during the test). This clenching and unclenching exercise should help you to feel very relaxed.

And Keep Breathing

Conscious attention to breathing is an excellent way of managing test stress (or any stress, for that matter). The majority of people who get into trouble during tests take shallow breaths. They breathe using only their upper chests and shoulder muscles, and may even hold their breath for long periods of time. Conversely, the test taker who by accident or design keeps breathing normally and rhythmically is likely to be more relaxed and in better control during the entire test experience.

So, now is the time to get into the habit of relaxed breathing. Do the next exercise to learn to breathe in a natural, easy rhythm. By the way, this is another technique you can use during the test to collect your thoughts and ward off excess stress. The entire exercise should take no more than three to five minutes.

With your eyes still closed, breathe in slowly and deeply through your nose. Hold the breath for a bit, and then release it through your mouth. The key is to breathe slowly and deeply by using your diaphragm (the big band of muscle that spans your body just above your waist) to draw air in and out naturally and effortlessly. Breathing with your diaphragm encourages relaxation and helps minimize tension. Try it and notice how relaxed and comfortable you feel.

QUICK TIPS AS YOU PREPARE FOR THE EXAM

- Be sure you know the schedule for the AP exams ahead of time. Your teacher should have this year's testing schedule. If you are taking other AP exams in addition to AP English Literature and Composition, you should know when during the two-week exam period these are going to be held so you can adjust your mental and physical energies accordingly.

- For those of you taking two or more AP exams, it will be a tough time, but not impossible. Just remember, "This too shall pass."

- Whatever you do, try to get enough sleep.

- If something serious interferes with any of the test times, be aware that each test *does* have an alternative test that you might take under extreme extenuating circumstances. This is not a desired alternative, but it is a possibility.

- No matter what else is going on at testing time, put it out of your mind. Your job, during the three hours of the exam, is to vindicate all that you have learned during the past year.

QUICK TIPS FOR THE DAYS JUST BEFORE THE EXAM

- The best test takers do less and less as the test approaches. Taper off your study schedule and take it easy on yourself. You want to be relaxed and ready on the day of the test. Give yourself time off, especially the evening before the exam. By then, if you've studied well, everything you need to know is firmly stored in your memory banks.

- Positive self-talk can be extremely liberating and invigorating, especially as the test looms closer. Tell yourself things such as, "I choose to take this test" rather than "I have to"; "I will do well" rather than "I hope things go well"; "I can" rather than "I cannot." Be aware of negative, self-defeating thoughts and images and immediately counter any you become aware of. Replace them with affirming statements that encourage your self-esteem and confidence. Create and practice visualizations that build on your positive statements.

- Get your act together sooner rather than later. Have everything (including choice of clothing) laid out days in advance. Most important, know where the test will be held and the easiest, quickest way to get there. You will gain great peace of mind if you know that all the little details—gas in the car, directions, etc.—are firmly in your control before the day of the test.

- Experience the test site a few days in advance. This is very helpful if you are especially anxious. If at all possible, find out what room your part of the alphabet is assigned to, and try to sit there (by yourself) for a while. Better yet, bring some practice material and do at least a section or two, if not an entire practice test, in that room. In this situation, familiarity doesn't breed contempt, it generates comfort and confidence.

- Forego any practice on the day before the test. It's in your best interest to marshal your physical and psychological resources for 24 hours or so. Even race horses are kept in the paddock and treated like princes the day before a race. Keep the upcoming test out of your consciousness; go to a movie, take a pleasant hike, or just relax. Don't eat junk food or tons of sugar. And—of course—get plenty of rest the night before. Just don't go to bed too early. It's hard to fall asleep earlier than you're used to, and you don't want to lie there thinking about the test.

HANDLING STRESS DURING THE TEST

The biggest stress monster will be the test itself. Fear not; there are methods of quelling your stress during the test.

- Keep moving forward instead of getting bogged down in a difficult question. You don't have to get everything right to achieve a fine score. The best test takers skip difficult material temporarily in search of the easier stuff. They mark the questions that require extra time and thought. This strategy buys time and builds confidence so you can handle the tough stuff later.

- Don't be thrown if other test takers seem to be working more furiously than you are. Continue to spend your time patiently thinking through your answers; it's going to lead to better results. Don't mistake the other people's sheer activity as signs of progress and higher scores.

- Keep breathing! Weak test takers tend to forget to breathe properly as the test proceeds. They start holding their breath without realizing it, or they breathe erratically or arrhythmically. Improper breathing interferes with clear thinking.

- Some quick isometrics during the test—especially if concentration is wandering or energy is waning—can help. Try this: Put your palms together and press intensely for a few seconds. Concentrate on the tension you feel through your palms, wrists, forearms, and up into your biceps and shoulders. Then, quickly release the pressure. Feel the difference as you let go. Focus on the warm relaxation that floods through the muscles. Now you're ready to return to the task.

- Here's another isometric that will relieve tension in both your neck and eye muscles. Slowly rotate your head from side to side, turning your head and eyes to look as far back over each shoulder as you can. Feel the muscles stretch on one side of your neck as they contract on the other. Repeat five times in each direction.

With what you've just learned here, you're armed and ready to do battle with the test. This book and your studies will give you the information you'll need to answer the questions. It's all firmly planted in your mind. You also know how to deal with any excess tension that might come along, both when you're studying for and taking the exam. You've experienced everything you need to tame your test anxiety and stress. You're going to get a great score.

COUNTDOWN TO THE TEST

Is it starting to feel like your whole life is a build-up to the AP English Literature test? As the test gets closer, you may find your anxiety is on the rise. You shouldn't worry. After the preparation you've received from this book, you're in good shape for the test.

Itinerary

To calm any pretest jitters you may have, here is a sane itinerary for the last week.

The Week Before the Test

Review the chapters in this book and in your textbook. Are there major holes in your preparation? If there are, choose a few of these areas to work on—but don't overload.

Take a full-length practice test. If you haven't done so already, take one or more of the practice tests in this book. These are good practice for the real thing.

Two Days Before the Test

Do your last studying—a few more passages, an essay outline, a look through the Key Terminology chapter—and then call it quits.

The Night Before the Test

Don't study. Get together the following items:

- A watch
- A few sharpened No. 2 pencils and some ballpoint pens
- Erasers
- Photo ID card

Know exactly where you're going and exactly how you're getting there.

Relax the night before the test. Read a good book, take a bubble bath, watch TV. Get a good night's sleep. Go to bed at a reasonable hour and leave yourself extra time in the morning.

The Morning of the Test

Eat breakfast. Make it something substantial, but not anything too heavy or greasy. Don't drink a lot of coffee if you're not used to it; bathroom breaks cut into your time.

Dress in layers so that you can adjust to the temperature of the test room.

Read something. Warm up your brain with a newspaper or a magazine. You shouldn't let the test questions be the first thing you read that day.

Be sure to get there early.

During the Test

Don't be shaken. If you find your confidence slipping, remind yourself how well you've prepared. You know the structure of the test; you know the instructions; you've studied for every question type.

Even if something goes really wrong, don't panic. If the test booklet is defective—two pages are stuck together or the ink has run—try to stay calm. Raise your hand, tell the proctor you need a new book. If you accidentally misgrid your answer page, again don't panic. Raise your hand, tell the proctor. She might be able to arrange for you to regrid your test after it's over, when it won't cost you any time.

Food or drinks are not allowed during the exam. Remember, however, that this is a three hour test. You may want to eat a piece of fruit or have a juice drink during the short break between the Multiple-Choice and Essay sections.

After the Test

Once the test is over, put it out of your mind. Feel free to start thinking about more interesting things than tests!

You might walk out of the test room thinking that you blew it. You probably didn't. You tend to remember the questions that stumped you, not the many that you knew.

If you want more help, or just want to know more about the AP exams, college admissions, or Kaplan test prep courses, give us a call at 1-800-KAP-TEST. We're here to answer your questions and to help you in any way that we can.

OK, you are ready. You've worked hard, studied diligently, now go in and shine!!

Good luck!

The AP English Literature & Composition Exam

Chapter Three: **Key Terminology**

- Key Literary Terms and Definitions

- Key Terminology Usage Examples

- Key Terminology Practice Set: Poetry Exercise and Prose Exercise

- Key Terminology Practice Set Answer Explanations

Every academic subject has a vocabulary that describes and identifies its inherent substance. This vocabulary, or jargon, is important for you to understand and define. More importantly, for the English Literature Advanced Placement Exam, you must apply your knowledge of the vocabulary to any piece of writing with which you may be presented.

Here are some common terms you may have to face on Test Day. You also may want to use this terminology—correctly!—in your essays. Review unfamiliar terms, then try your hand at the exercises at the end of this chapter. Refer to this section frequently as you work your way through this book.

Allegory—a prose or poetic narrative in which the characters, behavior, and even the setting demonstrates multilevels of meaning and significance. Often allegory is a universal symbol or personified abstraction such as Death portrayed as a black-cloaked "grim reaper" with a scythe and hourglass.

Alliteration—the sequential initial repetition of a similar sound, usually applied to consonants, usually heard in closely proximate stressed syllables. A common American children's alliteration is "Peter Piper picked a peck of pickled peppers."

Allusion—a reference to a literary or historical event, person, or place. For example, in Jane Smiley's novel, *1,000 Acres,* the father figure is Larry who attempts to divide his land among three daughters *à la* Shakespeare's *King Lear*.

Anaphora—the regular repetition of the same word or phrase at the beginning of successive phrases or clauses. A look at John F. Kennedy's inaugural speech gives us good examples of anaphora. Another older example of anaphora follows:

> This royal throne of kings, this sceptred isle,
> This earth of majesty, this seat of Mars,
> This other Eden, demi-paradise,
> This fortress built by nature for herself
> Against infection and the hand of war,
> This happy breed of men, this little world,
> This precious stone set in the silver sea,
> Which serves it in the office of a wall,
> Or as a moat defensive to a house
> Against the envy of less happier lands;
> This blessèd plot, this earth, this realm, this England . . .
> —John of Gaunt in Shakespeare's Richard II (2.1.40–50)

Anecdote—a brief story or tale told by a character in a piece of literature. For example, Chaucer's entire Canterbury Tales is a collection of anecdotes related by the Pilgrims on their journey.

Antagonist—any force that is in opposition to the main character, or protagonist. For example, Pap is antagonist to Huck in *The Adventures of Huckleberry Finn,* and the environment is an antagonist in Jack London's "To Build a Fire."

Antithesis—the juxtaposition of sharply contrasting ideas in balanced or parallel words, phrases, grammatical structure, or ideas. For example, Alexander Pope reminds us that "To err is human, to forgive divine."

Apostrophe—an address or invocation to something that is inanimate—such as an angry lover who might scream at the ocean in his or her despair. Many are familiar with the title line of a famous Christmas carol, which exemplifies apostrophe: "O little town of Bethlehem, how still we see thee lie…."

Archetype—recurrent designs, patterns of action, character types, themes or images which are identifiable in a wide range of literature; for instance, the *femme fatale,* that female character who is found throughout literature as the one responsible for the downfall of a significant male character.

Assonance—a repetition of identical or similar vowel sounds, usually those found in stressed syllables of close proximity. Samuel T. Coleridge used assonance when he wrote, "In Xanadu did Kubla Kahn…."

Asyndeton—a style in which conjunctions are omitted, usually producing a fast-paced, more rapid prose. For example, Caesar's famous lines, "I came, I saw, I conquered," are asyndeton.

Attitude—the sense expressed by the tone of voice and/or the mood of a piece of writing; the feelings the author holds towards his subject, the people in his narrative, the events, the setting or even the theme. It might even be the feeling he holds for the reader. In AP English exams, students are often asked to respond to the attitude of the writer, speaker, or narrator towards some aspect within the piece of writing that is being presented.

Ballad—a narrative poem that is, or originally was, meant to be sung. Repetition and refrain (recurring phrase or phrases) characterize the ballad. *Scarborough Fair* is an example of a traditional ballad updated for a modern audience.

Ballad stanza—a common stanza form, consisting of a quatrain (a stanza of four lines) that alternates four-beat and three-beat lines: one and three are unrhymed iambic tetrameter (four beats), and two and four are rhymed iambic trimeter (three beats):

> In Scarlet Town, where I was born
> There lived a fair maid dwellin';
> Made many a youth cry well-a-day,
> And her name was Barbara Allen.

Blank verse—the verse form that most resembles common speech, blank verse consists of unrhymed lines in iambic pentameter. Many of Shakespeare's plays are in blank verse, as is Milton's *Paradise Lost.*

Caesura—a pause in a line of verse, indicated by natural speech patterns rather than due to specific metrical patterns. Pope was able to keep his heroic couplets interesting by varying the position of the caesurae, as here:

> Alas how changed! || What sudden horrors rise!
> A naked lover || bound and bleeding lies!
> Where, where was Eloise? || Her voice, her hand,
> Her poniard, || had opposed the dire command.

Caricature—a depiction in which a character's characteristics or features are so deliberately exaggerated as to render them absurd. Political cartoons use visual caricature; writers, such as Charles Dickens, create verbal caricature—this can be found both in drawing and in print in *The Pickwick Papers.*

Chiasmus—a figure of speech by which the order of the terms in the first of two parallel clauses is reversed in the second. This may involve a repetition of the same words: "Pleasure's a sin, and sometimes sin's a pleasure"—Byron.

Colloquial—ordinary language, the vernacular. For example, depending upon where in the United States you live, a sandwich might be a hero, a sub, or a hoagie.

Conceit—a comparison of two unlikely things that is drawn out within a piece of literature, in particular an extended metaphor within a poem. Conceits might be the idea of tracing a love affair as a flower growing, budding, coming to fruition, and dying, for example. Hair might be spun gold; teeth like stars or pearls, etc.

Connotation—what is suggested by a word, apart from what it explicitly describes, often referred to as the implied meaning of a word. For example, the words *awesome* or *sweet* or *gay* have undergone a series of connotative alterations in the last couple of decades.

Consonance—the repetition of a sequence of two or more consonants, but with a change in the intervening vowels, such as *pi*tter-*pa*tter, *pi*sh-*po*sh, *cl*inging and *cl*anging. Shakespeare's *Midsummer's Night's Dream* includes the lines: "Or if there were a sympathy in choice/ War, death, or sickness did lay siege to it."

Couplet—two rhyming lines of iambic pentameter that together present a single idea or connection. The last two lines of all of Shakespeare's sonnets, such as XVIII, "So long as men can breathe or eyes can see/So long lives this and this gives life to thee," are couplets.

Dactylic—the metrical pattern, as used in poetry, in which each foot consists of a stressed syllable followed by two unstressed ones. Words such as *Can' a da, hol' i day, cel' e brate* are all examples of a dactylic foot.

Denotation—a direct and specific meaning, often referred to as the dictionary meaning of a word.

Dialect—the language and speech idiosyncrasies of a specific area, region, or group of people. For example, Minnesotans say "you betcha"; Southerners say "you all."

Diction—the specific word choice an author uses to persuade or convey tone, purpose, or effect. For example, Edgar A. Poe said, "I hadn't so much forgot as I couldn't bring myself to remember." This has far more impact on the reader than his just saying, "I chose not to remember."

Dramatic monologue—a monologue set in a specific situation and spoken to an imaginary audience. Another term for this could be *soliloquy*.

Elegy—a poetic lament upon the death of a particular person, usually ending in consolation. Perhaps the most famous elegy is Thomas Gray's poem, "Elegy Written in a Country Churchyard."

Enjambment—the continuation of a sentence from one line or couplet of a poem to the next. See poem, "The Sick Rose," under *symbolism*.

Epic—a poem that celebrates, in a continuous narrative, the achievements of mighty heroes and heroines, often concerned with the founding of a nation or developing of a culture; it uses elevated language and grand, high style. Prime examples of epic poetry include *The Iliad*, *The Odyssey*, and *Paradise Lost*. A more contemporary example could be George Lucas's *Star Wars*.

Exposition—that part of the structure that sets the scene, introduces and identifies characters, and establishes the situation at the beginning of a story or play.

Extended metaphor—a detailed and complex metaphor that extends over a long section of a work, also known as a *conceit*.

Falling action—that part of plot structure in which the complications of the rising action are untangled. This is also known as the *denouement*.

Farce—a play or scene in a play or book that is characterized by broad humor, wild antics, and often slapstick and physical humor. Shakespeare's *A Midsummer's Night's Dream* is filled with farce. The more contemporary *Catch-22* uses farce as did Peter Sellers in the *Pink Panther* or Monty Python's *Search for the Holy Grail*.

Foreshadowing—to hint at or present an indication of the future beforehand. In *Romeo and Juliet*, Romeo says, before meeting Juliet:

> . . . my mind misgives
> Some consequences yet hanging in the stars
> Shall bitterly begin his fearful date
> With this night's revels and expire term
> Of a despised life closed to my breast
> By some vile forfeit of untimely death.

Formal diction—language that is lofty, dignified, and impersonal. Such diction is often used in narrative epic poetry.

Flashback—retrospection, where an earlier event is inserted into the normal chronology of the narrative. Harper Lee's novel, *To Kill a Mockingbird*, is written as a flashback to specific events that took place in the adult narrator's childhood.

Free verse—poetry that is characterized by varying line lengths, lack of traditional meter, and non-rhyming lines. Walt Whitman's *Leaves of Grass* uses free verse.

Genre—a type or class of literature such as epic or narrative or poetry or belles letters.

Hyperbole—overstatement characterized by exaggerated language. "I'm starving!" is usually hyperbole.

Iambic—a metrical form in which each foot consists of an unstressed syllable followed by a stressed one. For example, the words *for gíve, re mórse, com páre, re péat* demonstrate the iambic foot.

Imagery—broadly defined, any sensory detail or evocation in a work; more narrowly, the use of figurative language to evoke a feeling, to call to mind an idea, or to describe an object. Basically, imagery involves any or all of the five senses.

Informal diction—language that is not as lofty or impersonal as formal diction; similar to everyday speech. Such diction might include such words as *OK, 'bye, hey, huh*?

In medias res—"in the midst of things"; refers to opening a story in the middle of the action, necessitating filling in past details by exposition or flashback.

Irony—a situation or statement characterized by significant difference between what is expected or understood and what actually happens or is meant. Irony is often humorous, and sometimes sarcastic when it uses words to imply the opposite of what they normally mean. Classical sarcastic irony is Jonathan Swift's *A Modest Proposal*.

Jargon—specialized or technical language of a trade, profession, or similar group. The computer industry, for example, has introduced much jargon into our vocabulary. Words such as *geek, crash, interface*, are all examples of jargon.

Juxtaposition—the location of one thing as being adjacent or juxtaposed with another. This placing of two items side by side creates a certain effect, reveals an attitude or accomplishes some purpose of the writer.

Limited point of view—a perspective confined to a single character, whether a first person or a third person; the reader cannot know for sure what is going on in the minds of other characters.

Litote—a figure of speech that emphasizes its subject by conscious understatement. For example, the understated "not bad" as a comment about something especially well done. George Orwell wrote "Last week I saw a woman flayed and you would hardly believe how much it altered her person for the worse."

Loose Sentence—a sentence grammatically complete, and usually stating its main idea, before the end. For example, "The child ran as if being chased by demons."

Lyric—originally designated poems meant to be sung to the accompaniment of a lyre; now any short poem in which the speaker expresses intense personal emotion rather than describing a narrative or dramatic situation. The *sonnet* and the *ode* are two types of lyric poetry.

Message—a misleading term for *theme*; the central idea or statement of a story, or area of inquiry or explanation; misleading because it suggests a simple, packaged statement that preexists and for the simple communication of which the story is written.

Metaphor—one thing pictured as if it were something else, suggesting a likeness or analogy between them. It is an implicit comparison or identification of one thing with another unlike itself without the use of a verbal signal such as *like* or *as*. Sometimes the term metaphor is used as a general term for figure of speech. Romeo exclaims over Juliet by using metaphor: "But soft what light through yonder window breaks. It is the east and Juliet is the sun."

Meter—the more or less regular pattern of stressed and unstressed syllables in a line of poetry. This is determined by the kind of "foot" (iambic or dactylic, for example) and by the number of feet per line (five feet = pentameter, six feet = hexameter, for example.)

Metonymy—a figure of speech in which an attribute or commonly associated feature is used to name or designate something as in "The White House announced today…."

Mood—a feeling or ambiance resulting from the tone of a piece as well as the writer/narrator's attitude and point of view. This effect is fabricated through descriptions of feelings or objects that establish a sense of fear, patriotism, sanctity, hope, etc. For example, many of Thomas Hardy's novels, such as *Jude the Obscure,* have been accused of establishing moods of relentless gloom, depression, and despair.

Motif—a recurrent device, formula, or situation that often serves as a signal for the appearance of a character or event. For example, in *The Great Gatsby*, the recurring image, or motif, of the color green is found throughout the novel.

Narrative structure—a textual organization based on sequences of connected events, usually presented in a straightforward, chronological framework.

Narrator—the "character" who "tells" the story, or in poetry, the *persona*.

Occasional poem—a poem written about or for a specific occasion, public or private. An *epithalamium* is a wedding poem, for example.

Ode—a lyric poem that is somewhat serious in subject and treatment, elevated in style and sometimes uses elaborate stanza structure, which is often patterned in sets of three. Odes are written to praise and exalt a person, characteristic, quality or object, for example, Poe's "To Helen," or Keats's "Ode to a Nightingale."

Omniscient point of view—also called unlimited focus: a perspective that can be seen from one character's view, then another's, then another's, or can be moved in or out of the mind of any character at any time. The reader has access to the perceptions and thoughts of all the characters in the story.

Onomatopoeia—a word capturing or approximating the sound of what it describes; "buzz" is a good example. The purpose of these words is to make a passage more effective for the reader or listener. In *Fahrenheit 451*, for example, Ray Bradbury uses onomatopoeia when he says, "Mildred rose and began to move about the room. Bang! Smash! Wallop, bing, bong, boom."

Overstatement—exaggerated language; also called *hyperbole*.

Oxymoron—a figure of speech that combines two apparently contradictory elements, as in "wise fool" or "jumbo shrimp."

Parable—a short fiction that illustrates an explicit moral lesson through the use of analogy. Many parables can be found in the Bible such as the stories of "The Prodigal Son" or "The Loaves and Fishes."

Paradox—a statement that seems contradictory but may actually be true. A popular paradox from the 1960s was when war protesters would "fight for peace."

Parody—a work that imitates another work for comic effect by exaggerating the style and changing the content of the original. In contemporary music, for example, Weird Al Yankovic has made his fortune writing parodies of popular songs.

Parallel structure—the use of similar forms in writing for nouns, verbs, phrases, or thoughts; for example, "Jane likes reading, writing, and skiing."

Pastoral—a poem (also called an ecologue, a bucolic, or an idyll) that describes the simple life of country folk, usually shepherds who live a timeless, painless (and sheepless) life in a world full of beauty, music, and love. *Jane Eyre* and *Wuthering Heights* are examples of pastoral literature.

Periodic sentence—a sentence which is not grammatically complete until the end. For example, "The child, who looked as if she were being chased by demons, ran."

Persona—the voice or figure of the author who tells and structures the story and who may or may not share the values of the actual author.

Personification—treating an abstraction or nonhuman object as if it were a person by endowing it with human qualities. William Wordsworth speaks of the stars as "Tossing their heads in sprightly dance" and Robert Browning describes "leaping waves" in his poem "Meeting at Night."

Petrarchan sonnet—also called Italian sonnet: a sonnet form that divides the poem into one section of eight lines (octave) and a second section of six lines (sestet), usually following the abba abba cde cde rhyme scheme though the sestet's rhyme varies.

> O Earth, lie heavily upon her eyes;
> Seal her sweet eyes weary of watching. Earth;
> Lie close around her; leave no room for mirth
> With its harsh laughter, nor for sounds of sighs.
> She hath no questions, she hath no replies,
> Hushed in and curtained with a blessed dearth
> Of all that irked her from hour of birth;
> With stillness that is almost Paradise.
>
> Darkness more clear than noonday holdeth her,
> Silence more musical than any song;
> Even her very heart has ceased to stir;
> Until the morning of Eternity
> Her rest shall not begin nor end, but be;
> And when she wakes she will not think it long.
>
> —Rossetti

Plot—the arrangement of the narration based on the cause-effect relationship of the events.

Protagonist—the main character in a work, who may or may not be heroic. For example, Guy Montag is the protagonist in *Fahrenheit 451*, Oedipus is the protagonist in *Oedipus Rex*, and Ralph is the protagonist in *Lord of the Flies*.

Quatrain—a poetic stanza of four lines, for example:

> Tyger! Tyger! burning bright
> In the forests of the night,
> What immortal hand or eye
> Could frame thy fearful symmetry?
> —From William Blake's "The Tyger"

Realism—the practice in literature of attempting to describe nature and life without idealization and with attention to detail. Henry James and Mark Twain are examples of authors in this school.

Refrain—A repeated stanza or line(s) in a poem or song.

Rising action—The development of action in a work, usually at the beginning. The first part of plot structure (see *falling action*).

Rhyme—the repetition of the same or similar sounds, most often at the ends of lines. The following stanza of Frost's "The Road Not Taken" shows the rhyme:

> I shall be telling this with a <u>sigh</u>
> Somewhere ages and ages <u>hence</u>
> Two roads diverged in a wood, and <u>I</u>
> I took the one less traveled,
> And that has made all the <u>difference.</u>

Rhythm—the modulation of weak and strong (stressed and unstressed) elements in the flow of speech.

Sarcasm—a form of verbal irony in which apparent praise is actually harshly or bitterly critical. For example, if a teacher says to a student who sneaks into class an hour late, "Nice of you to join us today," the teacher is being sarcastic.

Satire—a literary work that holds up human failings to ridicule and censure. Jonathan Swift and George Orwell both were masters of satire.

Scansion—the analysis of verse to show its meter.

Setting—the time and place of the action in a story, poem, or play. George Lucas's *Star Wars* opens by telling us that it was "A long time ago in a galaxy far, far away."

Shakespearean sonnet—also called an English sonnet: a sonnet form that divides the poem into three units of four lines each and a final unit of two lines, usually *abab cdcd efef gg*. Here's Shakespeare's 34th:

> Why didst thou promise such a beauteous day,
> And make me travel forth without my cloak,
> To let base clouds o'ertake me in my way,
> Hiding thy bravery in their rotten smoke?
> 'Tis not enough that through the cloud thou break,
> To dry the rain on my storm-beaten face,
> For no man well of such a salve can speak,
> That heals the wound, and cures not the disgrace:
> Nor can thy shame give physic to my grief;
> Though thou repent, yet I have still the loss:
> The offender's sorrow lends but weak relief
> To him that bears the strong offence's cross.
> Ah! but those tears are pearl which thy love sheds,
> And they are rich and ransom all ill deeds.

Shaped verse—another name for concrete poetry: poetry that is shaped to look like an object. John Hollander's "A State of Nature" is shaped to look like New York State.

Simile—a direct, explicit comparison of one thing to another, usually using the words *like* or *as* to draw the connection. See also *metaphor*. Charles Dickens wrote: "There was a steamy mist in all the hollows, and it had roared in its forlornness up the hill, like any evil spirit."

Soliloquy—a monologue in which the character in a play is alone and speaking only to himself or herself. A famous example of soliloquy is Hamlet's "To Be or Not to Be" speech.

Speaker—the person, not necessarily the author, who is the voice of a poem.

Stanza—a section of a poem demarcated by extra line spacing. Some distinguish a stanza, a division marked by a single pattern of meter or rhyme, from a verse paragraph, a division marked by thought rather than pattern, not unlike a paragraph in prose writing. Stanzas can be identified by the number of their lines:

Couplet—two lines

Tercet—three lines

Quatrain—four lines

Cinquain—five lines

Sestet—six lines

Heptatich—seven lines

Octave—eight lines

Stereotype—a characterization based on conscious or unconscious assumptions that some one aspect, such as gender, age, ethnic or national identity, religion, occupation, marital status, and so on, are predictably accompanied by certain character traits, actions, even values.

Stock character—one who appears in a number of stories or plays such as the cruel stepmother, the femme fatale, etc.

Structure—the organization or arrangement of the various elements in a work.

Style—a distinctive manner of expression; each author's style is expressed through his or her diction, rhythm, imagery, and so on. It is a writer's typical way of writing. Style includes word choice, tone, degree of formality, figurative language, rhythm, grammar, structure, sentence length, organization, and every other feature of a writer's use of language. For example, Hemingway wrote primarily with short, simple sentences while Joseph Conrad wrote long, rambling prose.

Symbolism—a person, place, thing, event, or pattern in a literary work that designates itself and at the same time figuratively represents or "stands for" something else. Often the thing or idea represented is more abstract, general, non- or superrational than the symbol, which is more concrete and particular. The poem "The Sick Rose" by William Blake, is full of symbolism:

> O Rose, thou art sick!
> The invisible worm
> That flies in the night
> In the howling storm,
> Has found out thy bed
> Of crimson joy,
> And his dark secret love
> Does thy life destroy.

Critics have written thousands of pages about the sexual and death symbolism of this poem (feel free to try your own interpretation!).

Synecdoche—When a part is used to signify a whole, as in *All hands on deck!* and *The rustler bragged he'd absconded with five hundred head of longhorns.* "Hands" stand for the whole of the sailors, and the rustler obviously took more than just the heads and the horns of the animals he was stealing.

Syntax—the way words are put together to form phrases, clauses, and sentences. Syntax is sentence structure and how it influences the way the reader receives a particular piece of writing.

Terza rima—a verse form consisting of three-line stanzas in which the second line of each rhymes with the first and third of the next. Shelley's "Ode to the West Wind," written in terza rima, begins:

O wild West Wind, thou breath of Autumn's being,	*a*
Thou, from whose unseen presence the leaves dead	*b*
Are driven, like ghosts from an enchanter fleeing	*a*
Yellow, and black, and pale, and hectic red.	*b*
Pestilence-stricken multitudes: O thou,	*c*
Who chariotest to their dark wintry bed . . .	*b*

Theme—a generalized, abstract paraphrase of the inferred central or dominant idea or concern of a work; the statement a poem makes about its subject.

Tone—the attitude a literary work takes toward its subject and theme; the tenor of a piece of writing based on particular stylistic devices employed by the writer. Tone reflects the narrator's attitude.

Tragedy—a drama in which a character (usually good and noble and of high rank) is brought to a disastrous end in his or her confrontation with a superior force. Often the protagonist's downfall is a direct result of a fatal flaw in his or her character. Examples of tragedy would include *Oedipus the King, Hamlet,* and *The Mayor of Casterbridge.*

Trochee—a metrical form in which each foot consists of stressed syllable followed by an unstressed one. Examples of a trochaic foot can be heard in the stressed/unstressed syllables of the following words: *car' wash, out' side, Day' ton, off' spring.*

Turning point—the third part of plot structure, the point at which the action stops rising and begins falling or reversing. Sometimes referred to as the *climax* of the story.

Villanelle—a verse form consisting of nineteen lines divided into six stanzas—five tercets (three-line stanzas) and one quatrain (four-line stanza). The first and third line of the first tercet rhyme, and this rhyme is repeated through each of the next four tercets and in the last two lines of the concluding quatrain.

Voice—the acknowledged or unacknowledged source of the words of the story; the speaker; the "person" telling the story or poem. When referring to voice in a literary passage, you should look closely at all the elements of the author's style and just how these elements come together in the particular piece of literature you are reading.

KEY TERMINOLOGY PRACTICE SET

Now try the following multiple-choice questions to test your understanding of literary terms in context. A poetry passage and a prose passage are followed by questions designed to hone your ability to recognize, define, and use literary terminology.

Poetry Exercise

Read this poem by A. E. Housman, and then answer the multiple-choice questions that follow.

> **"When I was one-and-twenty..."**
> When I was one-and-twenty
> I heard a wise man say,
> "Give crowns and pounds and guineas
> But not your heart away;
> (5) Give pearls away and rubies
> But keep your fancy free."
> But I was one-and-twenty,
> No use to talk to me.
> When I was one-and-twenty
> (10) I heard him say again,
> "The heart out of the bosom
> Was never given in vain;
> 'Tis paid with sighs a plenty
> And sold for endless rue."
> (15) And I am two-and-twenty,
> And oh, 'tis true, 'tis true.

1. The narrator's tone can BEST be described as

   (A) miserable

   (B) reminiscent

   (C) tragic

   (D) passionate

   (E) forceful

2. Lines 1 and 9 can BEST be described as a(n)

   (A) refrain

   (B) apology

   (C) repetition

   (D) parallel structure

   (E) rhetorical question

3. In line 12, the term *vain* means

   (A) proud

   (B) heroic

   (C) without direction

   (D) without purpose

   (E) unsuccessful

4. The metrical scansion of this poem shows it has the characteristics of

   (A) iambic pentameter

   (B) iambic hexameter

   (C) iambic trimeter

   (D) trochaic tetrameter

   (E) trochaic dimeter

5. The theme of this poem can be found in which lines?

    (A) "Give pearls away and rubies/But keep your fancy free." (5–6)

    (B) "But I was one-and-twenty,/No use to talk to me." (7–8)

    (C) "The heart out of the bosom/Was never given in vain" (11–12)

    (D) "'Tis paid with sighs a plenty/And sold for endless rue." (13–14)

    (E) "And I am two-and-twenty,/And oh, 'tis true, 'tis true." (15–16)

6. The repetition in the final line provides or enhances the poem's

    (A) refrain

    (B) syntactical weakness

    (C) tone of lamentation

    (D) lack of originality

    (E) sorrowful mood

7. This poem BEST reflects which underlying, universal theme?

    (A) one must be careful in love

    (B) one should not be so concerned with material possessions

    (C) with age comes wisdom that youth often ignores

    (D) without wisdom one cannot have wealth

    (E) if you don't at first succeed, try again next year

8. Although this poem is written in a single stanza, it could be divided into

    (A) two octaves in juxtaposition

    (B) alternating heroic couplets

    (C) leave as one single flowing stanza

    (D) four quatrains

    (E) three quatrains followed by a couplet

9. In line 14, the word *rue* refers to

    (A) sadness

    (B) regret

    (C) money

    (D) wisdom

    (E) an herb

10. The repetition of lines beginning with the short conjunctions *But* and *And* is an example of

    (A) parallelism

    (B) syntax error

    (C) poetic rhythm

    (D) assonance

    (E) anaphora

11. The following poetic devices are evident in this poem:

    (A) couplet, alliteration, conceit

    (B) assonance, metonymy, direct quotation

    (C) consonance, onomatopoeia, personification

    (D) metaphor, rhythm, caesura

    (E) symbol, litotes, allusion

12. The poem suggests an underlying conceit using imagery related to

    (A) unrequited love

    (B) fancy-free love

    (C) suffering from heartache

    (D) birthdays and aging

    (E) buying, spending, and exchanging goods

13. The last two lines of the poem serve all of the following purposes EXCEPT

    (A) reinforce the theme

    (B) project the narrator's tone

    (C) add a touch of humor

    (D) defy the wisdom of age

    (E) reintroduce the narrator

14. The wisdom of the "wise man" can BEST be summarized as

   (A) be careful in your love life

   (B) being poor materially is better than being unhappy in love

   (C) nothing is as bad as financial failure

   (D) one can learn from experiences and mistakes

   (E) with age will come wisdom and understanding

Prose Exercise

Read this passage by Edgar Allan Poe and then answer the multiple-choice questions that follow.

Our first meeting was at an obscure library in the Rue Montmartre, where the accident of our both being in search of the same very rare and very remarkable volume, brought us into closer
(5) communion. We saw each other again and again. I was deeply interested in the little family history which he detailed to me with all that candor which a Frenchman indulges whenever mere self is the theme. I was astonished too, at the vast
(10) extent of his reading; and, above all, I felt my soul enkindled within me by the wild fervor, and the vivid freshness of his imagination. Seeking in Paris the objects I then sought, I felt that the society of such a man would be to me a treasure beyond
(15) pride; and this feeling I frankly confided to him. It was at length arranged that we should live together during my stay in the city; and as my worldly circumstances were somewhat less embarrassed than his own, I was permitted to be at the expense
(20) of renting, and furnishing in a style which suited the rather fantastic gloom of our common temper, a time-eaten and grotesque mansion, long deserted through superstitions into which we did not inquire, and tottering to its fall in a retired and
(25) desolate portion of the Faubourg St. Germain.

Had the routine of our life at this place been known to the world, we should have been regarded as madmen—although, perhaps, as madmen of a harmless nature. Our seclusion was perfect. We
(30) admitted no visitors. Indeed the locality of our retirement had been carefully kept a secret from my own former associates; and it had been many years since Dupin had ceased to know or be known in Paris. We existed within ourselves alone.

(35) It was a freak of fancy in my friend (for what else shall I call it?) to be enamored of the Night for her own sake; and into this bizarrerie, as into all his others, I quietly fell; giving myself up to his wild whims with a perfect abandon. The sable
(40) divinity would not herself dwell with us always; but we could counterfeit her presence. At the first dawn of the morning we closed all the massy shutters of our old building; lighted a couple of tapers which, strongly perfumed, threw out only
(45) the ghastliest and feeblest of rays. By the aid of these we then busied our souls in dreams—reading, writing, or conversing, until warned by the clock of the advent of the true Darkness. Then we sallied forth into the streets, arm and arm, contin-
(50) uing the topics of the day, or roaming far and wide until a late hour, seeking, amid the wild lights and shadows of the populous city that infinity of mental excitement which quiet observation can afford.

(55) At such times I could not help remarking and admiring (although from his rich ideality I had been prepared to expect it) a peculiar analytic ability in Dupin. He seemed, too, to take an eager delight in its exercise—if not exactly in its dis-
(60) play—and did not hesitate to confess the pleasure thus derived. He boasted to me, with a low chuckling laugh, that most men, in respect to himself, wore windows in their bosoms, and was wont to follow up such assertions by direct and very star-
(65) tling proofs of his intimate knowledge of my own. His manner at these moments was frigid and abstract; his eyes were vacant in expression; while his voice, usually a rich tenor rose into a treble which would have sounded petulantly but for the
(70) deliberateness and entire distinctness of the enunciation. Observing him in these moods, I often dwelt meditatively upon the old philosophy of the Bi-Part soul, and amused myself with the fancy of a double Dupin—the creative and the resolvent.

1. Taken as it stands, this passage opens without preamble. The literary term for such an opening is

   (A) introduction
   (B) *in medias res*
   (C) symbolic
   (D) trochaic
   (E) retrospection

GO ON TO THE NEXT PAGE

2. *Night* and *Darkness*, as found in paragraph 3 are examples of what literary technique?

    (A) onomatopoeia

    (B) oxymoron

    (C) parody

    (D) personification

    (E) paradox

3. In the final paragraph, the narrator is speaking of Dupin in terms of being a(n) what?

    (A) personification

    (B) paradox

    (C) oxymoron

    (D) motif

    (E) protagonist

4. The first sentence of paragraph 3 displays obvious examples of

    (A) hyperbole

    (B) alliteration

    (C) simile

    (D) apostrophe

    (E) conceit

5. Upon first meeting his friend, the narrator indicates that Dupin was somewhat

    (A) shy and reluctant to talk

    (B) boisterous and genial

    (C) modest and retiring

    (D) egocentric and forthcoming

    (E) proper and reserved

6. In line 39, the word *freak* can best be defined as a(n)

    (A) scary person

    (B) extreme fright

    (C) unusual occurrence

    (D) idiosyncrasy

    (E) horrible dream

7. The tone of this passage can BEST be described as

    (A) melancholy and lamenting

    (B) distressed but factual

    (C) introspective but factual

    (D) distressed and annoyed

    (E) reminiscent and longing

8. The last paragraph juxtaposes the idea of

    (A) night and day

    (B) open mindedness and close mindedness

    (C) the narrator and his friend

    (D) the duplicitous natures of Dupin

    (E) the rational and the irrational

9. Night, for the narrator and Dupin, is symbolically referred to in all BUT which of the following terms?

    (A) total seclusion

    (B) sable divinity

    (C) massy shutters

    (D) true Darkness

    (E) deathlike sleep

10. The structure or movement of this passage can BEST be described as

    (A) general to specific

    (B) specific to general

    (C) chronological

    (D) space oriented

    (E) asynchronous

11. The sentence structures within this passage are mostly

    (A) simple and to the point
    (B) compound and loose in nature
    (C) compound and joined by appropriate conjunctions
    (D) fragments, not full sentences at all
    (E) compound, often utilizing *and* and the semicolon

12. One could describe the narrator of this passage as

    (A) arrogant and self-assured
    (B) timid and hesitant to tell his story
    (C) first person in presentation
    (D) erudite in his presentation
    (E) representative of an all-knowing story teller

13. The author relies on dashes to

    (A) show that he is unsure about his thoughts
    (B) display the academic nature of his writing
    (C) demonstrate his "searching" for the right word or phrase
    (D) incorporate parenthetical comments into the passage
    (E) utilize a unique and tricky piece of punctuation

14. The reader can BEST describe the diction of this passage as

    (A) antiquated and learned
    (B) simplistic and easy to follow
    (C) formal and somewhat technical
    (D) filled with colloquialisms and jargon
    (E) comfortably informal

KEY TERMINOLOGY PRACTICE SET ANSWERS AND EXPLANATIONS

The preceding terminology questions are not unlike some you will find on the AP English Literature multiple-choice section. If you are unfamiliar with any of the terms used, both in the correct response or the incorrect choices (distractors), go back to the glossary at the beginning of this chapter.

Poetry Exercise Answer Explanations

1. (B)

The narrator's tone can BEST be described as reminiscent. The title itself gives you the best clue: "<u>when</u> I was one-and-twenty." The other choices are too strong for the tone. Although the narrator seems mildly disturbed by his ignoring the wise man's words, his voice conveys lament or wistfulness, as he remembers that he had refused to listen to the advice of the older "wise man" and has only himself to blame for any heartache he may have incurred. Reminiscent is the *best* descriptor of this narrator's tone.

2. (A)

Lines 1 and 9 can BEST be described as a refrain. If you were tempted to answer (D), parallel structure, you would not be totally wrong. However, in this poem the narrator uses the repetition of "When I was one and twenty..." as a refrain, a specialized poetic form of parallel structure in this instance. Note that both questions 1 and 2 use the qualifier "BEST" in the question stem. You should not be surprised, therefore, that more than one response seems like it could work. You must decide which is *best*.

3. (D)

When the wise man says "The heart out of the bosom/Was never given in vain" he means that if a person gives one's heart, he or she cannot expect to do so without some sort of effect or purpose. We often hear people say something was done in vain, that is, to no effect or result. Here the narrator sets up a double negative, which implies that the heart is never given for no purpose. Therefore, from the selection of choices, (D) without purpose, is the correct response.

4. (C)

Since the lines in this poem are dominated by three iambic feet, iambic trimeter is the appropriate response to this question. The multiple-choice poetry questions usually do not go into great detail with scansion and rhyme scheme; however, it would be wise of you to know the basic patterns that are found in most poetry.

5. (B)

This question might throw you at first because every choice is wordy, and you must wade through so much you may become confused. *First* decide in your mind what the theme is. *Skim* the poem again if you are unsure. *Then look* for the one quotation that best fits your conclusion. *Do not* just jump in and try to unravel all the choices before you make some mental decisions first. The basic message of this poem is that the narrator was so sure of himself at age 21 that he did not heed what the wise man told him. Therefore, lines 7–8, answer (B), is the most appropriate response.

6. (C)

The best response to this question is "tone of lamentation." The repetition, "'tis true, 'tis true" enhances the narrator's regretful tone that has dominated most of the poem. The other response you might have considered would be (E), sorrowful mood. There is no doubt that this narrator is sorry he did not listen to the wiser man's advice, but the repetition of "'tis true" is in the spirit of a lament.

7. (C)

After reading through your choices, you may debate between (A) and (C), with age comes wisdom that youth often ignores. (A) is definitely a subtheme, but given the title and the humor in "And I am two-and-twenty," (C) is the BEST choice. You might wonder why this question is asked since question 5 also deals with the theme. Note, however, that question 5 asks which line reflects the theme of the poem while question 7 is asking you to take the idea of the poem and relate it to a wider, more universal concept.

8. (A)

Notice how lines 1 and 9 begin in the same manner. This poem could easily have been divided into two 8-line stanzas, making (A) two octaves in juxtaposition the best response to this question. Remember, juxtaposition means concurrent with or next to. It is a good word to include in your vocabulary, and it is often used in discussing literature. The thought presentation does not lend this poem to four quatrains (four-line stanzas), especially looking at the last potential division between lines 12 and 13. **(D)**. Because the poem is 16 lines long, answer **(E)** cannot be correct. You have already established in question 4 the iambic trimeter characteristic of the lines of this poem, which precludes **(B)** heroic couplets being the proper response, since a couplet must be iambic pentameter.

9. (B)

Although rue is the name of a plant used for medicinal purposes, as it is used in line 14 of this poem, the best definition of the word is choice **(B)** regret. None of the other responses is appropriate.

10. (A)

The repetition of lines beginning with the short conjunctions *But* and *And* is an example of **(A)** anaphora. Anaphora is the repetition of a word or phrase at the beginning of a line.

11. (B)

This question might take you more time than the others to answer. In each you are being asked to consider three different devices. The best way to respond to such a question is to do a process of elimination. (Do not hesitate to write in the test booklet.) By now you have already eliminated several of the possibilities because you have had to look at the poem several times to answer previous questions. Remember, with such a question, ALL THREE devices must be present for the answer to be correct. With that in mind, you should have chosen **(B)** assonance, metonymy, direct quotation. Assonance, repetition of similar vowels in close proximity, is evident in lines 3 (*crowns and pounds*) and 6 (*keep; free*); metonymy is present in line 11, the "heart" representing one's love; and the wise man's words are presented within the quotation marks.

12. (E)

Here you are being asked to remember the term *conceit*, which is identified under Key Terminology as a comparison of two unlikely things, in particular an extended metaphor within a poem. The conceit can be found in **(E)** buying, spending, and exchanging goods. This extended metaphor can be traces through lines 3–6 and is picked up again in lines 12–14.

13. (D)

This is another type of multiple-choice question that can consume precious clock time. You are more used to taking tests that have only one correct response. In this type of question, however, four of the five responses are actually correct. Only one is not correct. Again, you must attack by using process of elimination. In contrast to question 11, however, you are eliminating right responses rather than wrong ones. The correct response would therefore be **(D)** defy the wisdom of age. In fact, the last two lines (the narrator's words this time) regretfully admit that the wise man's words were true, after all.

14. (B)

The wisdom of the "wise man" can BEST be summarized as "being poor materially is better than being unhappy in love." Remember, you are being asked about the wisdom (the message given by) the "wise man." You might have been tempted to choose either **(D)** or **(E)**. These are certainly related to the thematic idea of the poem, but they are not what the wise man is really saying. The wise man urges the narrator to give everything away if he wants, suffer financial loss if he must, but warns him not to arbitrarily give away his heart, for he will pay the price if he does so unwisely. And the narrator finds out, "'tis true, 'tis true."

Prose Exercise Answer Explanations

1. (B)

in medias res. This term refers to a situation that has no introduction; the action begins in the middle of things, without prologue or lengthy lead-in.

2. (D)

The fact that the writer has chosen to capitalize both Night and Darkness is significant. Night is referred to as a female "sable divinity," thereby making **(D)** personification, the correct answer to this question.

3. (B)

By the end of the short passage, the narrator has described Dupin as being a curiosity and somewhat of an enigma. The only possible response, therefore, is **(B)**, paradox. Oxymoron is certainly a paradox in itself, but oxymoron refers to two words, such as baggy tights, and would not work well as a response to this question. The other choices are inaccurate as well.

4. (B)

The first sentence of paragraph 3 displays several obvious examples of alliteration: "It was a freak of fancy in my friend (for what else shall I call it?) ...wild whims...." A hyperbole **(A)** is an extreme exaggeration, a simile **(C)** a comparison using like or as, an apostrophe **(D)** addresses an inanimate object, and a conceit **(E)** is an extended metaphor. None of these other responses would be suitable for this question.

5. (D)

Upon first meeting his friend, the narrator indicates that Dupin was somewhat egocentric and forthcoming. This question is asking you to decipher subtle meaning and *connotation.* Lines 6–9 are where you must take your cues. "I was deeply interested in the little family history which he detailed to me with all that candor which a Frenchman indulges whenever mere self is the theme." The words *candor* and *detailed*, as well as the words *indulges* and *mere self* [being the] *theme* indicate that Dupin readily spoke to the narrator, and was expansive with his information since he was talking about himself.

6. (D)

In line 39, the word *freak* can best be defined as an idiosyncrasy. The word *freak* has many connotations in our language. However, line 39 reads "It was a freak of fancy in my friend...," and then the narrator goes on to tell us about the obsession Dupin seems to have with darkness and night. None of the other definitions for *freak* would be appropriate as a response.

7. (C)

The tone of this passage can BEST be described as introspective but factual. The narrator is remembering what happened; he gives us the details as he remembers them. However, you should be able to infer that he is also trying to figure something out as he is telling us the story. He seems to be musing, to be deciphering things as he goes along. We may suspect that he'll be distressed **(B)** later on, but at this point the tone is calm.

8. (D)

The last paragraph juxtaposes the idea of the duplicitous natures of Dupin. Here's that word again. If you didn't commit *juxtaposition* to memory in the practice questions for poetry, you'd be wise to do so now. This question, however, should not have been difficult. If you correctly identified Dupin as being a paradox in question 3, then you should have gotten this one without too much trouble. The narrator tells us that Dupin changes from being eager, boastful, and chuckling with laughter to a manner "frigid and abstract; his eyes were vacant in expression; while his voice, usually a rich tenor rose into a treble..." (lines 75–76). The narrator even reflects upon the possibility of the Bi-Part soul in relation to his friend.

9. (E)

Notice the BUT in the question stem and select carefully. Nowhere does the narrator make reference to the night as deathlike sleep.

10. (A)

The structure or movement of this passage can BEST be described as chronological. The AP English Literature and Composition Exam may ask you to consider the progression of a passage—beginning to end, retrospective (flashback), foreshadowing and present, etc. In this case, the narrator simply related things in the order in which they happened, at least as he remembers them happening.

11. (E)

The sentence structures within this passage are mostly compound, often utilizing *and* and the semicolon.

12. (C)

One could describe the narrator of this passage as first person in presentation. Although you might think the narrator erudite **(D)**, given the brevity of this passage, the most simple and least debatable response is that this is a first person ("I"-narrator) presentation.

13. (D)

The author relies on dashes to incorporate parenthetical comments into the passage. This passage uses parenthetical information liberally. This can be seen in lines 51–52, for example when the narrator says "we then busied our souls in dreams—reading, writing or conversing...." He uses the information after the dash to inform us just what he means by dreams. The passage contains several other examples of parenthetical structure. Remember, parenthetical comments could be those inserted inside parentheses.

14. (A)

The diction of this passage can BEST be described as antiquated and learned. The language of this passage is certainly not what you would hear in everyday conversation. You probably readily recognized that this is not a contemporary piece. Also, the setting of Paris gives the passage a sense of other-worldiness. It is hard for us to imagine anyone today saying that a run down old house in a deserted neighborhood as "tottering to its fall in a retired and desolate portion of [the town]." You might have been tempted to choose letter **(C)**, formal and somewhat technical. However, although the language can easily be identified as formal, it certainly does not fit the idea of technical.

Chapter Four: **Writing the Essays**

- Decipher the Prompt

- Structure the Presentation

- Use "Superior Language"

- Learn the Elements of a High Scoring Essay

- Practice

- Summing Up: Guidelines for an Effective Essay

If you've been in an AP English class, you are probably wondering what more can you learn about writing essays, since that seems to be all you do in your class. Actually, you've probably already learned the basics of good essay writing. This section will concentrate on those things that are most essential for you to remember when you write your AP essays.

DECIPHER THE PROMPT

Even though you will be writing under extreme time constraints (remember, two hours for three essays), you must still produce an essay that is worthy of you. The first thing, of course, is to read the essay prompt and the passage you are given. Then reread the essay prompt. Determine what you are being asked to do and how you are being asked to accomplish it. For example, if you are asked to write about *the effect of the changing attitude of the narrator in a passage by analyzing tone, syntax and diction*, then that is what you do. Identify the changing attitude—what is this change; what purpose does it serve in the piece? Then, how do the tone, syntax and diction show you this change? Finally, how does this change affect the passage (or poem) overall? What effect does this change have upon the narrator, or the reader?

Deciphering the steps of the prompt is your most important task. Even the very best written essay will not score well if you don't fulfill the expectations of the prompt.

STRUCTURE YOUR PRESENTATION

The next thing is to determine how you will present your information. Some students feel most comfortable choosing the three (or however many) specific items—tone, syntax, and diction—and writing about each one separately, looking at the passage or poem as a whole each time. After they have done that, these students usually discuss the attitude shift, often in the conclusion of their essays. That is not a bad way of presenting information. If you are comfortable with that approach, and the resulting essay flows well because you have blended each idea using good transitions, then write your essay in that manner. Some students, however, find that when they first talk just about tone then just about diction, etc. their resulting essay is too segmented and it seems not to flow. Nevertheless, many high scoring essays are written in just that manner. It all depends on how well the student has blended the sections to make a whole.

Other students let the movement of the passage determine the parts of their essay responses. Many even rely on *in the beginning*, then *in the middle, at the end*, and so on. However they see the passage moving, they use that movement to determine their body paragraphs. With each segment of the passage, these students talk about all three literary tools—diction, tone, and syntax—as they affect each part of the passage. This then leads to their discussion about the attitude shift, as they then pull everything together either in another body paragraph or in the conclusion.

A third alternative, and perhaps the most difficult but often most successful approach, is to let the idea of attitude shift dominate your entire essay. When you write your essay that way, tone, syntax, diction, as well as movement of the passage become secondary to the controlling idea of attitude shift. Usually such an essay is successful because the student takes time in the introduction to develop the idea of attitude shift as the dominating focus to the essay. This approach takes a lot of practice, and, perhaps, a bit of luck. Perhaps something will serendipitously occur to you after you have read the prompt and the passage, and before you know it the thoughts come almost faster than you can write!

By now you should realize that there just is not one sure-fire formula for writing upper half AP English essays. You have probably been writing essays all year, and by now you have recognized where your own strengths and weaknesses lie. Whatever your approach, perfect it with lots of practice, practice, practice.

STRIVE FOR "SUPERIOR CONTROL" OF LANGUAGE

In your essays, your control of language is important. Writing that is grammatical, concise, direct, and persuasive (that is, you persuade the reader you know what you are talking about), displays the "superior control of language" that readers look for in upper half responses.

- Grammar—your writing must follow the general rules of standard written English.
- Diction—your word choice is important. If homonyms confuse you, then review the ones that give you problems such as *effect/affect*, and *it's/its*. Also, do not flaunt large or erudite vocabulary if it is not natural to your writing style. If you are trying to impress the reader, such practice *may obfuscate more than elucidate what you are articulating.* You get the idea.

- Syntax—refers to sentence structure. Be sure your sentences are constructed so that your ideas are clear and understandable. Vary your sentence structure, sometimes using simple sentences and other times using compound and complex structures.

PLAN AND WRITE

Give yourself a hand by roughing out your ideas first. Your test booklet will have plenty of room for you to jot down ideas and organize your thoughts. If you do not come up with anything solid within the first six to eight minutes, start writing anyway. Start with your introduction and let the prompt itself be your guide. Whatever you do, *never* leave an essay blank. Say something. There is no redeeming a score if you fail to answer one of the essay questions. Also, you can begin with any of the three essays you wish. If one of the three grabs your attention, begin there. Once you have something down on paper, your anxiety will lessen and before you know it ideas for the other responses will occur to you.

DON'T SWEAT THE DETAILS

Do not obsess over every little thing. If you cannot remember how to spell a word, or even the name of a character (for the open-ended question), just keep going. Even the top scoring essays are not without flaws. The essay readers understand that you are writing first-draft essays. They will not be looking to take points off for minor errors, provided you don't make them consistently. If your essays are littered with misspellings, and grammar mistakes, however, the reader may conclude that you have a serious communication problem and score your response accordingly.

ELEMENTS OF THE HIGH-SCORING ESSAY

To write an effective essay, you must be concise, forceful and as correct as you can be. An effective essay wastes no words, makes its point in a clear, direct way, and conforms to the generally accepted rules of grammar and form.

Essays are rated higher if they:
- Develop a central idea or thesis
- Synthesize the ideas and move to a logical conclusion
- Present ideas cohesively and logically
- Are written clearly

The first of these involves having a central idea or thesis that unifies your essay; the second and third mean tying all your ideas together with logic, unity and coherence; and the last means to present all your wonderful ideas in a manner that is forthright and demonstrates your knowledge, understanding, and confidence. Remember, these essays are basically first drafts that will be graded. They must be complete and well organized, but also easy for a reader to see that you have mastered the skills a college freshman has upon completion of an introductory English lit and comp course.

Basically, your AP essays are like any other writing. You want to have a good introduction. Try to get the reader's attention immediately. Make the introduction clear and concise, but do not belabor it. The AP reader certainly wants to know what you plan to do, but the reader is more interested in whether you have successfully done what you say you are going to do. For the third, open-ended essay, you can assume the reader is familiar with the work you have chosen. There is no need to summarize it in the introduction or anywhere else in your essay.

The body of your essay is the most crucial part of your response. Make sure that your ideas flow smoothly. Use transitions to hold your ideas together. Don't just tell the reader, show what you mean with references to line numbers and a few well-chosen (and short!) quotations from the passage. Be sure to describe, explain, and discuss your ideas thoroughly. Stay focused. If it seems that you might be rambling on or talking off-topic, pause a minute and reign in your ideas. You do not have time to ramble all over in your body paragraphs, and extraneous material will not enhance your essay score.

Finally, your conclusion is important. Whether you have a lengthy, separate conclusion in which you bring the controlling idea or thesis full circle, or you actually have pulled most everything together in your last body paragraph and you are just adding a short two-three sentence finale, bringing closure to the essay is very important. Because readers are always well aware that your essay is not much more than a rough draft, they recognize that introductions may often be a bit sluggish until the writer warms up to his or her subject. Consequently, readers are more forgiving of slow starting essays with pokey introductions than they are of unfinished, incomplete or let-down conclusions that fail to tie together the essence of the student's response.

PRACTICE

In the following chapters are numerous sample prompts relating to poetry and prose passages. Try your hand at them, as well as at the essay prompts in the three practice tests. In the Answer Explanations for Practice Tests I–III are sample student essays and commentaries on them from the perspective of AP scoring. Take a hint from these to know what to do on the free-response section—and what *not* to do.

SUMMING UP

The important thing to remember is that you would not even be looking at this book if you hadn't already spent much time and effort getting this far. You have written so many essays, you probably think you could do so in your sleep. Just remember a few basic questions as you write your essay and you will be fine.

- Did you read the prompt carefully—both before and after reading the passage?
- Did you read the passage carefully, annotating anything that might relate to the prompt?
- Did you address the tasks the prompt has set up for you?
- Is your essay organized? If you have to add information later, do so neatly using an asterisk.

- Have you (neatly) done some on-the-spot revision where necessary?
- Have you presented and developed your ideas as fully as possible? Using references to the passage where applicable?
- Have you used language effectively?

If you are feeling overwhelmed, just take each suggestion separately; do not try to incorporate everything you've been told all at once. Remember, you've come a long way from the first time you scribbled on wide-line paper with an extra fat pencil clutched tightly in your little hand. You can do it. Take a deep breath and remember to exhale. Read the prompt; read the passage; read the prompt again; and go for it!

Chapter Five: **Poetry on the Exam**

- How Poetry Appears on the Exam
- Poetry in the Essay Section
- Poetry Essay Practice Prompts
- Poetry in the Multiple-Choice Section

Poetry makes its chief appeal to the emotion and to the imagination of the reader or listener. Its primary purpose is to awaken emotion, to inspire the reader, or to give pleasure. Poetic style includes its physical arrangement, its word choice, and its form. It is usually written in lines and stanzas; its diction calls for unusual expression and figurative language. Poetry can take many forms, but often it is musical and/or metrical.

HOW POETRY APPEARS ON THE EXAM

On the Advanced Placement English Literature and Composition Exam, the poetry that is presented, either in the multiple-choice or the essay section, is often not poetry that you will readily find in most high school literature books. There is a reason for this. The AP Test Development Committee tries to avoid using those poems that students will have already explored. The most obvious reason for this, of course, is the equity issue. The AP English Literature and Composition guideline for teachers does not designate any specific list of literature that a student must have covered before taking the exam. Therefore, if a poem on the exam were one that normally would be covered in the curriculum of some students, but not other students, some would have an unfair advantage over others. Contrariwise, foreknowledge of a piece of literature can inhibit a student's ability to respond. Sometimes certain past lessons, activities, or preconceived notions actually interfere with the student's ability to take a fresh look at the poem. The Test Development Committee feels that presenting literature that students may be less likely to have experienced seems to work the best for all.

When a poem is used as one of the four or five passages in the multiple-choice section, it will be followed by some very specific questions that will ask you to consider a number of things about the poem. Of course, some questions will simply verify that you have comprehended the basic meaning of the poem. In addition, you will be asked general questions about the poem such as what type of poem it is, what its meter might be, or who the narrator probably is. Moreover, the multiple-choice questions will ask you more detailed questions about meaning, inference, point of view, narrator's attitude, and so on. You will see some examples of these types of questions in the practice sets in this section.

If by chance you already know the poem, keep that knowledge in a special place within your mind. Use the information if it will help you. Disregard that knowledge if it causes you confusion. More likely, you may already be familiar with the author of a poem used on the exam, especially on the poetry essay question. That knowledge may help you out. However, do not assume that just because Emily Dickinson has authored a poem, for example, that you should automatically start writing about death imagery. If such information is indeed relevant to your essay response, that is good. If it is not, do not let your prior knowledge of the author miscolor your analysis of the poem—this time you may just be faced with an exception to Dickinson's "usual."

POETRY IN THE ESSAY SECTION

On the AP Exam, you must be able to analyze a poem. Analysis means to break it down, look at it from many angles. In your essay response, however, this does not mean that you should be rephrasing or summarizing it. True, you will have to make references to specific lines, and possibly even to entire sections of the given poem, but any sort of retelling of the poem must be used as support for your analysis, not in lieu of your analysis. You can see the difference in the following example of a poem by Oliver Wendell Holmes.

The Last Leaf

I saw him once before,
As he passed by the door,
  And again
The pavement stones resound,
(5) As he totters o'er the ground
  With his cane.

They say that in his prime,
Ere the pruning-knife of Time
  Cut him down
(10) Not a better man was found
By the Crier on his round
  Through the town.

But now he walks the streets,
And looks at all he meets
(15) Sad and wan,
And he shakes his feeble head,
That it seems as if he said,
"They are gone."

The mossy marbles rest
(20) On the lips that he has prest
  In their bloom,
And the names he loved to hear
Have been carved for many a year
  On the tomb.

(25) My grandmamma has said—
Poor old lady, she is dead
  Long ago—
That he had a Roman nose,
And his cheek was like a rose
(30) In the snow;

But now his nose is thin,
And it rests upon his chin
  Like a staff,
And a crook is in his back,
(35) And a melancholy crack
  In his laugh.

I know it is a sin
For me to sit and grin
  At him here;
(40) But the old three-cornered hat,
And the breeches, and all that,
  Are so queer!

And if I should live to be
The last leaf upon the tree
(45) In the spring,
Let them smile, as I do now,
At the old forsaken bough
  Where I cling.

Summary

The narrator of this poem is talking about an old man that he (or she) has seen, not for the first time. In watching the old man, the narrator notices that he can barely totter along. When the old man meets people, he seems confused. He speaks of people who are long dead.

Apparently the narrator's deceased grandmother once knew the old man. She said he had been a handsome young man. Now, however, his looks are gone. His nose is narrow, his back is hunched and his chin sags upon his chest. Those he once knew and loved are long buried.

The narrator admits that the old man's looks make him laugh. He is oddly dressed, with a strange hat and funny looking pants. (Sounds like he's on his way to a golf game!)

Nevertheless, the narrator admits at the end that he would like to live a long time too. And if the narrator is fortunate enough to be an old man, then he doesn't care if others smile at him the way he does at the old man.

Analysis

This seems to be a simple poem at first, but there is more to it than just a narrator who impolitely gets a laugh out of watching a very old man make his way.

The narrator speaks of the tottering old man as if he is something to ridicule. However, everyone—"They," the Crier and even the narrator's old grandmamma—says that this old man was a good, respectable, and well-loved person in his prime.

The narrator tells us that all of the old man's former "loves" are deceased—the names he loved to hear have long been carved upon the marble stone that covers the lips and cheeks of those he once kissed and cared for.

Much imagery is used in this poem—it is easy to see the old man as he totters on his cane. A sense of sadness is evoked by the "sad and wan" looks he gives other with his rheumy eyes. His once patrician nose is thin, while his elegant countenance is bent and unsteady. Melancholy can be heard in his laugh. There is also a provocative image of Time with a pruning knife.

The best part of the poem, however, is the irony at the end when the narrator, though laughing now, says that he hopes that he too can be so old. Then others will smile at yet another last leaf upon the tree.

Notice the difference between summary and analysis. Admittedly, the analysis above is a brief one. Both the analysis and the summary are written as if a student had been asked to write something quickly in response to reading the Holmes poem. Nevertheless, you should be able to detect the differences between the two. The first one tells you what you have read. The next one explains what you have read. It is analysis that the AP Exam expects from you. Use summary or paraphrase only in support of your analysis.

Let's look at another poem, John Keats's "To Autumn":

To Autumn

Season of mists and mellow fruitfulness,
  Close bosom-friend of the maturing sun;
Conspiring with him how to load and bless
  With fruit the vines that round the thatch-eves run;
(5) To bend with apples the moss'd cottage-trees,
  And fill all fruit with ripeness to the core;
   To swell the gourd, and plump the hazel shells
With a sweet kernel; to set budding more,
  And still more, later flowers for the bees,
(10) Until think they warm days will never cease,
   For summer has o'er-brimm'd their clammy cells.

Who hath not seen thee oft amid thy store?
  Sometimes whoever seeks abroad may find.
Thee sitting careless on a granary floor,
(15) Thy hair soft-lifted by the winnowing wind;
Or on a half-reap'd furrow sound asleep,
  Drowsed with the fume of poppies, while thy hook
   Spares the next swath and all its twined flowers:
And sometimes like a gleaner thou dost keep
(20) Steady thy laden head across a brook;
  Or by a cider-press, with patient look,
   Thou watchest the last oozings, hours by hours.

Where are the songs of Spring? Ay, where are they?
  Think not of them, thou hast thy music too,—
(25) While barred clouds bloom the soft-dying day,
  And touch the stubble-plains with rosy hue;
Then in a wailful choir the small gnats mourn
  Among the river sallows, borne aloft
   Or sinking as the light wind lives or dies;
(30) And full-grown lambs loud bleat from hilly bourn.
  Hedge-crickets sing; and now with treble soft
  The redbreast whistles from a garden-croft,
  And gathering swallows twitter in the skies.

In reading this poem, you might make the following annotations:

To Autumn

Season of mists and mellow fruitfulness,	*Addresses Autumn, using*
Close bosom-friend of the maturing sun;	*descriptors, not by name*
(5) Conspiring with him how to load and bless	*How is sun mature?*
With fruit the vines that round the thatch-eves run;	*Vivid visual images*
To bend with apples the moss'd cottage-trees,	
And fill all fruit with ripeness to the core;	*Images of bountiful harvest—*
To swell the gourd, and plump the hazel shells	*swell & plump—everything is full*
(10) With a sweet kernel; to set budding more,	*Lots of infinitive verbs*
And still more, later flowers for the bees,	
Until they think warm days will never cease,	*Clammy—as in sticky, like honey?*
For summer has o'er-brimm'd their clammy cells.	*Why mention summer here?*
Who hath not seen thee oft amid thy store?	*Who is* thy*?*
(15) Sometimes whoever seeks abroad may find.	*Must still be addressing Autumn.*
Thee sitting careless on a granary floor,	
Thy hair soft-lifted by the winnowing wind;	*Is this Autumn's hair?*
Or on a half-reap'd furrow sound asleep,	
Drowsed with the fume of poppies, while thy hook	*Sounds like early Fall*
(20) Spares the next swath and all its twined flowers:	*—flowers still in bloom, sun's hot*
And sometimes like a gleaner thou dost keep	
Steady thy laden head across a brook;	*Autumn has its own personality*
Or by a cider-press, with patient look,	
Thou watchest the last oozings, hours by hours.	*Activities of the fall season*
(25) Where are the songs of Spring? Ay, where are they?	*Begins with another question.*
Think not of them, thou hast thy music too,—	*Just enjoy sounds of the present.*
While barred clouds bloom the soft-dying day,	
And touch the stubble-plains with rosy hue;	
Then in a wailful choir the small gnats mourn	
(30) Among the river sallows, borne aloft	
Or sinking as the light wind lives or dies;	*These are all examples of*
And full-grown lambs loud bleat from hilly bourn.	*Autumn's music.*
Hedge-crickets sing; and now with treble soft	
The redbreast whistles from a garden-croft,	*These are not as hopeful as*
And gathering swallows twitter in the skies.	*Spring's sounds. Is there more going on here than what it says?*

Discussion

John Keats wrote this poem in the fall of 1819. Interestingly, this was only two years before his own untimely death at the young age of 26. Despite the unexpectedness of his own early death (drowned at sea), many scholars and followers of Keats attribute to him an uncanny sense of prescience in some of his poetry. Whatever the case, you will discover in this poem, despite its overwhelming imagery of life, warmth, and fullness, there seems to also be an underlying suggestion that this affluence will not last forever.

The marginal notes to the right of the poem suggest the sort of commentary that you should automatically be doing as you read poetry analytically. While you may not have time to go into such depth on the exam, you can make notes in your exam booklet as you read, or make some mental notes to yourself.

This poem is an *ode*, and our Key Terminology glossary tells you that an ode is "a lyric poem that is somewhat serious in subject and treatment, elevated in style and sometimes uses elaborate stanza structure, which is often patterned in sets of three." "To Autumn," you can readily note, contains these characteristics. This poem is certainly more elaborate and formal than "The Last Leaf" by Holmes. Not only are there just three stanzas, but if you look at the progression of these stanzas, you can see that the first directly addresses Autumn. The second describes Autumn by identifying it with many of the characteristic activities and idiosyncrasies of the season as if they were activities and characteristics of the personified Autumn. Finally, stanza three discusses the music of Autumn. Although it opens with a mention of Spring, the poet quickly directs us to appreciate Autumn's music. This last suggests that things are not as uplifting as might be if the poem were discussing the music of Spring, instead of the music of fall the bountiful, but also dying season.

Reading for Meaning

When you read for meaning, you should be sure that your reading includes the following:

- **Question** what you are reading. Ask yourself if you are consciously understanding what you are reading.
- **Comment** and reflect in your mind upon the ideas that are being presented in the passage.
- **Pause briefly** and think about what you have just read.
- **Evaluate** what you have read.
- Note **quotations** that are particularly challenging or unusual. You can do this by simply underlining or annotating a section of the text.
- **Recognize** words; attempt to figure out meaning from context.

It is true that you will not have time to stop and consciously do all of these things on the AP Exam itself. Nevertheless, you will have time to do at least some of them. In the meantime, these are helpful habits to incorporate into your reading. Then, when you are under timed conditions such as the AP exam, these habits come naturally.

After Reading for Meaning, you are ready to begin close analysis. The following chart should help you with analyzing this poem or any prose passage you may come across. Of course, this is a lot of detail, you say. How are you expected to do all that and write an essay and do it all in minutes? The reality is that you are not. The detailed breakdown you see next is, like the above suggestions for Reading for Meaning, is a practice activity. With practice, you will find yourself more able to do this sort of analysis automatically, almost simultaneously with your close reading of a passage or poem.

To Autumn

Observations	Examples from Text	Effect on Reader
1. Author's purpose: Why is the piece being written? What response does the writer wish to evoke from the reader?	Sounds almost like a prayer to fall, as if he reveres the season.	The poem gives an over- dose of plenty. It's mesmerizing— like warm sun.
2. Audience How is the audience indicated? Is the audience directly addressed? Does the writer use "you"?	It's an address (ode) to Autumn. No indication of a human audience. *You* is the sun, not "we" the humans.	Reader has to have experienced similar feelings, or he/she will be left out.
3. Style of Language Is it formal, colloquial, archaic, dialect, poetic, abstract, concrete? Is sarcasm, satire, parody evident?	Old fashioned style—*reap'd, watchest, Ay,* *borne aloft, thee,* and *thatch*.	Old way of speech makes poem hard to understand. The whole poem has a sense of archaic and countryside ritual.
4. Diction What words stand out? Are there significant connotations? What words give you TONE clues?	*Close-bosom friend, hath-thee-Ay,* *wailful choir, bleat*. What are "river sallows"?	Old fashioned is off-putting. Words are unfamiliar and odd, give the poem a prayerlike sound.
5. Syntax Is there unusual word order, periodic sentences, parallel construction? Any other sentence structure oddities?	First stanza is not even a sentence—just one long fragment! Asks a lot of questions!	Lack of sentences in first stanza makes it hard to read. Notice how most of the questions are answered. That helps.
6. Selection of Detailf What details seem important? What do these details reveal? Do they establish any pattern? Any details seem to be "missing"?	Details!! He doesn't just say it's been a good growing year. Says nothing about idea that winter (death) is next—wonder why?	I got the idea right away—almost overkill here. Makes poem tedious. I think that the fact that winter isn't mentioned must be very important.
7. Imagery To what senses does the writer appeal? Is there a pattern to the imagery used? Does any one sense predominate? Is their any shift in emphasis?	All senses are tapped—sight, sound, smell & taste: *bend w/ apples, plump hazel nuts,* *hair soft lifted, cider press, oozing honey,* *loud bleat, twitter in the sky.*	Again, it seems like too much, but maybe that's the idea. Images at the end seem less quiet than earlier tranquil dozing, almost raucous.

Observations	Examples from Text	Effect on Reader
8. Figurative Language Check for symbols, similes, metaphors, analogies, oxymoron, hyperbole, metonomy, paradox.	Autumn is a symbol of nearing death? Lots of metaphors—*close bosom friend, maturing sun,* etc. Oxymoron = *wailful choirs.* Paradox = *clammy cells.*	Figurative language seems to be this poem's strong point. I find something new every time I read it.
9. Structure Any significant organizational pattern? Any shifts or significant deviations?	Three stanzas of 11 lines each. Really weird rhyme scheme—unusual.	Formal ode structure establishes sense of time and purpose? Rhymes may be significant; is there a reason for this?—curious.
10. Tone What word(s) describe the writer's attitude toward the subject and the audience? Do "feelings" shift w/in the piece?	The writer is obviously drugged by the opulence of this season. I sense a shift in the last stanza, is he not saying something?	Unless reader can identify w/ writer's almost reverent attitude, it is hard to "get involved." I think he's avoiding what's ahead.

After you have investigated a number of poems with this close scrutiny, you will find it much easier to respond to a passage on the Advanced Placement English Literature and Composition Exam.

POETRY ESSAY PRACTICE PROMPTS

The particular Oliver Wendell Holmes poem you've read in the previous section could well lend itself to a poem used in the essay section of the exam. The narrator's shift in attitude is what makes that poem special. An essay response where you might be asked to discuss the author's sudden change in attitude and the possible reasons for this shift would be very possible for an essay prompt using this poem as its focus.

With perhaps only two exceptions in all the years that the AP English Literature Exam has existed, it has included one essay question on poetry. Most of the time the test will ask you to deal with one particular poem such as "The Sow," "One Art," "The Centaur," "The Death of a Toad," "The Broken Heart," and many others.

Sometimes, however, the AP English Literature Exam will present two poems for you to write about by comparing and/or contrasting some aspect(s) such as their particular points of view, the two author's purposes, attitudes, etc. This was the case in 1994 with two poems about Helen of Troy—"To Helen" by Edgar Allan Poe and "Helen" by Hilda Doolittle. In 2000 students were asked to respond to two very different points of view about Ulysses and the Sirens, and back in 1988 students were asked to respond to "Bright Star" by John Keats and "Choose Something Like a Star" by Robert Frost.

In the next part of this section about poetry, you will find once again "The Last Leaf" and "To Autumn" reproduced. This will be followed by a discussion about typical questions that could be asked in a poem essay question and what possible avenues you might take in responding to such a question.

The Last Leaf

I saw him once before,
As he passed by the door,
   And again
The pavement stones resound,
(5) As he totters o'er the ground
   With his cane.

They say that in his prime,
Ere the pruning-knife of Time
   Cut him down
(10) Not a better man was found
By the Crier on his round
   Through the town.

But now he walks the streets,
And looks at all he meets
(15) Sad and wan,
And he shakes his feeble head,
That it seems as if he said,
"They are gone."

The mossy marbles rest
(20) On the lips that he has prest
   In their bloom,
And the names he loved to hear
Have been carved for many a year
   On the tomb.

(25) My grandmamma has said—
Poor old lady, she is dead
   Long ago—
That he had a Roman nose,
And his cheek was like a rose
(30) In the snow;

But now his nose is thin,
And it rests upon his chin
   Like a staff,
And a crook is in his back,
(35) And a melancholy crack
   In his laugh.

I know it is a sin
For me to sit and grin
   At him here;
(40) But the old three-cornered hat,
And the breeches, and all that,
   Are so queer!

And if I should live to be
(45) The last leaf upon the tree
   In the spring,
Let them smile, as I do now,
At the old forsaken bough
   Where I cling.

To Autumn

Season of mists and mellow fruitfulness,
   Close bosom-friend of the maturing sun;
Conspiring with him how to load and bless
   With fruit the vines that round the thatch-eves run;
(5) To bend with apples the moss'd cottage-trees,
   And fill all fruit with ripeness to the core;
   To swell the gourd, and plump the hazel shells
With a sweet kernel; to set budding more,
   And still more, later flowers for the bees,
(10) Until they think warm days will never cease,
   For summer has o'er-brimm'd their clammy cells.

Who hath not seen thee oft amid thy store?
   Sometimes whoever seeks abroad may find.
Thee sitting careless on a granary floor,
(15) Thy hair soft-lifted by the winnowing wind;
Or on a half-reap'd furrow sound asleep,
Drowsed with the fume of poppies, while thy hook
Spares the next swath and all its twined flowers:
And sometimes like a gleaner thou dost keep
(20) Steady thy laden head across a brook;
   Or by a cider-press, with patient look,
   Thou watchest the last oozings, hours by hours.

Where are the songs of Spring? Ay, where are they?
   Think not of them, thou hast thy music too,—
(25) While barred clouds bloom the soft-dying day,
   And touch the stubble-plains with rosy hue;
Then in a wailful choir the small gnats mourn
   Among the river sallows, borne aloft
   Or sinking as the light wind lives or dies;
(30) And full-grown lambs loud bleat from hilly bourn.
   Hedge-crickets sing; and now with treble soft
   The redbreast whistles from a garden-croft,
   And gathering swallows twitter in the skies.

There are a number of ways these two poems might be presented together as the essay question in poetry. The first might read something like:

> *Read the following two poems carefully. Then write a well-organized essay in which you discuss their similarities and differences. In your essay be sure to consider both the theme and style of each poem.*

Another prompt might read:

> *Both of the following poems describe the same thematic idea. After reading each poem carefully, identify this underlying theme. Then, in a well-organized essay, analyze the specific stylistic differences between these two poems. Be sure to consider point of view, imagery, poetic presentation, structure and other such poetic devices when comparing the two poems.*

Yet another prompt could read:

> *Read the following poems carefully, then write a well-organized essay in which you compare/contrast how the formal elements such as structure, syntax diction, and imagery reveal the speakers' attitudes towards old age.*

Finally:

> *Read the following two poems carefully. Considering such elements as speaker, diction, imagery, form, and tone, write a well-organized essay in which you compare the speakers' views about being old.*

No doubt, you can see a pattern to the possibilities for prompts that require you to compare or contrast two different poems. The earlier part of this poetry section, in which we explored reading for meaning and close analysis of poem, should enable you to formulate answers to such prompts.

There is little doubt that both of these poems deal with the idea of growing old, or being old. You may wonder how you are supposed to identify with such a concept. Use the poems to help you respond. Look closely at what each poet is saying. Pay particular attention to HOW each poet presents his ideas. Is not a last leaf going to appear in autumn? Isn't autumn that time of year just prior to the death of a year? Despite the fact that these two poems look very different, and read much differently, they really are addressing the same thing.

Now that you have a better idea of how you can decode a poem, you should have no problem responding to a prompt very similar to the ones presented above. If you are still unsure, refer to the section on key terminology in this book, beginning on page 17, and review those terms relevant to poetry analysis. In particular, you would want to look at the two poems' stanza structure, rhyme scheme, imagery, detail, language, tone, and attitude of the two narrators. Also, see the Answers and Explanations for the Practice Tests at the end of this book for examples of student responses to essay questions about poetry.

POETRY IN THE MULTIPLE-CHOICE SECTION

The Multiple Choice section of the Advanced Placement English Literature and Composition Exam consists of four or five passages with questions following these passages. It is rare that one of these passages is not a poem.

You will not have the time to do an in-depth analysis of a poem on the multiple-choice section—remember, you have about 12–15 minutes per passage. On the multiple-choice section of the test, you will have to read quickly for meaning, and attack the questions, returning to the poem for the information you need to answer each one.

You can, however, familiarize yourself with the types of questions you may face; this, in turn, will help you with your reading skills, since you will know what types of things to be on the lookout for. We'll start some typical types of questions, working with our old friends "To Autumn" and "The Last Leaf."

"To Autumn:"

1. In this poem, the narrator describes Autumn as all of the following EXCEPT

    (A) season of mist

    (B) season of mellow fruitfulness

    (C) asleep in a half-reaped furrow

    (D) hair being lifted by a breeze

    (E) the season before the winter

Answer: (E)

Autumn is never described as the season before winter. You can easily infer that from the passage (as well as from prior knowledge), but nowhere does the narrator give that description directly. (A) and (B) are in line 1. Line 15 mentions the hair, (D), while line 16 describes Autumn snoozing in the furrow. Remember that this type of question can be tricky. What you are given are four correct responses and only one incorrect response. That means you must often go through a process of elimination to discover the correct response.

2. The unspoken message that seems to underlie this poem is

    (A) Autumn promotes feelings of patience, torpor and great satisfaction.

    (B) We must enjoy what we have at the moment, not pine for the past nor worry about what is ahead.

    (C) Spring was a great time with its own special music, but Autumn has music all of its own.

    (D) The maturing sun warms the land and increases the narrator's sense of lassitude.

    (E) The summer has lasted so long into Autumn that the bees are finding themselves overwhelmed by increased honey making.

Answer: (B)

It is important to note that the question asks specifically for the unspoken message. In fact, all of the other responses are actually mentioned in the poem, either directly or by way of similar imagery. For example, letter (A) can be identified throughout stanzas one and two in all the comments about successful fruition, lazy drowziness, and patient watching and waiting. The last stanza covers letter (C). The bit about the bees is evident in lines 9–11.

3. Which of the following images does NOT refer to the satisfactory fruition of the season?

 (A) to bend with apples the moss'd cottage-trees

 (B) o'er-brimmed their clammy cells

 (C) now with treble soft the redbreast whistles

 (D) full-grown lambs loud bleat

 (E) swell the gourd and plump the hazel shells

Answer: (C)

All of the other responses make a specific reference to abundance and fruition at the end of the growing season. Although the redbreast (bird) singing is among the images, it does not relate to the culmination of growth typical of the Autumn season.

4. Which of the following combinations is NOT present within this Keats poem?

 (A) iambic pentameter, 11-line stanzas, and litote

 (B) eye rhyme, rhetorical question, and parallel structure

 (C) ear rhyme, metaphor, and hyperbole

 (D) alliteration, consonance, and assonance

 (E) oxymoron, onomatopeia, and personification

Answer: (A)

This poem does not contain litote, that is, deliberate understatement. The other two parts of (A) are, however correct: the meter is iambic pentamenter and the stanzas contain 11 lines. (B) is all correct: eye rhyme can easily be seen in lines 13 and 15. There are several rhetorical questions, and parallel structure is evident especially in the first stanza with all the repetitions of infinitive verbs such as to *load* and *bless*, to *bend*, [to] *fill* with fruit, to *swell* and to *plump*, and to *set* the budding more. As for letter (C), of course there is much ear rhyme present. Metaphors permeate the stanzas and the narrator's enthusiasm and exaggeration can be identified as nothing but hyperbole. Alliteration (D) is everywhere, for example line 6; consonance (repetition of consonant sounds within words) and assonance (repetition of vowel sounds within words) are also present as in line 9 for consonance: *still more, later flowers*, and line 3 for assonance: *conspiring with him how to load and bless*. Oxymoron (E) is found in line 27, "wailful choir," the lambs "bleat" in onomatopeia, and all of Autumn is personified by this poem.

This type of question is time consuming, but not necessarily difficult unless you are unable to recognize poetic devices. If such a question seems to be taking up too much of your time (especially if such a question is early in the multiple-choice questions), you might want to circle it in the test booklet. Leave a blank space on the scoring sheet, and go back to it after you have responded to the rest of the multiple-choice questions. Never let one question use up too much of your time. Get the rest of the questions completed first, then go back to tackle the more difficult or time consuming questions.

Multiple-choice questions become much easier for you to respond to correctly when you have practiced reading for meaning and close analysis so that they become second nature for you. Now, try your hand at these questions about "The Last Leaf."

"The Last Leaf"

5. Which of the following is NOT true about the poem, "The Last Leaf"?

(A) It is a metrical poem with a structured rhyme scheme.
(B) It is a ballad composed of a series of sestets.
(C) Its lines are not all of the same metrical length.
(D) It is a reflection of one's own mortality.
(E) Its narrator is amused by the sight of the tottering old man.

Answer: (B)

Yes, the poem is composed of a series of sestets. However, the poem is NOT a ballad.

As with question 1 about "To Autumn," this is an EXCEPT question. It is important for you to be very aware of this type of question. First, you may find this question challenging simply because it gives you four out of five responses that are correct. You are used to finding only ONE correct response among incorrect ones. This question actually gives you a wrong response that you must identify. Look out for this type of question.

In addition, the answer (the incorrect statement) is actually partially true. This is also an important test idiosyncrasy you must be on the lookout for. An entire response must be correct (in this case, both parts of the response have to be untrue) in order for the response to be correct. A half-correct answer is not ever going to be the right one for you to choose.

6. The narrator's attitude can BEST be described as

(A) consistent throughout the poem
(B) reflective at the beginning of the poem, moving to the objective
(C) amused by the entire episode
(D) extremely objective by the end of the poem
(E) moving from objective observation to self contemplation

Answer: (E)

You should not find this question too problematic. The poem certainly does not begin in a reflective mode (B). In fact, it opens in a chatty, descriptive mode. Nor is the narrator's attitude the same (A) throughout the poem. There is definite change that takes place. In fact, it is rare in any piece of good literature that the attitude of the narrator or a significant character does not vary. Although the narrator certainly is amused (C) by the vision of the old man, this is not an ongoing amusement on the part of the narrator. Like (A), letter (D) is incorrect. The end of the poem finds the narrator being very reflective of his own inevitable aging (E). In fact, he hopes that he, too, can be like the old man—the last leaf upon the tree.

7. The imagery in stanza four can be BEST described as a(n)

   (A) description of a graveyard

   (B) memories of former lovers

   (C) reference to the demise of all who were cared for

   (D) an old man's befuddled memories

   (E) an alliterative depiction of some old tombs

Answer: (C)

The imagery in this stanza should not be looked at as limited to just former lovers (B). In fact, the old man seems to have lost all whom he loved or cared for, making (C) the correct response. Notice that actually an argument might be made for any of these responses. However, when you are dealing with imagery, you know that you are not necessarily to take anything literally. It is not uncommon for a question that asks for your BEST response to offer more than one "correct" response. What you must do is decide which, among the correct responses is the BEST response.

8. "The Last Leaf" demonstrates the following collection of poetic devices

   (A) end rhyme, iambic pentameter, alliteration

   (B) personification, apostrophe, direct quotation

   (C) uniform stanzas, simile, allegory

   (D) alternating rhyme, sestet, free verse

   (E) hyperbole, heroic couplet, metaphor

Answer: (C)

It is true that parts of (A) are true because the poem is end rhymed and you can readily find alliteration such as in line 19, "mossy marble." Personification (B) is certainly evident as Time does its gardening, and direct quotations cannot be overlooked. However, it does not contain an apostrophe, that is a formal address to an inanimate object. The only part of (D) that is correct is that the poem is comprised of eight sestets. Finally, (E) has only one correct part, that is metaphor. Comparison (also making allegory in (C) correct) is certainly made between the man and the last leaf, or one might argue that the last leaf is his tenuous hold on life and it is the tree itself that represents the old man. Also, although the rhyme scheme within the sestets appears in pairs with each set of longer lines, these lines are not iambic pentameter as is a characteristic of a heroic couplet.

No matter what poem you are given to read—whether it be in the multiple-choice section of the exam or a poem for you to analyze and respond to in essay form, or just a poem you read in your

English class, you will find most or all of the following guidelines helpful. Try to incorporate as many as you can in your first reading of a poem, then use the rest as you answer the questions.

SUMMING UP: GUIDELINES FOR READING A POEM

- Check out the poem's title. In many instances the title alone can tell you a lot about the poem.
- Read the poem carefully; be sure you have a good understanding of the literal meaning of the poem. As you read it, mentally paraphrase what you are reading.
- After you have a handle on what it means literally, you must look at it again for its figurative meaning. Are there underlying metaphors? Which words have special connotations? Are there special references or allusions in the poem?
- What imagery do you find? Be very conscious of what "feeling" words the author is using.
- Is there special diction or syntax to consider? Do any of the words give you information about when the poem might have been written (assuming you do not have that information available to you)? How are the sentences structured? Be particularly aware of the author's use of punctuation.
- Is there a change in the poem? Can you detect any shifts—in narrator, or the tone, or the mood of the piece? Sometimes you can detect this by the setup of the stanzas. Other times you have to look closely at the action within the poem to see if there has been a shift. Sometimes shifts are earmarked by a change in pronoun or a change in verb tense.
- Has the poet used any specific poetic techniques that are important to the analysis? For instance, in John Donne's "A Valediction Forbidding Mourning," the poet's use of conceit—the narrator and his lover's affection explained as a geometry compass used for drawing circle—is the essence of the entire poem. If such a conceit were ignored, analysis would be impossible.
- Are there any details that particularly strike you as worth noting? Can you identify an author's style by these details? And, is that even significant? For example, e. e. cummings and his penchant for using only lower case letters.
- Finally, especially significant for the AP Exam, what is the *tone* of the poem? How do you know that? And then, what is the narrator's *attitude* in the poem? Can you guess at the effect the poem is supposed to have? Can you detect any difference in attitude between the narrator and the poet him/herself? Is that significant?

Perhaps you are feeling overwhelmed by all of this right now. However, if you have been in an Advanced Placement English class this year, no doubt you have already had to do analysis on this level. If you have not had the fortune of such a class, then just take each suggestion on its own merit. Give yourself time to think about the previous suggestions. Look at a couple poems on your own, or access some of the previous AP tests from the College Board website, www.college-board.com/ap, and practice, practice, practice.

Chapter Six: **Prose on the Exam**

- How Prose Appears on the Exam
- Prose in the Essay Section
- Prose Essay Practice Prompts
- Prose in the Multiple-Choice Section
- Prose Multiple-Choice Practice Set and Answer Explanations
- Summing Up: Guidelines for Reading Prose

Like Moliere's gentleman, we all "talk prose." In prose fiction, including novels, short stories, and plays, elements like character development, plot, setting, and narrative structure come into play to a much greater degree than in poetry, although many poetic devices are also used. In prose non-fiction, argument and analysis of an issue come to the fore. Like poetry, prose is a big part of the AP English Literature exam.

PROSE ON THE AP ENGLISH LITERATURE EXAM

The AP exam will test your skills at reading and analyzing prose fiction, with excerpts from novels, short stories, and drama; there may also be the occasional nonfiction excerpt from literary biography or criticism. As in the poetry selections, you are likely to see passages from books not covered in the typical AP course, in the interests of fairness to all students taking the test.

A number of multiple-choice question passages are prose, and the essay section has one passage that is prose analysis (the others are the poetry passage and the open-ended question). This chapter of the book discusses some of the expectations of prose analysis questions. It includes short stories by Kate Chopin and James Joyce to read and analyze. In addition, you will find essay prompts and multiple-choice questions having to do with the prose passages.

PROSE IN THE ESSAY SECTION

With only one or two exceptions, the Advanced Placement Literature and Composition Exam always has had an essay question on prose analysis. The prompts associated with the prose passages might take a form similar to any of the following:

- *Write an essay in which you demonstrate how the narrator of this passage establishes his attitude toward _____.*

- *The following are passages by two different authors. Read the passages carefully, then write a well-organized essay in which you compare the different attitudes of the writers by analyzing the diction and choice of details of each.*

- *Read the passage carefully. Then write an essay that explains how the writer enables us to understand _____. Pay particular attention to such literary devices as tone, word choice, and figurative language.*

- *The following passage comes from _____. Write a carefully constructed essay in which you analyze the narrative techniques and other resources of language that the author uses to characterize the main character of the piece.*

The prose analysis questions ask you to pay particular attention to author's attitude and tone and the methods/techniques the author uses to express the attitudes. Sometimes you will be given a particular idea to focus on; other times you will have to work out the focus of the passage for yourself. Whatever the case, you will need to be particularly tuned into literary devices such as diction, images, details, nuances of connotation, tone, mood, attitude. Of course you must also be conscious of such basic things such as setting, plot, character, and theme.

Usually the passages are not too lengthy, for the test development committee realizes that you only have two hours in which to read, synthesize, and respond to the essays. The committee takes all these things into consideration as they choose the passages and prompts that best go together on each exam. Nevertheless, a passage might be as lengthy as a page. Only occasionally has it been longer.

The following very short Kate Chopin short story, "Story of an Hour," is printed here in its entirety, although it is a bit longer than what you might typically find as a prose passage. It is best in its entirety, however, and it is therefore presented as a total package for your enjoyment and close reading/writing practice.

Knowing that Mrs. Mallard was afflicted with a heart trouble, great care was taken to break to her as gently as possible the news of her husband's death.

(5)   It was her sister Josephine who told her, in broken sentences; veiled hints that revealed in half concealing. Her husband's friend Richards was there, too, near her. It was he who had been in the newspaper office when intelligence of the railroad disas-

(10) ter was received, with Brently Mallard's name leading the list of "killed." He had only taken the time to assure himself of its truth by a second telegram, and had hastened to forestall any less careful, less tender friend in bearing the sad message.

(15)   She did not hear the story as many women have heard the same, with a paralyzed inability to accept its significance. She wept at once, with sudden, wild abandonment, in her sister's arms. When the storm of grief had spent itself she went away to her

(20) room alone. She would have no one follow her.

There stood, facing the open window, a comfortable, roomy armchair. Into this she sank, pressed down by a physical exhaustion that haunted her body and seemed to reach into her soul.

(25)   She could see in the open square before her house the tops of trees that were all aquiver with the new spring life. The delicious breath of rain was in the air. In the street below a peddler was crying his wares. The notes of a distant song which

(30) some one was singing reached her faintly, and countless sparrows were twittering in the eaves.

There were patches of blue sky showing here and there through the clouds that had met and piled one above the other in the west facing her window.

(35)   She sat with her head thrown back upon the cushion of the chair, quite motionless, except when a sob came up into her throat and shook her, as a child who has cried itself to sleep continues to sob in its dreams.

(40)   She was young, with a fair, calm face, whose lines bespoke repression and even a certain strength. But now there was a dull stare in her eyes, whose gaze was fixed away off yonder on one of those patches of blue sky. It was not a glance of

(45) reflection, but rather indicated a suspension of intelligent thought.

There was something coming to her and she was waiting for it, fearfully. What was it? She did not know; it was too subtle and elusive to name.

(50) But she felt it, creeping out of the sky, reaching toward her through the sounds, the scents, the color that filled the air.

Now her bosom rose and fell tumultuously. She was beginning to recognize this thing that was

(55) approaching to possess her, and she was striving to beat it back with her will—as powerless as her two white slender hands would have been.

When she abandoned herself a little whispered word escaped her slightly parted lips. She said it

(60) over and over under her breath: "free, free, free!" The vacant stare and the look of terror that had followed it went from her eyes. They stayed keen and bright. Her pulses beat fast, and the coursing blood warmed and relaxed every inch of her body.

(65)   She did not stop to ask if it were or were not a monstrous joy that held her. A clear and exalted perception enabled her to dismiss the suggestion as trivial.

She knew that she would weep again when she

(70) saw the kind, tender hands folded in death; the face that had never looked save with love upon her, fixed and gray and dead. But she saw beyond that bitter moment a long procession of years to come that would belong to her absolutely. And she opened and

(75) spread her arms out to them in welcome.

There would be no one to live for during those coming years; she would live for herself. There would be no powerful will bending hers in that blind persistence with which men and women believe they

(80) have a right to impose a private will upon a fellow-creature. A kind intention or a cruel intention made the act seem no less a crime as she looked upon it in that brief moment of illumination.

And yet she had loved him—sometimes. Often

(85) she had not. What did it matter! What could love, the unsolved mystery, count for in face of this possession of self-assertion which she suddenly recognized as the strongest impulse of her being!

"Free! Body and soul free!" she kept whispering.

(90)   Josephine was kneeling before the closed door with her lips to the keyhole, imploring for admission. "Louise, open the door! I beg, open the door—you will make yourself ill. What are you doing Louise? For heaven's sake open the door."

(95) "Go away. I am not making myself ill." No; she was drinking in a very elixir of life through that open window.

Her fancy was running riot along those days ahead of her. Spring days, and summer days, and *(100)* all sorts of days that would be her own. She breathed a quick prayer that life might be long. It was only yesterday she had thought with a shudder that life might be long.

She arose at length and opened the door to her *(105)* sister's importunities. There was a feverish triumph in her eyes, and she carried herself unwittingly like a goddess of Victory. She clasped her sister's waist, *(110)* and together they descended the stairs. Richards stood waiting for them at the bottom.

Some one was opening the front door with a latchkey. It was Brently Mallard who entered, a little travel-stained, composedly carrying his grip- *(115)* sack and umbrella. He had been far from the scene of accident, and did not even know there had been one. He stood amazed at Josephine's piercing cry; at Richards' quick motion to screen him from the view of his wife.

(125) But Richards was too late.

When the doctors came they said she had died of heart disease—of joy that kills.

The short story has been reprinted below with some marginal notes. These annotations should give you an idea of the sort of thing you should be considering, if only subconsciously, as you read a prose passage. If you were just reading this short story as a short story, and not as a passage to write about, what could you say about it? What is the plot? What is the setting—the time, the place? What are the conflicts? Who are the characters? What is the theme? How does this story possibly apply to your world?

Story of an Hour

Knowing that <u>Mrs. Mallard</u> was afflicted with a heart trouble, great care was taken to break to her as gently as possible the news of her husband's death.

It was her sister Josephine who told her, in broken sentences; veiled hints that revealed in half concealing. Her husband's friend Richards was there, too, near her. It
(5) was he who had been in the newspaper office when intelligence of the railroad disaster was received, with Brently Mallard's name leading the list of "killed." He had only taken the time to assure himself of its truth by a second telegram, and had hastened to forestall any less careful, less tender friend in bearing the sad message.

She did not hear the story as many women have heard the same, with a paralyzed
(10) inability to accept its significance. She wept at once, with sudden, wild abandonment, in her sister's arms. When the storm of grief had spent itself she went away to her room alone. She would have no one follow her.

There stood, facing the <u>open window</u>, a comfortable, roomy armchair. Into this she sank, pressed down by a physical exhaustion that haunted her body and seemed to
(15) reach into her soul.

She could see in the open square before her house the tops of trees that were all aquiver with the new spring life. The delicious breath of rain was in the air. In the street below a peddler was crying his wares. The notes of a distant song which some one was singing reached her faintly, and countless sparrows were twittering in the eaves.
(20) There were patches of <u>blue sky</u> showing here and there through the clouds that had met and piled one above the other in the west facing her window.

She sat with her head thrown back upon the cushion of the chair, quite motionless, except when a sob came up into her throat and shook her, as a child who has cried itself to sleep continues to sob in its dreams.
(25) She was young, with a fair, calm face, whose lines bespoke repression and even a certain strength. But now there was a dull stare in her eyes, whose gaze was fixed away off yonder on one of those patches of blue sky. It was not a glance of reflection, but rather indicated a suspension of intelligent thought.

There was something coming to her and she was waiting for it, fearfully. What was it?
(30) She did not know; it was too subtle and elusive to name. But she felt it, creeping out of the sky, reaching toward her through the sounds, the scents, the color that filled the air.

Now her bosom rose and fell tumultuously. She was beginning to recognize this thing that was approaching to possess her, and she was striving to beat it back with her will—as powerless as her two white slender hands would have been.
(35) When she abandoned herself a little whispered word escaped her slightly parted lips. She said it over and over under her breath: "free, free, free!" The vacant stare and the look of terror that had followed it went from her eyes. They stayed keen and bright. Her pulses beat fast, and the coursing blood warmed and relaxed every inch of her body.

She did not stop to ask if it were or were not a <u>monstrous joy</u> that held her. A clear
(40) and exalted perception enabled her to dismiss the suggestion as trivial.

She knew that she would weep again when she saw the kind, tender hands folded in death; the face that had never looked save with love upon her, fixed and gray and dead. But she saw beyond that bitter moment a long procession of years to come that would belong to her absolutely. And she opened and spread her arms out to them in welcome.
(45) There would be no one to live for during those coming years; she would live for herself. There would be no powerful will bending hers in that blind persistence with

---

Note she is Mrs. Mallard here. Later she will be referred to by first name.

Mallard is a male duck—as if she is just the female counterpart of the husband—a Mrs. Male species?

Open window implies some sort of release, not closed in or restrained in any way.

Rain = water = baptism to new life?

Blue sky as a symbol of good (or better) times?

What's happening? What is she realizing?

Unable to avoid the inevitable.

Exaltation, no sadness.

Oxymoron reflects the irony.

An epiphany or turning point?

KAPLAN
Test Prep and Admissions

which men and women believe they have a right to impose a private will upon a fellow-creature. A kind intention or a cruel intention made the act seem no less a crime as she looked upon it in that brief <u>moment of illumination</u>.

(50)   And yet she had loved him—sometimes. Often she had not. What did it matter! What could love, the unsolved mystery, count for in face of this possession of self-assertion which she suddenly recognized as the strongest impulse of her being!

This is important! Critical to the story.

<u>"Free! Body and soul free!" she kept whispering.</u>

Josephine was kneeling before the closed door with her lips to the keyhole, implor-
(55) ing for admission. "<u>Louise</u>, open the door! I beg, open the door—you will make yourself ill. What are you doing Louise? For heaven's sake open the door."

"Go away. I am not making myself ill." No; she was drinking in a very elixir of life through that open window.

The ultimate paradox.

Her fancy was running riot along those days ahead of her. Spring days, and summer
(60) days, and all sorts of days that would be her own. She breathed a quick prayer that life might be long. It was only yesterday she had thought with a shudder that life might be long.

She arose at length and opened the door to her sister's importunities. There was a feverish triumph in her eyes, and she carried herself unwittingly like a <u>goddess of</u>

Victorious in her new-found freedom.

(65) <u>Victory</u>. She clasped her sister's waist, and together they descended the stairs. Richards stood waiting for them at the bottom.

Some one was opening the front door with a latchkey. It was Brently Mallard who entered, a little travel-stained, composedly carrying his grip-sack and umbrella. He had been far from the scene of accident, and did not even know there had been one. He
(70) stood amazed at Josephine's piercing cry; at Richards' quick motion to screen him from the view of his wife.

This is the ultimate ironic oxymoron. Note "heart disease."

But Richards was too late.

When the doctors came they said she had died of <u>heart disease—of joy that kills</u>.

Discussion

Now that this short story has been summarily analyzed and annotated for you, you should be able see how several of the suggested prompts might be answered. A few characteristics have been noted about the main character, Louise Mallard, and several significant items have been annotated concerning underlying meaning and significant plot movement. The entire point of the AP English Literature and Composition Exam is that students are able to respond successfully to any prompt, regardless of what passage they are presented. Extensive reading and continuous writing practice is the best way to prepare for any question with which you may be presented. Whether you are asked to discuss Louise Mallard's shift in attitude toward the death of her husband, or the author's attitude toward the repressed situation of women shortly after the turn of the 20th century, you will be ready.

Imagery abounds in this passage—the name Mallard is the family name. Since a mallard is actually a reference to the male of that duck species, being Mrs. Mallard suggests the second-class nature of the wife's position. Louise goes to her room and sits by an open window—not closed, barred, or heavily curtained. In fact several times the story mentions the blue sky and the rain. Blue skies traditionally represent good (or at least better) times. Rain is cleansing, perhaps suggesting the beginning of a new life. Of course Louise herself, yet a young woman, experiences an emotional realization—an epiphany perhaps—arousing in her a recognition of future possibilities. These are just a few of the images you should pick up from reading this story.

The structure of the passage/short story is also interesting. Notice that the paragraphs are extremely short, almost journalistic in nature. It is probable that Chopin used this structure to enhance the sense that this story is a montage of feelings, as a flood of sensual and emotional impressions overwhelm Louise. Another feature of this story is how quickly the action begins and how abruptly it concludes. In one swoop, Louise's future opens to her, but just as suddenly it is removed.

Diction and word *connotation* are another aspect of this story worth investigating. Of course, the obvious things such as taking a train, receiving a telegram and carrying a grip are terminology identifying the setting of the story. More importantly, however, are the author's skillful word combinations and suggestions, which help establish the tone of the entire story. Refer to the annotated passage for the line numbers of the following citations. Louise "wept at once…with wild abandonment" (line 10) in a sudden, but rather brief "storm of grief," (line 11) similar, perhaps to the storm that had so recently brought the cleansing rains that washed the air and the streets outside her window. Someone outside her window is "singing" (line 19) and "countless sparrows were twittering in the eaves" (line 19). These words suggest that life outside is liberated, happy, and something to look forward to. In fact, despite her "powerless" (line 34) struggle against the "something" (line 29) that is dawning upon her, she murmurs the words "free, free, free!" (line 36) like the mantra of a praying monk. The story describes her as having a "monstrous joy" (line 39) and arriving at an "exalted perception" (line 40) and experiencing a "moment of illumination" (line 49). Louise may have loved her husband, but her will was not her own. Now she can "live for herself" (lines 45–46) without any "bending" (line 46) to her husband's "private will" (line 47). All of these words lead up to the pivotal phrase in the story where Louise repeats again, "Free! Body and soul free!" (line 53). Now all the days ahead of her will "belong to her absolutely" (line 44). In this frame of mind, then, she opens her locked door and descends the stairs "in feverish triumph [like] the goddess Victory" (lines 64–65). But alas, her triumph is to be short lived as her oblivious but quite-alive husband enters the front door. With ultimate ingenuity, Kate

Chopin brings on the finale with the best of her clever diction, for the words in last lines are so well chosen: The doctors declare that Louise Mallard has died of "heart disease"; her demise was a result of "joy that kills" (line 73).

This last line, of course should lead you right into the consideration of the underlying *irony* within this story. We know from the onset that Mrs. Mallard suffers from a weak heart. Yet, after all that has developed within this very concise but full story, it is unlikely that the "joy" is what kills her, but rather the abruptness of its unexpected extinction. That, of course, is what makes this story so very successful.

Conflict alters throughout this short story. At first we see Louise in conflict with the emotions evoked by her husband's sudden death. How she responds, and how polite society might expect her to respond are a bit different, and we can see that in her very brief "storm of grief" (line 11). In addition, she wishes to be alone, shunning the ministrations of her sister and her husband's friend, Richard. As she settles into the peacefulness of her room, we see Louise at odds with her own burgeoning emotions. Unbidden, her "fancy runs riot" (line 59). She is described as "powerless" (line 34) as she "strives to beat [her feelings] back" (line 33). Eventually she comes to terms with her feelings and her situation. She sees herself not as a bereft widow, but as a liberated free-willed female. Finally, in triumph—over herself and over society of that time, she opens the door and enters into a new world. Unexpectedly, however, conflict rears its ugly head once again when her husband (not dead at all) enters the house, unaware of what has happened. This last conflict, of course, is what undoes her "weak heart."

Tone and *attitude* evolve from such things as *images, diction, conflict and syntax*, as well as the *ironic finale* of this particular story. All authors use these elements and others to craft their own distinct writing. Increasing the breadth of your reading, taking time before the test to decode passages in a manner such as above, and writing about the passages you analyze—these are practice activities that will help you the most on the AP prose analysis essays. The more comfortable and adept you become at writing prose analysis, the more assured you can be of receiving an upper half score on the prose analysis essay.

Reading for Meaning

When you read prose for meaning you should be sure that your reading includes the following:

- **Question** what you are reading. Ask yourself if you are consciously understanding what you are reading.
- **Comment and reflect** in your mind the ideas that are being presented in the passage.
- **Predict** what may be coming up based on what you've already read.
- **Pause** briefly and think about what you have just read.
- **Evaluate** what you have read.
- **Note** quotations that are particularly challenging or unusual. You can do this by simply underlining or annotating a section of the text.
- **Recognize** words; attempt to figure out meaning from context.

It is true that you will hardly have time to do all of these things on the AP Exam itself, but you will be able to do some of them. In the interim, these are helpful habits to incorporate into your reading. Then, when you are under timed conditions such as the AP exam, these habits come naturally.

PROSE ESSAY PRACTICE PROMPTS: "STORY OF AN HOUR"

Now let us make some conjectures about some possible prompts and how you might best read the short story in order to respond to these prompts.

- *Read the following passage carefully. Then, in a well-organized essay discuss how the tone of the passage changes. Pay particular attention to literary elements such as diction and syntax and how they help the reader to recognize the changes in tone.*

- *Authors of short stories, novels and plays take some time to decide upon just the right title for their literary works. In this short story, "Story of an Hour," by Kate Chopin, discuss this title as appropriate for the piece. Be sure to consider not only what happens within the story, but also how the title relates to the phrase "brief moment of illumination" that the main character experiences.*

- *The following short story is the story about the death of a husband. Read the passage carefully; in a well organized essay explain how the main character's attitude towards her husband's death changes within the story. Be sure to discuss how literary devices such as tone, diction, imagery, and figurative language help us to realize the main character's attitude.*

- *Some critics have called the following short story an ultimate irony. Read the passage carefully, and in a well-constructed essay explain how Kate Chopin, the author, has so successfully developed this irony within the story.*

- *Write a carefully constructed essay in which you analyze the literary techniques and other resources of language that the author uses to characterize Louise Mallard.*

- *The essence of successful literature is the element of conflict. Read the following short story by Kate Chopin. In a well-organized essay, discuss the various elements of conflict within the passage and how these conflicts enhance the story.*

PROSE ANALYSIS

After reading prose for meaning, you are ready to begin analysis. The following chart should help you with any prose passage you may come across. Of course, this is a lot of detail, you say. How are you expected to do all that and write an essay and do it all in 40 minutes? The reality is that you are not. The detailed breakdown you see next is, like the above suggestions for reading for meaning, is a practice activity. With practice, you will find yourself more able to do this sort of analysis automatically, almost simultaneously with your close reading of a passage.

Read the following excerpt from the short story "Araby," by James Joyce, and study the analysis chart that follows.

North Richmond Street, being blind, was a quiet
street except at the hour when the Christian
Brothers' School set the boys free. An uninhabited
house of two storeys stood at the blind end,
(5) detached from its neighbours in a square ground.
The other houses of the street, conscious of decent
lives within them, gazed at one another with
brown imperturbable faces. . . .

When the short days of winter came, dusk fell
(10) before we had well eaten our dinners. When we
met in the street the houses had grown sombre.
The space of sky above us was the colour of ever-
changing violet and towards it the lamps of the
street lifted their feeble lanterns. The cold air
(15) stung us and we played till our bodies glowed.
Our shouts echoed in the silent street. The career
of our play brought us through the dark muddy
lanes behind the houses, where we ran the gauntlet of the rough tribes from the cottages, to the
(20) back doors of the dark dripping gardens where
odours arose from the ashpits, to the dark odorous stables where a coachman smoothed and
combed the horse or shook music from the buckled harness. When we returned to the street, light
(25) from the kitchen windows had filled the areas. If
my uncle was seen turning the corner, we hid in
the shadow until we had seen him safely housed.
Or if Mangan's sister came out on the doorstep to
call her brother in to his tea, we watched her from
(30) our shadow peer up and down the street. We waited to see whether she would remain or go in and,
if she remained, we left our shadow and walked
up to Mangan's steps resignedly. She was waiting
for us, her figure defined by the light from the
(35) half-opened door. Her brother always teased her
before he obeyed, and I stood by the railings looking at her. Her dress swung as she moved her
body, and the soft rope of her hair tossed from
side to side.
(40) Every morning I lay on the floor in the front
parlour watching her door. The blind was pulled
down to within an inch of the sash so that I could
not be seen. When she came out on the doorstep
my heart leaped. I ran to the hall, seized my books
(45) and followed her. I kept her brown figure always
in my eye and, when we came near the point at
which our ways diverged, I quickened my pace

and passed her. This happened morning after
morning. I had never spoken to her, except for a
(50) few casual words, and yet her name was like a
summons to all my foolish blood.

Her image accompanied me even in places the
most hostile to romance. On Saturday evenings
when my aunt went marketing I had to go to carry
(55) some of the parcels. We walked through the flaring streets, jostled by drunken men and bargaining women, amid the curses of labourers, the shrill
litanies of shop-boys who stood on guard by the
barrels of pigs' cheeks, the nasal chanting of
(60) street-singers, who sang a come-all-you about
O'Donovan Rossa, or a ballad about the troubles
in our native land. These noises converged in a
single sensation of life for me: I imagined that I
bore my chalice safely through a throng of foes.
(65) Her name sprang to my lips at moments in
strange prayers and praises which I myself did not
understand. My eyes were often full of tears (I
could not tell why) and at times a flood from my
heart seemed to pour itself out into my bosom. I
(70) thought little of the future. I did not know
whether I would ever speak to her or not or, if I
spoke to her, how I could tell her of my confused
adoration. But my body was like a harp and her
words and gestures were like fingers running upon
(75) the wires.

One evening I went into the back drawing-
room in which the priest had died. It was a dark
rainy evening and there was no sound in the
house. Through one of the broken panes I heard
(80) the rain impinge upon the earth, the fine incessant
needles of water playing in the sodden beds. Some
distant lamp or lighted window gleamed below
me. I was thankful that I could see so little. All my
senses seemed to desire to veil themselves and,
(85) feeling that I was about to slip from them, I
pressed the palms of my hands together until they
trembled, murmuring: 'O love! O love!' many
times.

Araby

Observations	Examples from Text	Effect on Reader
1. Author's purpose: Why is the piece being written? What response does the writer wish to evoke from the reader?	Sounds like exposition—setting the scene for what might take place later.	This passage gives a good sense of setting. It also arouses interest in what may happen.
2. Audience How is the audience indicated? Is the audience directly addressed? Does the writer use "you"?	No indication of a human audience.	Reader gets some sense of setting and may be curious about the narrator.
3. Style of Language Is it formal, colloquial, archaic, dialect, poetic, abstract, concrete? Is sarcasm, satire, parody evident?	Straightforward, no pretense. Rather formal for a child-narrator.	"Child" narrator is most likely now older due to unchildlike language.
4. Diction What words stand out? Are there significant connotations? What words give you TONE clues?	Good use of subject-verb combinations such as *houses gazed, houses had grown somber, bodies glowed, noises converged.*	Words create images, give the reader a good "feel" for what the narrator is telling us about.
5. Syntax Is there unusual word order, periodic sentences, parallel construction? Any other sentence structure oddities?	Variety of sentence structure; a few simple statements, but most are compound and complex. Nice parallelism (anaphora) in paragraph 3 in the repetition of "I."	Easy to follow, sentences seem to flow, keeping the reader interested.
6. Selection of Detail What details seem important? What do these details reveal? Do they establish any pattern? Any details seem to be "missing"?	Narrator doesn't just say he's smitten. Paragraphs 4 and 5 show us just how badly he is enamored by this girl.	It's easy to understand what the narrator is telling us. Details help me feel like I am right there watching and spying with the narrator.

Observations	Examples from Text	Effect on Reader
7. Imagery To what senses does the writer appeal? Is there a pattern to the imagery used? Does any one sense predominate? Is there any shift in emphasis?	Most senses are included, sight, sound, smell, feel—*imperturbable faces, bodies glowed, nasal chanting, body like a harp.*	The abundance of imagery reminds the reader that this is a memoir of an older person recalling childhood experiences.
8. Figurative Language Check for symbols, similes, metaphors, analogies, oxymoron, hyperbole, metonomy, paradox.	Paragraph 4 is loaded: a simple marketing trip becomes a religious ritual. Personification, metaphor seem to dominate	Figurative language controls this passage. From the jingle of the horse harness to the litany of the vendors, the author drowns us in figurative language.
9. Structure Any significant organizational pattern? Any shifts or significant deviations?	No significant structure other than an overall, panoramic to the more specific view	Reader gets overall picture then is enmeshed in the story
10. Tone What word(s) describe the writer's attitude toward the subject and the audience? Do "feelings" shift w/in the piece?	First and foremost, the tone is nostalgic. By paragraph 4, however, the tone shifts to reverential, even religious in nature	At first the reader assumes a reminiscent story from child-hood. By the end of this selection, the narrator seems obsessive.

This reading prose for meaning is just a starting activity for close reading. Now read the entire short story *Araby* by James Joyce. Following the short story is a closer look at prose analysis of this particular passage, focusing particularly on setting and point of view. In addition, the short story is followed by some multiple-choice questions that will test your understanding of the passage based on your mastery of close reading skills.

North Richmond Street, being blind, was a quiet street except at the hour when the Christian Brothers' School set the boys free. An uninhabited house of two storeys stood at the blind end,
(5) detached from its neighbours in a square ground. The other houses of the street, conscious of decent lives within them, gazed at one another with brown imperturbable faces.

The former tenant of our house, a priest, had
(10) died in the back drawing-room. Air, musty from having been long enclosed, hung in all the rooms, and the waste room behind the kitchen was littered with old useless papers. Among these I found a few paper-covered books, the pages of
(15) which were curled and damp: *The Abbot*, by Walter Scott, *The Devout Communicant*, and *The Memoirs of Vidocq*. I liked the last best because its leaves were yellow. The wild garden behind the house contained a central apple-tree and a few
(20) straggling bushes, under one of which I found the late tenant's rusty bicycle-pump. He had been a very charitable priest; in his will he had left all his money to institutions and the furniture of his house to his sister.

(25) When the short days of winter came, dusk fell before we had well eaten our dinners. When we met in the street the houses had grown sombre. The space of sky above us was the colour of ever-changing violet and towards it the lamps of the
(30) street lifted their feeble lanterns. The cold air stung us and we played till our bodies glowed. Our shouts echoed in the silent street. The career of our play brought us through the dark muddy lanes behind the houses, where we ran the gauntlet of
(35) the rough tribes from the cottages, to the back doors of the dark dripping gardens where odours arose from the ashpits, to the dark odorous stables where a coachman smoothed and combed the horse or shook music from the buckled harness.
(40) When we returned to the street, light from the kitchen windows had filled the areas. If my uncle was seen turning the corner, we hid in the shadow until we had seen him safely housed. Or if Mangan's sister came out on the doorstep to call
(45) her brother in to his tea, we watched her from our shadow peer up and down the street. We waited to see whether she would remain or go in and, if she

remained, we left our shadow and walked up to Mangan's steps resignedly. She was waiting for us,
(50) her figure defined by the light from the half-opened door. Her brother always teased her before he obeyed, and I stood by the railings looking at her. Her dress swung as she moved her body, and the soft rope of her hair tossed from side to side.

(55) Every morning I lay on the floor in the front parlour watching her door. The blind was pulled down to within an inch of the sash so that I could not be seen. When she came out on the doorstep my heart leaped. I ran to the hall, seized my books
(60) and followed her. I kept her brown figure always in my eye and, when we came near the point at which our ways diverged, I quickened my pace and passed her. This happened morning after morning. I had never spoken to her, except for a
(65) few casual words, and yet her name was like a summons to all my foolish blood.

Her image accompanied me even in places the most hostile to romance. On Saturday evenings when my aunt went marketing I had to go to
(70) carry some of the parcels. We walked through the flaring streets, jostled by drunken men and bar-gaining women, amid the curses of labourers, the shrill litanies of shop-boys who stood on guard by the barrels of pigs' cheeks, the nasal chanting of
(75) street-singers, who sang a come-all-you about O'Donovan Rossa, or a ballad about the troubles in our native land. These noises converged in a single sensation of life for me: I imagined that I bore my chalice safely through a throng of foes.
(80) Her name sprang to my lips at moments in strange prayers and praises which I myself did not understand. My eyes were often full of tears (I could not tell why) and at times a flood from my heart seemed to pour itself out into my bosom. I
(85) thought little of the future. I did not know whether I would ever speak to her or not or, if I spoke to her, how I could tell her of my confused adoration. But my body was like a harp and her words and gestures were like fingers running
(90) upon the wires.

One evening I went into the back drawing-room in which the priest had died. It was a dark rainy evening and there was no sound in the house. Through one of the broken panes I heard

(95) the rain impinge upon the earth, the fine incessant needles of water playing in the sodden beds. Some distant lamp or lighted window gleamed below me. I was thankful that I could see so little. All my senses seemed to desire to veil themselves (100) and, feeling that I was about to slip from them, I pressed the palms of my hands together until they trembled, murmuring: "O love! O love!" many times.

At last she spoke to me. When she addressed the (105) first words to me I was so confused that I did not know what to answer. She asked me was I going to Araby. I forgot whether I answered yes or no. It would be a splendid bazaar; she said she would love to go.

(110) "And why can't you?" I asked.

While she spoke she turned a silver bracelet round and round her wrist. She could not go, she said, because there would be a retreat that week in her convent. Her brother and two other boys were (115) fighting for their caps, and I was alone at the railings. She held one of the spikes, bowing her head towards me. The light from the lamp opposite our door caught the white curve of her neck, lit up her hair that rested there and, falling, lit up the hand (120) upon the railing. It fell over one side of her dress and caught the white border of a petticoat, just visible as she stood at ease.

"It's well for you," she said.

"If I go," I said, "I will bring you something."

(125) What innumerable follies laid waste my waking and sleeping thoughts after that evening! I wished to annihilate the tedious intervening days. I chafed against the work of school. At night in my bedroom and by day in the classroom her image came (130) between me and the page I strove to read. The syllables of the word Araby were called to me through the silence in which my soul luxuriated and cast an Eastern enchantment over me. I asked for leave to go to the bazaar on Saturday night. (135) My aunt was surprised, and hoped it was not some Freemason affair. I answered few questions in class. I watched my master's face pass from amiability to sternness; he hoped I was not beginning to idle. I could not call my wandering (140) thoughts together. I had hardly any patience with the serious work of life which, now that it stood

between me and my desire, seemed to me child's play, ugly monotonous child's play.

On Saturday morning I reminded my uncle that I wished to go to the bazaar in the evening. He (145) was fussing at the hallstand, looking for the hatbrush, and answered me curtly:

"Yes, boy, I know."

As he was in the hall I could not go into the front parlour and lie at the window. I felt the (150) house in bad humour and walked slowly towards the school. The air was pitilessly raw and already my heart misgave me.

When I came home to dinner my uncle had not yet been home. Still it was early. I sat staring at the (155) clock for some time and, when its ticking began to irritate me, I left the room. I mounted the staircase and gained the upper part of the house. The high, cold, empty, gloomy rooms liberated me and I went from room to room singing. From the (160) front window I saw my companions playing below in the street. Their cries reached me weakened and indistinct and, leaning my forehead against the cool glass, I looked over at the dark house where she lived. I may have stood there for an (165) hour, seeing nothing but the brown-clad figure cast by my imagination, touched discreetly by the lamplight at the curved neck, at the hand upon the railings and at the border below the dress.

When I came downstairs again I found Mrs. (170) Mercer sitting at the fire. She was an old, garrulous woman, a pawnbroker's widow, who collected used stamps for some pious purpose. I had to endure the gossip of the tea-table. The meal was prolonged beyond an hour and still my uncle did (175) not come. Mrs. Mercer stood up to go: she was sorry she couldn't wait any longer, but it was after eight o'clock and she did not like to be out late, as the night air was bad for her. When she had gone I began to walk up and down the room, clenching (180) my fists. My aunt said:

"I'm afraid you may put off your bazaar for this night of Our Lord."

At nine o'clock I heard my uncle's latchkey in the hall door. I heard him talking to himself and (185) heard the hallstand rocking when it had received the weight of his overcoat. I could interpret these signs. When he was midway through his dinner I

asked him to give me the money to go to the
bazaar. He had forgotten.

(190)　　"The people are in bed and after their first sleep
now," he said.

I did not smile. My aunt said to him energeti-
cally:

"Can't you give him the money and let him go?
(195) You've kept him late enough as it is."

My uncle said he was very sorry he had forgotten. He said he believed in the old saying: "All
work and no play makes Jack a dull boy." He asked
me where I was going and, when I told him a sec-
(200) ond time, he asked me did I know The Arab's
Farewell to his Steed. When I left the kitchen he
was about to recite the opening lines of the piece
to my aunt.

I held a florin tightly in my hand as I strode
(205) down Buckingham Street towards the station. The
sight of the streets thronged with buyers and glar-
ing with gas recalled to me the purpose of my
journey. I took my seat in a third-class carriage of
a deserted train. After an intolerable delay the
(210) train moved out of the station slowly. It crept
onward among ruinous houses and over the twin
kling river. At Westland Row Station a crowd of
people pressed to the carriage doors; but the
porters moved them back, saying that it was a spe-
(215) cial train for the bazaar. I remained alone in the
bare carriage. In a few minutes the train drew up
beside an improvised wooden platform. I passed
out on to the road and saw by the lighted dial of a
clock that it was ten minutes to ten. In front of me
(220) was a large building which displayed the magical
name.

I could not find any sixpenny entrance and,
fearing that the bazaar would be closed, I passed
in quickly through a turnstile, handing a shilling
(225) to a weary-looking man. I found myself in a big
hall girded at half its height by a gallery. Nearly all
the stalls were closed and the greater part of the
hall was in darkness. I recognized a silence like
that which pervades a church after a service. I
(230) walked into the centre of the bazaar timidly. A few
people were gathered about the stalls which were
still open. Before a curtain, over which the words
Café Chantant were written in coloured lamps,
two men were counting money on a salver. I lis-
(235) tened to the fall of the coins.

Remembering with difficulty why I had come, I
went over to one of the stalls and examined porce-
lain vases and flowered tea-sets. At the door of the
stall a young lady was talking and laughing with
(240) two young gentlemen. I remarked their English
accents and listened vaguely to their conversation.

"O, I never said such a thing!"

"O, but you did!"

"O, but I didn't!"

(245)　"Didn't she say that?"

"Yes. I heard her."

"O, there's a… fib!"

Observing me, the young lady came over and
asked me did I wish to buy anything. The tone of
(250) her voice was not encouraging; she seemed to have
spoken to me out of a sense of duty. I looked
humbly at the great jars that stood like eastern
guards at either side of the dark entrance to the
stall and murmured:

(255)　"No, thank you."

The young lady changed the position of one of
the vases and went back to the two young men.
They began to talk of the same subject. Once or
twice the young lady glanced at me over her
(260) shoulder.

I lingered before her stall, though I knew my
stay was useless, to make my interest in her wares
seem the more real. Then I turned away slowly
and walked down the middle of the bazaar. I
(265) allowed the two pennies to fall against the six-
pence in my pocket. I heard a voice call from one
end of the gallery that the light was out. The
upper part of the hall was now completely dark.

Gazing up into the darkness I saw myself as a
(270) creature driven and derided by vanity; and my
eyes burned with anguish and anger.

Discussion

"Araby" is one of James Joyce's celebrated short stories. He is known for rambling, stream of con-sciousness from his characters. This particular stylistic quality of Joyce makes reading his works a challenging task indeed. Nevertheless, you should find this particular story, from a series of stories he wrote, called *The Dubliners*, not an overwhelming challenge to read and understand.

You probably quickly deduced that this is not an American short story. Just the British spellings should be enough to make that evident to you. In addition, the setting is not reminiscent of an American town. Nevertheless, the situation is not unlike those you might have found in small town America in the '30s, '40s, and early '50s. This would be especially true if such an American town were influenced by only one or two strong religious denominations. Joyce's stories are totally influ-enced by the strong domination of the Irish Catholic church.

Tone and Point of View

Although the story is told in first person viewpoint of the young adolescent male narrator, this nar-rator is mature well beyond the experience of this story. This mature man reminisces about his youthful hopes, desires, and frustrations. Because of the maturity of the voice, an ironic view is presented of the institutions and people surrounding the boy. This ironic view would be impossible for the immature, emotionally involved mind of the boy himself. You might remember that in *To Kill a Mockingbird*, Harper Lee creates a similar narrator when the older Scout tells us her story in a similar manner. In both of these literary pieces, the narrator consistently maintains full sensitivity to the youthful trials and anguish. From the first to last, the reader can recognize the earlier dreams of the child narrators in these literary pieces.

The opening of "Araby," which sets the scene, prepares the reader for the conflict that exists between the loveliness of the ideal and the drabness of the actual. Descriptive words show the narrator's consciousness of the boy's response to beauty and the response of the neighborhood people who seem blind to any sort of loveliness. Notice the narrator tells us about the "blind" houses, inhabited by "decent" people who stare unseeingly at one another (paragraph 1). He describes the house as drab and the barrenness of the garden is contrasted with the former owner's (a priest) worldliness. The narrator challenges us to reconcile the nice furniture and secu-lar literature left by the former owner to the unproductive garden with its "few straggling bushes" (paragraph 2).

When a neighboring girl transfixes the boy narrator, she represents for him (as we infer from the "older" voice of the narrator) all that is pure and good and beautiful. She is the ideal, the embodi-ment of all his boyish dreams of the burgeoning physical as well as the incarnation of all that is holy and sacred. He is alone as a boy with his view of impossible loveliness among the reality of dirty streets, empty carriage cars, and a tawdry bazaar. This is irony at its subtle best.

By using the boy/man narrator, the author allows the reader to see the ironic discrepancies between what is real and what is only imagined. Despite the dead house on a dead street in a dying city, the young boy, not unlike Don Quixote, is stubbornly determined to "bear his chalice safely through a throng of foes" (lines 78–79). It is this very throng—screaming street vendors, apathetic bazaar clerks, and junky trinkets—that eventually betray the narrator's self deception. His living dream is illusory at best, and he curses himself for the vain folly that it could be any more than what it is.

Imagery and Figurative Language

Try as he might, James Joyce could never shake his Irish Catholic heritage. It is impossible not to see this influence in his writing. "Araby" is no exception.

The setting itself physically resembles a church. North Richmond Street is composed of two rows of houses with "brown imperturbable (pewlike?) faces" (line 8), leading down to the tall "uninhabited house" (empty altar?) in lines 3–4. Even the narrator's garden contains a central image, that of the apple tree. It seems that all else in this "garden of paradise" is gone except for a "few straggling bushes" (lines 19–20).

Moral decay is everywhere—the Garden of Eden behind the house has perished. The boy's own feelings toward the girl seem to be greatly confused. Sometimes he supplicates her with prayer, other times his newly found sexual desires emerge. She seems haloed by (holy?) light in the doorway, but he continues to spy on her through closed curtains. He bears his chalice through the throngs like a holy acolyte, but his adoration for her is entangled with his desire to please her with materialistic charms or trinkets.

Much like Holden Caulfield, this narrator wishes to keep things pure and idealistic. He looks on from afar, but when he does speak to his "sacred Virgin" it is not about love and holiness, but about a materialistic local bazaar. And the bazaar itself reflects the confusion: it is not a local church fete, but a far-away and mysterious, materialistic place called Araby, reminiscent of shifting whispering sands, not drab and dingy streets that smell of the local ash pit.

The boy narrator becomes a crusader to the mysterious east (Araby) where he finds not the Holy Grail, but a dark, dank stall filled with junky trinkets and people who do not even "see" him. In the end he realizes the folly of it all. "Gazing up into the darkness I saw myself as a creature driven and derided by vanity; and my eyes burned with anguish and anger" (lines 269–271).

Setting

Most students, when asked to discuss the setting of a work of literature, will answer that it consists of the time and place. It is, in fact, much more than that. The complicated world of the setting is essential to the understanding of a work of fiction: It reveals the atmosphere or mood of the work. It often yields clues to the tone that will eventually emerge. Setting may function either alone or in conjunction with other functions: 1) establish mood and atmosphere; 2) foreshadow events; 3) serve as a symbol; 4) reflect the emotional conditions of the characters in the work; 5) introduce or enrich the theme of a work; and 6) reveal characters' attributes. See how the setting anticipates the rest of the story in "Araby": "North Richmond Street, being blind, was a quiet street except at the hour when the Christian Brothers School set the boys free. An uninhabited house of two stories stood at the blind end, detached from its neighbors in a square ground. The other houses on the street, conscious of decent lives within them, gazed at one another with brown imperturbable faces." In fact, it is just this "blindness" that disturbs the narrator. It is not until he can "see" for himself how hopeless his dreams are that he can see that he is the one who has been blind, not the others in the story. At the end of the story, the main character, who has been wandering through a dim, poorly lighted bazaar, is left in the "dark" when someone turns the lights off. It is not until then that he realizes how vain and silly he has been. With the turning off of the lights, it seems that he can at once see things for what they truly are. All of this relates to the literary concept of setting.

Needless to say, volumes have been written on just this one short story. It is truly packed with complex secrets to be unraveled. As mentioned before, no passage on an Advanced Placement English Literature and Composition will be this lengthy. Nevertheless, this story does offer readers a wealth of ideas to contemplate.

PROSE IN THE MULTIPLE-CHOICE SECTION

The Multiple-Choice Section of the Advanced Placement English Literature and Composition Exam consists of four or five passages with questions following these passages. You'll definitely be seeing prose in this section.

You will not have the time to do an in-depth analysis of a passage on the multiple-choice section—remember, you have about 12–15 minutes per passage. On the multiple-choice section of the test, you will have to read for meaning, and use your close analysis and annotation habits, circling, underlining, and evaluating as you read. Then you will attack the questions, returning to the passage for the information you need to answer each one.

The best strategy for preparing for this section of the test is to familiarize yourself with the types of questions you may face; this in turn will help you with your reading skills, since you will know what types of things to be on the lookout for. Below you will find a selection of AP-type multiple-choice questions based on the full-length story "Araby" that we've just read and discussed. Refer to the complete version for the correct line and paragraph citations as you do the exercises.

"Araby"

1. The tone of "Araby" is BEST described by the words

    (A) sentimental and romantic
    (B) reminiscent and ironic
    (C) optimistic and humorous
    (D) religious and sanctimonious
    (E) satirical and irreverent

Answer: (B)

The overall tone of Araby is reminiscent and ironic. The diction and sense of hindsight indicate a narrator who is looking back at this incident from his youth. Irony comes into play in the contrast between the boy's romantic vision, that of a crusader carrying a chalice (lines 78–79), filled with an "Eastern enchantment" (line 133) that Araby casts over him, and the final disappointment of the sordid, "useless" (line 262) trip to the bazaar. Looking at the other answers, the boy's vision of Mangan's sister is ideally romantic, but the piece's overall tone is too harsh to be sentimental (A); remember that both terms must be right for a correct answer. There's nothing optimistic or humorous in the tone from the stolid beginning (C), and the story ends on a note of anguish. While religion certainly sets the tone of the piece, the tone is not smug (D). Irony is a better characterization of the tone than satire; the boy's sufferings are not pilloried by the author, and the tone is not irreverent.

2. Lines 6–8, "The other houses of the street, conscious of decent lives within them, gazed at one another with brown imperturbable faces," demonstrate

   (A) chiasmus
   (B) personification
   (C) alliteration
   (D) simile
   (E) asyndeton

Answer: (B)

The houses are given the human qualities of consciousness and sight ("gazed at one another"), as well as faces, making personification the best answer. Chiasmus is a figure of speech in which the order of the terms in two parallel clauses is reversed, as in "Ask not what your country can do for you; ask what you can do for your country"(A). Alliteration is the repetition of initial sounds, usually in close proximity (C). There are no similes, comparisons using *as* or *like,* in this sentence (D). An asyndeton is a style in which conjunctions are omitted, as in Caesar's "I came, I saw, I conquered" (E). Be sure to refer to the Key Terminology chapter for definitions of any terms you might not understand.

3. The sentence "The career of our play brought us through the dark muddy lanes behind the houses, where we ran the gauntlet of the rough tribes from the cottages, to the back doors of the dark dripping gardens where odours arose from the ashpits, to the dark odorous stables where a coachman smoothed and combed the horse or shook music from the buckled harness" (lines 32–39) contains

   (A) alliteration and parallel structure
   (B) metaphor and simile
   (C) imagery and rhetoric
   (D) irony and exposition
   (E) idiom and synechdoche

Answer: (A)

This rich sentence shows alliteration in the "dark dripping" gardens, and uses parallel structure ("to the back . . .to the dark . . .") to create a rhythmic feeling; the repetition of "dark" three times enhances this effect. Metaphor is certainly present ("rough tribes," "shook music"), but there is no simile here, eliminating (B). While imagery abounds in this sentence, the sentence is not rhetorical; it is not arguing a point (C). An argument can be made that the first few paragraphs of the story are expository, but irony is absent in this highly sensory sentence (D). "Ran the gauntlet" is an idiom, but synechdoche, the use of a part for a whole ("to give one's heart" for "to love," for example) is absent.

4. The word *litanies* in line 73 most nearly means

    (A) repetitive chant

    (B) echoes

    (C) wails

    (D) bellows

    (E) grunts

Answer: (A)

As used in this line, a litany is best denoted by a repetitive chant. The word also means a type of prayer, adding to the religious imagery of the story.

5. The narration of "Araby" is

    (A) omniscient

    (B) third person

    (C) first person

    (D) limited third person

    (E) limited first person

Answer: (C)

The narration is first person; the narrator relates the story using "I." It is not a limited first person (E); besides the young protagonist, there is another older and more knowing voice present as well.

6. Religious imagery occurs in all of the following lines EXCEPT:

    (A) line 16

    (B) line 72

    (C) line 79

    (D) line 81

    (E) line 104

Answer: (B)

Be careful with the EXCEPT questions, which can catch a hurried test taker. Line 72 has no religious imagery; all the others do. The words *The Devout Communicant*, meaning a committed believer, occur in a book title in line 16 (A). *Chalice*, line 79, is a reference to the Holy Grail (B). Line 81 has the word *prayers* in it (C), and in line 182, the boy's aunt refers to the "night of Our Lord" (E).

7. In line 220, the word *building* refers to

    (A) the train station

    (B) the bazaar

    (C) "ruinous houses" (line 211)

    (D) the marketplace

    (E) the Christian Brothers School

Answer: (B)

The "magical name" of the building is the clue to this detail question; this is the long-awaited bazaar. Be careful with detail questions; the testmaker will put in distorted details from the text next to the right answer, like the choices here.

8. Which is a subject NOT treated in this story?

   (A) the contrast between the material and the spiritual

   (B) a young man's burgeoning sexuality

   (C) the drabness of life without ideals

   (D) the class divisions of society

   (E) man's illusions and disappointment

Answer: (D)

The story centers on working class people, but there's no political discussion in the story other than the marketplace "ballad about the troubles in our native land" (lines 76–79). All the other subjects are explored. The author draws a striking contrast between the material setting and all the characters other than the boy and Mangan's sister; these two are set apart by spiritual imagery throughout the piece (A). The boy is highly aware of the girl's body, as well as the feelings in his own (B). (C) and (E), the drabness and disappointment of the long-awaited bazaar, are also treated.

BOOKS SUGGESTED IN PAST LITERATURE EXAMS

The College Board and the Advanced Placement English Literature Exam require no particular books or plays that you must read. However, the following is a list of titles that have been suggested in recent AP English Literature and Composition Exams to students responding to Essay Question 3. This is the open-ended question where students are asked to respond to a prompt using a book or play, of suitable literary merit, of their own choosing.

The Loved One	*The Scarlet Letter*	*Major Barbara*
Metamorphosis	*The Awakening*	*The Importance of Being Ernest*
A Prayer for Owen Meany	*The Color Purple*	*A Raisin in the Sun*
Emma	*The Sun Also Rises*	*Shakespeare's plays*
Huckleberry Finn	*Jude the Obscure*	*Candide*
Tom Sawyer	*Tess of the D'Ubervilles*	*The Eumenides*
Gulliver's Travels	*Wuthering Heights*	*Oedipus Rex*
Robinson Crusoe	*Their Eyes Were Watching God*	*Zoot Suit*
1984	*House on Mango Street*	*Fences*
Brave New World	*Slaughterhouse Five*	*A Doll's House*
Native Son	*The Great Gatsby*	*M. Butterfly*
Black Boy	*Sula*	*Medea*
House of Spirits	*Beloved*	*Antigone*
Pride and Prejudice	*Cry, the Beloved Country*	*Saint Joan*
Lord of the Flies	*Light in August*	*Hedda Gabler*

A Separate Peace	Love Medicine	Streetcar Named Desire
The Trial	Moll Flanders	The Glass Menagerie
Wide Sargasso Sea	No-No Boy	Death of a Salesman
Moby-Dick	Obasan	Rosencrantz and Guildenstern Are Dead
Grapes of Wrath	The Bluest Eye	Waiting for Godot
Frankenstein	Heart of Darkness	The Sandbox
Catch-22	The Portrait of a Lady	J.B.
As I Lay Dying	All the Pretty Horses	Lady Windemere's Fan
The House of the Seven Gables	I Know Why the Caged Bird Sings	Murder in the Cathedral
A Passage to India	Sons and Lovers	Who's Afraid of Virginia Woolf?
Things Fall Apart	Fathers and Sons	Our Town
Invisible Man	Great Expectations	The Hairy Ape
Crime and Punishment	The Handmaid's Tale	The Dollmaker

SUMMING UP: GUIDELINES FOR READING PROSE

The skills you've applied to analyzing poetry can serve you well as you read from a range of prose works.

- Check out the work's title. As with a poem, the title alone can tell you a lot about the piece.
- Who is the narrator? Is the narration first person, omniscient, third person? What is the point-of-view?
- What is the setting? Is it significant? What is the plot?
- After you have a handle on what the piece means literally, you must look at it again for its figurative meaning. Are there underlying metaphors? Which words have special connotations? Are there special references or allusions in the work?
- What imagery do you find? Be very conscious of what "feeling" words the author is using.
- Is there special diction or syntax to consider? How are the sentences structured? Be particularly aware of the author's use of punctuation.
- Is there a change in the piece? Can you detect any shifts—in narrator, or the tone, or the mood of the piece?
- Are there any details that particularly strike you as worth noting? Can you identify an author's style by these details? For e.g, Hemmingway's use of simple, direct sentences, Henry James' complex sentence structure?
- Finally, especially significant for the AP Exam, what is the tone of the piece? How do you know that? And then, what is the narrator's attitude in the piece? Can you guess at the effect the piece is supposed to have? Can you detect any difference in attitude between the narrator and the writer him/herself? Is that significant?

Give yourself time to think about the previous suggestions. Read with a discerning eye and ear keeping these questions in mind, and need we say practice, practice, practice?

Practice Tests and Explanations

Before taking these practice tests, find a quiet place where you can work uninterrupted for three hours or so. Make sure you have a comfortable desk, several No. 2 pencils, and a few ballpoint pens.

These practice tests include a multiple-choice section and a free-response section consisting of three essay questions. Use the answer grid that follows to record your multiple-choice answers. Write the essays on the pages provided; use additional sheets if needed.

Once you start the practice tests, don't stop until you've finished the multiple-choice section. You may then take a ten-minute break before proceeding to the essay section.

You'll find the answer key, scoring information, and explanations following the tests.

Good luck!

Practice Test One Answer Sheet

1 (A)(B)(C)(D)(E)   22 (A)(B)(C)(D)(E)   43 (A)(B)(C)(D)(E)

2 (A)(B)(C)(D)(E)   23 (A)(B)(C)(D)(E)   44 (A)(B)(C)(D)(E)

3 (A)(B)(C)(D)(E)   24 (A)(B)(C)(D)(E)   45 (A)(B)(C)(D)(E)

4 (A)(B)(C)(D)(E)   25 (A)(B)(C)(D)(E)   46 (A)(B)(C)(D)(E)

5 (A)(B)(C)(D)(E)   26 (A)(B)(C)(D)(E)   47 (A)(B)(C)(D)(E)

6 (A)(B)(C)(D)(E)   27 (A)(B)(C)(D)(E)   48 (A)(B)(C)(D)(F)

7 (A)(B)(C)(D)(E)   28 (A)(B)(C)(D)(E)   49 (A)(B)(C)(D)(E)

8 (A)(B)(C)(D)(E)   29 (A)(B)(C)(D)(E)   50 (A)(B)(C)(D)(E)

9 (A)(B)(C)(D)(E)   30 (A)(B)(C)(D)(E)   51 (A)(B)(C)(D)(E)

10 (A)(B)(C)(D)(E)   31 (A)(B)(C)(D)(E)   52 (A)(B)(C)(D)(E)

11 (A)(B)(C)(D)(E)   32 (A)(B)(C)(D)(E)   53 (A)(B)(C)(D)(E)

12 (A)(B)(C)(D)(E)   33 (A)(B)(C)(D)(E)   54 (A)(B)(C)(D)(E)

13 (A)(B)(C)(D)(E)   34 (A)(B)(C)(D)(E)   55 (A)(B)(C)(D)(E)

14 (A)(B)(C)(D)(E)   35 (A)(B)(C)(D)(E)   56 (A)(B)(C)(D)(E)

15 (A)(B)(C)(D)(E)   36 (A)(B)(C)(D)(E)   57 (A)(B)(C)(D)(E)

16 (A)(B)(C)(D)(E)   37 (A)(B)(C)(D)(E)   58 (A)(B)(C)(D)(E)

17 (A)(B)(C)(D)(E)   38 (A)(B)(C)(D)(E)

18 (A)(B)(C)(D)(E)   39 (A)(B)(C)(D)(E)

19 (A)(B)(C)(D)(E)   40 (A)(B)(C)(D)(E)

20 (A)(B)(C)(D)(E)   41 (A)(B)(C)(D)(E)

21 (A)(B)(C)(D)(E)   42 (A)(B)(C)(D)(E)

Practice Test One

Section I: Multiple-Choice Questions

Time: 1 hour
Number of questions: 58
Percent of total grade: 45

Directions: This section contains selections from literary works with questions on their content, style, form, and purpose. Read each selection, then choose the best answer from the five choices in each test item and fill in the corresponding oval on the answer sheet.

Note: Pay particular attention to the requirements of questions that contain the words **NOT, LEAST,** or **EXCEPT.**

GO ON TO THE NEXT PAGE

Questions 1–13. Read the following poem carefully before you mark your answers.

To Be of Use

The people I love the best
jump into work head first
without dallying in the shallows
and swim off with sure strokes almost out of sight.
(5) They seem to become natives of that element
the black sleek heads of seals
bouncing like half-submerged balls.

I love people who harness themselves, an ox to a heavy cart,
Who pull like water buffalo, with massive patience,
(10) Who strain in the mud and the muck to move things forward,
Who do what has to be done, again and again.

I want to be with people who submerge
in the task, who go into the fields to harvest
and work in a row and pass the bags along,
(15) who are not parlor generals and field deserters
but move in common rhythm
when the food must come in or the fire be put out.

The work of the world is common as mud.
Botched it smears the hands, crumbles to dust.
(20) But the thing worth doing well done
has a shape that satisfies, clean and evident.
Greek amphoras for wine or oil,
Hopi vases that held corn, are put in museums
but you know they were made to be used.
(25) The pitcher cries for water to carry
and the person for work that is real.

1. The animal references in stanzas I and II could BEST be identified as

   (A) personification

   (B) a fable

   (C) understatement

   (D) extended metaphor

   (E) verisimilitude

2. Which of the following is NOT present in the first stanza?

   (A) metaphor

   (B) third person limited narrator

   (C) assonance

   (D) simple sentences

   (E) alliteration

3. The narrator's attitude toward parlor generals and field deserters can BEST be described as one of

   (A) derision

   (B) tolerance

   (C) admiration

   (D) impatience

   (E) compassion

4. This poem can best be characterized as an example of

   (A) a lyrical ballad

   (B) a fable

   (C) free verse

   (D) mock heroic

   (E) iambic pentameter

5. The speaker perceives work chiefly in terms of

   (A) bestial toil

   (B) generals and followers

   (C) a harvest worth gathering

   (D) satisfaction and worthwhileness

   (E) forbearance and endurance

6. "The pitcher cries for water" (line 25) is most simply a reference to its

   (A) thirst and longing

   (B) appropriateness as a museum treasure

   (C) sentimentality

   (D) yearning and despair

   (E) pragmatic purpose

7. The tone of this poem is one of

   (A) condescension and contempt

   (B) respect and admiration

   (C) jealousy and envy

   (D) deference and humility

   (E) wistfulness and nostalgia

8. The narrator references the amphora and Hopi vases because they are

   (A) costly

   (B) valuable

   (C) practical

   (D) beautiful

   (E) unusual

GO ON TO THE NEXT PAGE

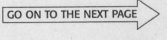

9. Many lines within this poem, such as those in stanza III, are not *end stopped*, but they demonstrate

   (A) run-on structures

   (B) enjambment

   (C) heroic couplets

   (D) Petrarchan rhyme

   (E) juxtaposition

10. The theme of the poem is BEST expressed by the lines

   (A) "...but move in a common rhythm/when the food must come in or the fire be put out" (lines 16–17).

   (B) "I love people who harness themselves..." (line 8).

   (C) "I want to be with people who submerge/in the task" (lines 12–13).

   (D) "The people I love the best/jump into work head first..." (lines 1–2).

   (E) "The pitcher cries for water to carry/and a person for work that is real" (lines 25–26).

11. The BEST example of irony in this poem can be found in the following phrase

   (A) "The people I love the best/jump into work head first" (lines 1–2).

   (B) "I want to be with people who submerge/in the task" (lines 12–13).

   (C) "Botched it smears the hands, crumbles to dust" (line 19)

   (D) "Hopi vases that held corn, are put in museums/but you know they were made to be used" (lines 23–24).

   (E) "The pitcher cries for water to carry/and a person for work that is real" (lines 25–26).

12. In line 5, the word *element* can BEST be understood to represent

   (A) swimming seals

   (B) bouncing balls

   (C) patient water buffalo

   (D) toiling oxen

   (E) meaningful work

13. The repeated phraseology used in the third stanza can be identified as

   (A) alliteration

   (B) anaphora

   (C) apposition

   (D) apostrophe

   (E) assonance

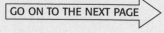
GO ON TO THE NEXT PAGE

Questions 14–23: Read the following passage carefully before you mark your answers.

There is a canal two rods wide along the northerly and westerly sides of the pond, and wider still at the east end. A great field of ice has cracked off from the main body. I hear a song
(5) sparrow singing form the bushes on the shore. He too is helping to crack it. How handsome the great sweeping curves in the edge of the ice, answering somewhat to those of the shore, but more regular! It is unusually hard, owing to the recent severe but
(10) transient cold, and all watered or waved like a palace floor. But the wind slides eastward over its opaque surface in vain, till it reaches the living surface beyond. It is glorious to behold this ribbon of water sparkling in the sun, the bare face of the
(15) pond full of glee and youth, as if it spoke the joy of the fishes within it, and of the sands on its shore.

The change from storm and winter to serene and mild weather, from dark and sluggish hours
(20) to bright and elastic ones, is a memorable crisis which all things proclaim. It is seemingly instantaneous at last. Suddenly an influx of light filled my house, though the evening was at hand, and the clouds of winter still overhung it, and the eaves
(25) were dripping with sleety rain. I looked out the window, and lo! where yesterday was cold gray ice there lay the transparent pond already calm and full of hope as in a summer evening reflecting a summer evening sky in its bosom, though none
(30) was visible overhead. The pitch pines and shrub oaks about my house, which had so long drooped suddenly resumed their several characters, looked brighter, greener, and more erect and alive, as if effectually cleansed and restored by the rain. I
(35) know that it would not rain any more. You may tell by looking at any twig of the forest, aye, at your very woodpile, whether its winter is past or not. As it grew darker, I was startled by the honking of geese flying low over the woods, like weary
(40) travelers getting in late from southern lakes, and indulging at last in unrestrained complaint and mutual consolation. Standing at my door, I could hear the rush of their wings; when, driving toward my house, they suddenly spied my light, and with
(45) hushed clamor wheeled and settled in the pond.

In the morning I watched the geese from the door through the mist, sailing in the middle of the pond, fifty rods off, large and tumultuous. But when I stood on the shore they at once rose up
(50) with great flapping of wings at the signal of their commander, and when they had got into rank circled about over my head, twenty-nine of them, and then steered straight to Canada, with a regular honk from the leader at intervals. A plump of
(55) ducks rose at the same time and took the route to the north in the wake of their noisier cousins.

For a week I heard the circling groping clangor of some solitary goose in the foggy mornings, seeking its companion, and still peopling the
(60) woods with the sound of a larger life than they could sustain. In April the pigeons were seen again flying express in small flocks, and in due time I heard the martins twittering over my clearing, though it had not seemed that the township con-
(65) tained so many that it could afford me any, and I fancied that they were peculiarly of the ancient race that dwelt in hollow trees ere white men came. In almost all climes the tortoise and the frog are among the precursors and herald of this sea-
(70) son, and birds fly with song and glancing plumage, and plants spring and bloom, and winds blow to correct this slight oscillation of the poles and preserve the equilibrium of Nature.

As every season seems best to us in its turn, so
(75) the coming in of spring is like creation of Cosmos out of Chaos and the realization of the Golden Age.

GO ON TO THE NEXT PAGE

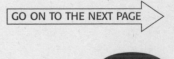

14. From the passage one can infer that the

    (A) geese are back
    (B) pond is melting
    (C) woodpile is low
    (D) martins are singing
    (E) mornings are foggy

15. The overall purpose of this passage seems to be the narrator's

    (A) desire to sound poetic
    (B) need to explain the unexpected sunshine in his house
    (C) description of the bird life around him
    (D) celebration of the oncoming season
    (E) delight to see the pond water

16. What is the predominant literary device used throughout this passage?

    (A) restrained description
    (B) personification
    (C) bombastic narration
    (D) hyperbole
    (E) rhetorical question

17. The tone of this passage can BEST be described as

    (A) colloquial
    (B) informative
    (C) unrestrained
    (D) audacious
    (E) poetic

18. The narrator describes the water as all of the following EXCEPT

    (A) a canal two rods wide
    (B) a ribbon
    (C) a transparent pond
    (D) a reflection of the sky
    (E) a mirror of his soul

19. The geese are BEST characterized through a series of

    (A) similes and metaphors
    (B) comic descriptors
    (C) emotional reflections
    (D) unrelated impressions
    (E) aural and visual images

20. The geese are described as all of the following EXCEPT

    (A) weary travelers
    (B) precursors of the season
    (C) regimental in action
    (D) cranky and commiserating
    (E) raucous relatives

21. Which is a subject NOT treated in this passage?

    (A) the connectedness of people to nature
    (B) the innocence of mankind
    (C) the cyclical certainty of nature
    (D) the glory of a long-awaited event
    (E) the animals heralding a change

22. One thing that is syntactically consistent within this passage is the

    (A) use of periodic sentences
    (B) scarcity of prepositional phrases
    (C) artful handling of rhetorical question
    (D) lack of simple sentences
    (E) overuse of parallelism

23. The word *plump* in line 54 most closely compares to the term

    (A) chubby
    (B) fat
    (C) full
    (D) clutch
    (E) club

GO ON TO THE NEXT PAGE ▷

Questions 24–33: Read the following passage carefully before you mark your answers.

Ambush

Very gradually, in tiny slivers, day began to break through the fog, and from my position in the brush I could see ten or fifteen meters up the trail. The mosquitoes were fierce. I remember
(5) slapping at them…then looking up and seeing the young man come out of the fog. He wore black clothing and rubber sandals and a gray ammunition belt. His shoulders were slightly stooped, his head cocked to the side listening to something. He
(10) seemed at ease. He carried his weapon in one hand, muzzle down, moving without any hurry up the center of the trail. There was no sound at all—none that I can remember. In a way, it seemed, he was part of the morning fog, or my own imagina-
(15) tion, but there was also the reality of what was happening in my stomach. I had already pulled the pin on a grenade. I had come up to a crouch. It was entirely automatic. I did not hate the young man; I did not see him as the enemy; I did not
(20) ponder issues of morality or politics or military duty. I crouched and kept my head low. I tried to swallow whatever was rising from my stomach, which tasted like lemonade, something fruity and sour. I was terrified. There were no thoughts
(25) about killing. The grenade was to make him go away—just evaporate—and I leaned back and felt my mind go empty and then fill up again. I had already thrown the grenade before telling myself to throw it. The brush was thick and I had to lob
(30) it high, not aiming, and I remember the grenade seeming to freeze above me for an instant, as if a camera had clicked and I remember ducking down and holding my breath and seeing little wisps of fog rise from the earth. The grenade
(35) bounced once and rolled across the trail. I did not hear it, but there must've been a sound, because the young man dropped his weapon and began to run, just two or three quick steps, then he hesitated, swiveling to his right, and he glanced down at
(40) the grenade and tried to cover his head but never did. It occurred to me then that he was about to die. I wanted to warn him. The grenade made a popping noise—not soft but not loud either—not what I'd expected—and there was a puff of dust
(45) and smoke—a small white puff—and the young man seemed to jerk upward as if pulled by invisible wires. He fell on his back. His rubber sandals had been blown off. There was no wind. He lay at the center of the trail, his right leg bent beneath
(50) him, his one eye shut, his other eye a huge star-shaped blue.

All I could do was gape at the fact of the young man's body. Even now, I haven't finished sorting it out. Sometimes I forgive myself, other times I
(55) don't. In the ordinary hours of life I try not to dwell on it, but now and then, when I'm reading a newspaper or just sitting alone in a room, I'll look up and see the young man coming out of the morning fog. I'll watch him walk toward me, his
(60) shoulders slightly stooped, his head cocked to the side, and he'll pass within a few yards of me and suddenly smile at some secret thought and then continue up the trail to where it bends back into the fog.

24. The narrator in "Ambush" responds to his difficult situation by

(A) becoming paralyzed by fear
(B) continuing up the trail into the fog
(C) shooting his rifle
(D) throwing a grenade
(E) screaming while attacking

25. The narrator experiences all the following sensations EXCEPT

(A) a desire to warn the enemy of his danger
(B) difficulty in his ability to swallow
(C) extreme anger upon seeing his enemy
(D) an upset stomach
(E) a lack of real hatred

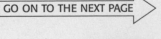
GO ON TO THE NEXT PAGE

26. The syntactical variance of sentence lengths in the first paragraph BEST accomplishes which of the following?

   (A) confuses the reader because of the irregular rhythm

   (B) lulls the reader into a sense of security

   (C) punctuates the tenseness of the situation

   (D) demonstrates the writer's ability to vary his style

   (E) reflects the writing style of the era

27. This passage could be said to begin

   (A) in a sinister manner

   (B) *in medias res*

   (C) melodramatically

   (D) passively

   (E) ironically

28. The narrator's actions can BEST be described as

   (A) planned and deliberate

   (B) arbitrary and random

   (C) reactionary and pragmatic

   (D) reflective and subjective

   (E) heroic and laudable

29. The narrator's attitude toward the dead enemy can BEST be described as

   (A) fear and anger

   (B) regret and rationalization

   (C) fraternity and humanity

   (D) courage and patriotism

   (E) satisfaction and pride

30. All of the following are present in the passage EXCEPT

   (A) onomatopoeia

   (B) foreshadowing

   (C) idiomatic expression

   (D) metaphor

   (E) rationalization

31. The theme of this passage can BEST be summed up with which of the following statements?

   (A) "Do unto others as you would want them to do to you."

   (B) "War makes man do things he would not do otherwise."

   (C) "Act first; regret later."

   (D) "Look out for yourself; no one else will."

   (E) "All is just in love and war."

32. The last sentence of the first paragraph describes the dead man using all of the following literary devices EXCEPT

   (A) parallelism

   (B) anaphora

   (C) metaphor

   (D) simile

   (E) imagery

33. The most likely reason for the use of dashes in lines 43–45 is to

   (A) demonstrate the writer's syntactical skills

   (B) reveal the narrator's emotional horror

   (C) eliminate the need for conjunctions

   (D) reveal the writer's lack of control

   (E) provide structural variety to the paragraph

GO ON TO THE NEXT PAGE

Questions 34–43: Read the following passage carefully before you mark your answers.

"To-morrow at twelve o'clock I regain my freedom and the right to associate with other men, but before I leave this room and see the sunshine, I think it necessary to say a few words to you.

(5) With a clear conscience I tell you, as before God, who beholds me, that I despise freedom and life and health, and all that in your books is called the good things of the world.

"For fifteen years I have been intently studying
(10) earthly life. It is true I have not seen the earth nor men, but in your books I have drunk fragrant wine, I have sung songs, I have hunted stags and wild boars in the forests, have loved women. . . . Beauties as ethereal as clouds, created by the
(15) magic of your poets and geniuses, have visited me at night, and have whispered in my ears wonderful tales that have set my brain in a whirl. In your books I have climbed to the peaks of Elburz and Mont Blanc, and from there I have seen the sun
(20) rise and have watched it at evening flood the sky, the ocean, and the mountain-tops with gold and crimson. I have watched from there the lightning flashing over my head and cleaving the storm-clouds. I have seen green forests, fields, rivers,
(25) lakes, towns. I have heard the singing of the sirens, and the strains of the shepherds' pipes; I have touched the wings of comely devils who flew down to converse with me of God. . . . In your books I have flung myself into the bottomless pit,
(30) performed miracles, slain, burned towns, preached new religions, conquered whole kingdoms. . . .

"Your books have given me wisdom. All that the unresting thought of man has created in the ages is compressed into a small compass in my brain. I
(35) know that I am wiser than all of you.

"And I despise your books, I despise wisdom and the blessings of this world. It is all worthless, fleeting, illusory, and deceptive, like a mirage. You may be proud, wise, and fine, but death will wipe
(40) you off the face of the earth as though you were no more than mice burrowing under the floor, and your posterity, your history, your immortal geniuses will burn or freeze together with the earthly globe.

(45) "You have lost your reason and taken the wrong path. You have taken lies for truth, and hideousness for beauty. You would marvel if, owing to strange events of some sorts, frogs and lizards suddenly grew on apple and orange trees instead
(50) of fruit, or if roses began to smell like a sweating horse; so I marvel at you who exchange heaven for earth. I don't want to understand you.

"To prove to you in action how I despise all that you live by, I renounce the two millions of which I
(55) once dreamed as of paradise and which now I despise. To deprive myself of the right to the money I shall go out from here five hours before the time fixed, and so break the compact. . . ."

GO ON TO THE NEXT PAGE

34. The main idea of this passage is BEST stated in which of the following pair of paragraphs?

    (A) paragraphs I and II
    (B) paragraphs II and IV
    (C) paragraphs I and IV
    (D) paragraphs III and VI
    (E) paragraphs I and VI

35. During the narrator's confinement, he used to accomplish all of the following EXCEPT

    (A) escape to a world of fantastical adventures
    (B) physically escape
    (C) escape to a world of philosophical turmoil
    (D) listen to sounds beyond his confinement
    (E) virtually escape to heaven and to hell

36. The tone of paragraph IV can BEST be described as

    (A) contemptuous
    (B) condescending
    (C) cantankerous
    (D) charismatic
    (E) choleric

37. The narrator's attitude towards his fellow man can BEST be described as one of

    (A) admiration and envy
    (B) understanding and longing
    (C) enmity and disgust
    (D) dislike and disappointment
    (E) anger and resentment

38. The tone of paragraph V can BEST be described as

    (A) demanding
    (B) didactic
    (C) disdainful
    (D) derogatory
    (E) determined

39. The presentation of several independent clauses in lines 11–13 with no intervening conjunction(s) and lack of proper punctuation is an example of

    (A) asyndenton and anaphora
    (B) apostrophe and assonance
    (C) apposition and repetition
    (D) assonance and addition
    (E) alliteration and absolutism

40. Paragraphs III and IV BEST demonstrate an example of

    (A) complementary ideas
    (B) antithesis
    (C) imbalance and parallelism
    (D) satisfaction
    (E) insecurity and diffidence

41. One can infer that the narrator had

    (A) been away at school for a long time
    (B) recently returned from a long journey
    (C) once valued money a great deal
    (D) been a mountain climber
    (E) suffered unimaginable hardships

42. The theme the narrator expresses can BEST be summarized as

    (A) Gambling will only lead to unhappiness.
    (B) Man is too taken with his own importance.
    (C) Some things are just not worth understanding.
    (D) Money is not everything.
    (E) Money is man's downfall.

43. The narrator's feelings about mankind are BEST demonstrated in which of the following paragraphs?

    (A) I
    (B) II
    (C) III
    (D) IV
    (E) V

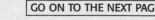
GO ON TO THE NEXT PAGE

Questions 44–58: Read the following poem carefully before you mark your answers.

Remembrance

Cold in the earth—and the deep snow piled above thee.
Far, far removed, cold in the dreary grave!
Have I forgot, my only Love, to love thee
Severed at last by Time's all-severing wave?

(5) Now, when alone, do my thoughts no longer hover
Over the mountains, on that northern shore,
Resting their wings where heath and fern leaves cover
Thy noble heart forever, ever more?

Cold in the earth—and fifteen wild Decembers,
(10) From those brown hills, have melted into spring;
Faithful indeed is the spirit that remembers
After such years of change and suffering!

Sweet Love of youth, forgive, if I forget thee,
While the world's tide is bearing me along;
(15) Other desires and other hopes beset me,
Hopes which obscure, but cannot do thee wrong!

No later light has lightened up my heaven,
No second morn has ever shone for me;
All my life's bliss from thee dear life has given,
(20) All my life's bliss is in the grave with thee.

But, when the days of golden dreams had perished,
And even Despair was powerless to destroy,
Then did I learn how existence could be cherished,
Strengthened, and fed without the aid of joy.

(25) Then did I check the tears of useless passion—
Weaned my young soul from yearning after thine;
Sternly denied its burning wish to hasten
Down to that tomb already more than mine.

And even yet, I dare not let it languish,
(30) Dare not indulge in memory's rapturous pain;
Once drinking deep of that divinest anguish,
How could I seek the empty world again?

44. This poem is BEST identified as a(n)

    (A) ballad

    (B) apostrophe

    (C) elegy

    (D) lyric

    (E) sonnet

45. This poem's structure is specifically that of

    (A) *aabb* rhyme scheme throughout

    (B) blank verse

    (C) free verse

    (D) alternating rhymed couplets

    (E) alternating rhymed lines within quatrains

46. The metaphor present in the second stanza concerns

    (A) northern mountains

    (B) noble heart

    (C) heath and fern

    (D) winged thoughts

    (E) hovering birds

47. Which stanza contains examples of <u>all</u> of the following: alliteration, assonance, anaphora, and consonance?

    (A) I

    (B) IV

    (C) V

    (D) VI

    (E) VIII

48. The reader can infer from this passage that the narrator has

    (A) continued to weep for a loved one

    (B) found new joy to live for

    (C) never stopped yearning

    (D) lamented a death for 15 years

    (E) been unfaithful to the departed

49. The narrator's diction within the last two stanzas is that of a(n)

    (A) sorrowful child

    (B) desperate mourner

    (C) ominous portender

    (D) passionate young woman

    (E) struggling disciplinarian

50. The narrator's tone in stanzas IV and V can BEST be described as

    (A) apology and acquittal

    (B) lamentation and sorrow

    (C) resignation and determination

    (D) reminiscence and nostalgia

    (E) desperation and despair

51. In line 29, the word *it* refers to

    (A) "tears of useless passion" (line 25)

    (B) "my life's bliss" (line 20)

    (C) "days of golden dreams" (line 21)

    (D) "my young soul" (line 26)

    (E) "memory's rapturous pain" (line 30)

52. The narrator's present attitude toward what might have been is one of

   (A) wistful regret

   (B) despair and anguish

   (C) passionate remorse

   (D) blissful reminiscence

   (E) change and suffering

53. The underlying theme of this poem can BEST be summarized as

   (A) "Time heals all wounds."

   (B) "Absence makes the heart grow fonder."

   (C) "Out of sight, out of mind."

   (D) "Out of sight but not out of mind."

   (E) "Faith heals all wounds."

54. Stanzas I and VIII can BEST be said to

   (A) capture the message of the poem

   (B) bring the poem full circle

   (C) imply blissful, unrequited passion within the narrator

   (D) demonstrate the narrator's therapeutic healing

   (E) remonstrate with the narrator's suicidal notion

55. The final stanza of this poem has at least two examples of

   (A) metaphor

   (B) oxymoron

   (C) synecdoche

   (D) onomatopoeia

   (E) conceit

56. The reader can infer from stanza IV that

   (A) a new love has entered the narrator's life

   (B) the narrator has worse things to cope with than another's death

   (C) one's existence can only be strengthened by feeding it with joy

   (D) life, even after great loss, can and should continue

   (E) the narrator was destroyed by Despair

57. The narrator makes reference to all of the following EXCEPT

   (A) the passing of 15 years

   (B) new hopes and desires that obscure memory

   (C) memories like winged spirits

   (D) the inability to live without the departed

   (E) fear of the soul's indulgence in rapturous pain

58. The reader can infer from the last stanza that the narrator

   (A) has conquered the urge to remember

   (B) cannot control the urge to indulge in self pity

   (C) refuses to be kept down by melancholy

   (D) weaned his or her soul from useless passionless yearning

   (E) dare not allow his or her soul to drink too deeply of anguished memories for fear of not being able to function in the world

IF YOU FINISH BEFORE TIME IS CALLED, YOU MAY CHECK YOUR WORK ON THIS SECTION ONLY. DO NOT TURN TO ANY OTHER SECTION IN THE TEST.   **STOP**

Section II: Essay Questions

Time: 2 hours
Number of questions: 3
Percent of total grade: 55

Directions: This section contains three essay questions. Answer all three questions, budgeting your time carefully.

GO ON TO THE NEXT PAGE

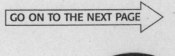

Question 1

Suggested Time: 40 minutes. Your response will count as one-third of your total score on the essay portion of the exam.

1. Read the following poem carefully. Then, in a well-organized essay, analyze how the speaker uses the varied imagery of the poem to reveal his attitude toward what he has found and how it affects him, paying particular attention to the shifting point of view of the narrator.

Between the World and Me

And one morning while in the woods I stumbled suddenly upon the thing
Stumbled upon it in a grassy clearing guarded by scaly oaks and elms
And the sooty details of the scene rose, thrusting themselves between the world and me....

There was a design of white bones slumbering forgottenly upon a cushion of ashes.
(5) There was a charred stump of a sapling pointing a blunt finger accusingly at the sky.
There were torn tree limbs, tiny veins of burnt leaves, and a scorched coil of greasy hemp;
A vacant shoe, an empty tie, a ripped shirt, a lonely hat, and a pair of trousers stiff with black blood.
And upon the trampled grass were buttons, dead matches. Butt-ends of cigars and cigarettes, peanut
    shells, a drained gin-flask and a whore's lipstick;
(10) Scattered traces of tar, restless array of feathers, and the lingering smell of gasoline.
And through the morning air the sun poured yellow surprise into the eye sockets of the stony
    skull....

And while I stood my mind was frozen within cold pity for the life that was gone.
The ground gripped my feet and my heart was circled by icy walls of fear—
(15) The sun died in the sky; a night wind muttered in the grass and fumbled the leaves in the trees; the
    woods poured forth the hungry yelping of hounds; the darkness screamed with thirsty voices; and
        the witnesses rose and lived:
The dry bones stirred, rattled, lifted, melting themselves into my bones.
The grey ashes formed flesh firm and black, entering into my flesh.

(20) The gin-flask passed from mouth to mouth, cigars and cigarettes glowed, the whore smeared lipstick
    red upon her lips,
And a thousand faces swirled around me, clamoring that my life be burned.....
And then they had me, stripped me, battering my teeth into my throat till I swallowed my own
    blood.

(25) My voice was drowned in the roar of their voices, and my black wet body slipped and rolled in their
    hands as they bound me to the sapling.
And my skin clung to the bubbling hot tar, falling from me in limp patches.
And the down and quills of the white feathers sank into my raw flesh, and I moaned in my agony.
Then my blood was cooled mercifully, cooled by a baptism of gasoline.
(30) And in a blaze of red I leaped to the sky as pain rose like water, boiling my limbs
Panting, begging I clutched childlike, clutched to the hot sides of death.
Now I am dry bones and my face a stony skull staring in yellow surprise at the sun....

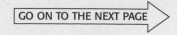

Write Your Essay Here

_____

_____

_____

_____

_____

_____

_____

_____

_____

_____

_____

_____

_____

_____

_____

_____

GO ON TO THE NEXT PAGE ▷

_____

_____

_____

_____

_____

_____

_____

_____

_____

_____

_____

_____

_____

_____

_____

_____

_____

GO ON TO THE NEXT PAGE ▷

KAPLAN
Test Prep and Admissions

_____

_____

_____

_____

_____

_____

_____

_____

_____

_____

_____

_____

_____

_____

_____

_____

_____

GO ON TO THE NEXT PAGE

_____

_____

_____

_____

_____

_____

_____

_____

_____

_____

_____

_____

_____

_____

_____

_____

_____

_____

GO ON TO THE NEXT PAGE →

KAPLAN
Test Prep and Admissions

Question 2

<u>**Suggested Time**</u>: 40 minutes. Your response will count as one-third of your total score on the essay portion of the exam.

2. In the following two passages, Virginia Woolf describes two different meals that she was served during a university visit. The first meal was served at the men's college, while the second meal was served at the women's college. Read the two passages carefully, then write a well-organized essay in which you explain how formal elements such as structure, syntax, diction, and imagery reveal not only the speaker's response to the two meals, but also discuss possible conclusions a reader might draw about the narrator's attitude, based upon these descriptions.

I. It is a curious fact that novelists have a way of making us believe that luncheon parties are invariably memorable for something very witty that was said, or for something very wise that was done. But
(5) they seldom spare a word for what was eaten. It is part of the novelist's convention not to mention soup and salmon and ducklings, as if soup and salmon and ducklings were of no importance whatsoever, as if nobody ever smoked a cigar or drank a
(10) glass of wine. Here, however, I shall take the liberty to defy that convention and to tell you that the lunch on this occasion began with soles, sunk in a deep dish, over which the college cook had spread a counterpane of the whitest cream, save that it was brand-
(15) ed here and there with brown spots like the spots on the flanks of a doe. After that came the partridges, but if this suggests a couple of bald, brown birds on a plate you are mistaken. The partridges, many and various, came with all their retinue of sauces and sal-
(20) ads, the sharp and sweet, each in its order, their potatoes, thin as coins but not so hard; their sprouts, foliated as rosebuds but more succulent. And no sooner had the roast and its retinue been done with than the silent serving man, the Beadle himself perhaps in a
(25) milder manifestation, set before us, wreathed in napkins, a confection which rose all sugar from the waves. To call it pudding and so relate it to rice and tapioca would be an insult. Meanwhile the wineglasses had flushed yellow and flushed crimson; had
(30) been emptied; had been filled. And thus by degrees was lit, halfway down the spine, which is the seat of the soul, not that hard little electric light which we call brilliance, as it pops in and out upon our lips, but the more profound, subtle and subterranean
(35) glow, which is the rich yellow flame of rational intercourse. No need to hurry. No need to sparkle. No need to be anybody but oneself… How good life seemed, how sweet its rewards, how trivial this

grudge or that grievance, how admirable friendship
(40) and the society of one's kind….
II. Everybody was assembled in the big diningroom. Dinner was ready. Here was the soup. It was a plain gravy soup. There was nothing to stir the fancy in that. One could have seen through the transpar-
(45) ent liquid any pattern that there might have been on the plate itself. But there was no pattern. The plate was plain. Next came beef with its attendant greens and potatoes—a homely trinity, suggesting the rumps of cattle in a muddy market, and sprouts
(50) curled and yellowed at the edge, and bargaining and cheapening, and women with string bags on Monday morning. There was no reason to complain of human nature's daily food, seeing that the supply was sufficient and coal-miners doubtless were sitting
(55) down to less. Prunes and custard followed. And if any one complains that prunes, even when mitigated by custard, are an uncharitable vegetable (fruit they are not), stringy as a miser's heart and exuding a fluid such as might run in misers' veins who have
(60) denied themselves wine and warmth for eighty years and yet not given to the poor, he should reflect that there are people whose charity embraces even the prune. Biscuits and cheese came next, and here the water jug was liberally passed round, for it is the
(65) nature of biscuits to be dry, and these were biscuits to the core. That was all. The meal was over. Everybody scraped their chairs back; the swingdoors swung violently to and fro; soon the hall was emptied of every sign of food and made ready no
(70) doubt for breakfast the next morning.

GO ON TO THE NEXT PAGE ⟩

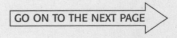

Write Your Essay Here

_____

_____

_____

_____

_____

_____

_____

_____

_____

_____

_____

_____

_____

_____

_____

_____

_____

GO ON TO THE NEXT PAGE

_____

_____

_____

_____

_____

_____

_____

_____

_____

_____

_____

_____

_____

_____

_____

_____

_____

GO ON TO THE NEXT PAGE

_____

_____

_____

_____

_____

_____

_____

_____

_____

_____

_____

_____

_____

_____

_____

_____

_____

_____

GO ON TO THE NEXT PAGE ▷

KAPLAN
Test Prep and Admissions

GO ON TO THE NEXT PAGE

Question 3

<u>Suggested Time</u>: 40 minutes. Your response will count as one-third of your total score on the essay portion of the exam.

3. Margaret Thatcher, former Prime Minister of Great Britain, once said, "In politics, if you want anything said, ask a man; if you want anything done, ask a woman."

    Novels and plays often portray circumstances that reflect Margaret Thatcher's sentiment. Select a novel or play that includes a situation in which a woman is the strongest character, best able to carry out necessary action. In a well-written, focused essay, discuss how this idea contributes to the meaning as well as the outcome of the work as a whole. You may choose a work from the list below or another novel or play of literary merit.

> *Anna Karenina*
> *Antigone*
> *Antony and Cleopatra*
> *Auntie Mame*
> *The Awakening*
> *The Color Purple*
> *The Dollmaker*
> *A Doll's House*
> *The Glass Menagerie*
> *The Handmaid's Tale*
> *Hedda Gabler*
> *House of Spirits*
> *Jane Eyre*
> *The Joy Luck Club*
> *Love Medicine*
> *Macbeth*
> *Medea*
> *Memoirs of a Geisha*
> *Moll Flanders*
> *Obasan*
> *Pigs in Heaven*
> *The Scarlet Letter*
> *Sula*
> *Tess of the D'Ubervilles*

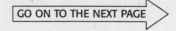
GO ON TO THE NEXT PAGE

Write Your Essay Here

_____

_____

_____

_____

_____

_____

_____

_____

_____

_____

_____

_____

_____

_____

_____

_____

GO ON TO THE NEXT PAGE ➤

_____

_____

_____

_____

_____

_____

_____

_____

_____

_____

_____

_____

_____

_____

_____

_____

_____

_____

_____

GO ON TO THE NEXT PAGE →

GO ON TO THE NEXT PAGE >

_____

_____

_____

_____

_____

_____

_____

_____

_____

_____

_____

_____

_____

_____

_____

_____

STOP

Practice Test One: **Answer Key**

1. D	21. B	41. C
2. B	22. D	42. B
3. A	23. D	43. E
4. C	24. D	44. C
5. D	25. C	45. E
6. E	26. C	46. D
7. B	27. B	47. C
8. C	28. B	48. D
9. B	29. B	49. E
10. E	30. C	50. A
11. D	31. C	51. D
12. E	32. D	52. A
13. B	33. B	53. D
14. C	34. E	54. B
15. D	35. B	55. C
16. B	36. A	56. D
17. E	37. C	57. D
18. E	38. C	58. E
19. E	39. A	
20. B	40. B	

Answers and Explanations

SECTION I: MULTIPLE CHOICE QUESTIONS

Questions 1–13

To Be of Use

The people I love the best
jump into work head first
without dallying in the shallows
and swim off with sure strokes almost out of sight.
(5) They seem to become natives of that element
the black sleek heads of seals
bouncing like half-submerged balls.

I love people who harness themselves, an ox to a heavy cart,
Who pull like water buffalo, with massive patience,
(10) Who strain in the mud and the muck to move things forward,
Who do what has to be done, again and again.

I want to be with people who submerge
in the task, who go into the fields to harvest
and work in a row and pass the bags along,
(15) who are not parlor generals and field deserters
but move in common rhythm
when the food must come in or the fire be put out.

The work of the world is common as mud.
Botched it smears the hands, crumbles to dust.
(20) But the thing worth doing well done
has a shape that satisfies, clean and evident.
Greek amphoras for wine or oil,
Hopi vases that held corn, are put in museums
but you know they were made to be used.
(25) The pitcher cries for water to carry
and the person for work that is real

1. (D)

The use of the seals, oxen, and buffalo is a purposeful comparison between these performing and working creatures and people who perform meaningful labor, an extended metaphor of the first two stanzas. Personification (A) gives human characteristics or qualities to an inanimate object or animal; you might be tempted by this answer choice, but note that the animals here are not given human characteristics; just the opposite. Although fables (B) often contain animals as allegorical characters, in this poem animals are referred to in their normal sense. Understatement (C), the deliberate attenuation of meaning sometimes designed to produce the opposite effect, doesn't occur in these stanzas. Verisimilitude (E) is the quality or characteristic of being true or real. It is not relevant to this question.

2. (B)

Please note: you are asked to identify something that is NOT found in stanza one. The narrator is indicated as first person from line 1 on; the second and third stanzas begin with *I*. Lines 6–7 actually contain a double metaphor (A): people to seals, seals to bouncing balls. Although several lines show evidence of assonance (C), the repetition of vowel sounds in a sequence of words with different endings, lines 5–6 have the best examples of assonance in the first stanza: "*seem…/sleek…seals.*" Despite the length of the two sentences that comprise the first stanza, each sentence is actually a simple sentence in its creation (D), with multiple prepositional phrases. Alliteration, the repetition of initial consonant sounds (E), is clearly present in lines 4, 6, and 7.

3. (A)

The narrator clearly has little tolerance for anyone who is not fully engaged in his or her work and no respect for armchair generals or anyone who might desert the field of battle. Derision therefore conveys the narrator's contempt. In light of the correct answer, the narrator feels no charity towards either the general or the deserter ((B) and (C)). Although one might argue that the author's no-tolerance tone shows impatience (D), the question asks for the BEST response, which is derisiveness—note the scornful phrases *parlor* general and *deserters*. No indication whatsoever of narrator compassion (E) for these types is evident.

4. (C)

Free verse is characterized by varying line lengths, lack of traditional meter, and nonrhyming lines, which certainly describes this poem. A ballad (A) is a common stanza form that usually consists of quatrains that alternate four-beat and three-beat lines with a specific rhyme scheme. Despite the mention of animals in this poem, they are not used allegorically, ruling out fable (B). This poem is not a satire or spoof of anything serious and thus not mock heroic (D). One may find a few regular meters here and there within this poem, but no meter dominates the lines; the poem is not in iambic pentameter (E).

5. (D)

The narrator lauds labor that she perceives as worthwhile and beneficial to all. Although animals are mentioned in the first half of the poem (A), the poet is really talking about human toil. The poet has nothing but disdain for the general in the parlor (B). Although a harvest is mentioned (C), it is only one example of labor. A suggestion of endurance and patience can be found in this poem, but the chief idea is "the thing worth doing well done" (line 20).

6. (E)

The pitcher's purpose is to hold water. It "cries" to do the job for which it was intended. Water is referred to metaphorically in line 25; (A) is off the mark. The pitcher is a museum piece, but the quotation is not a reference to a museum treasure (B). The tone of the quotation is not sentimental (C). One might think the "cry" is yearning (D), but the water reference is metaphorical.

7. (B)

The poet demonstrates respect and admiration for those who perform common labor for the common good. The only tone of contempt (A) is for those like the general and the deserter; no condescension is present. Neither jealousy nor envy (C) is present in the tone of this poem. Although the poet defers to those who labor honestly, humility (D) is not evident, nor are wistfulness or nostalgia (E).

8. (C)

It is the fact that these items have a useful purpose that the poet has chosen to feature them in this poem. The poet is not concerned with the value of these antiquities ((A) and (B)). The beauty of these items lies in their practicality, not necessarily their physical beauty (D). The only thing unusual about these antiquities is that they are kept from performing the task for which they were created (E).

9. (B)

When a sentence continues on to the next line of a poem, without a natural pause or stop, that is enjambment. Although the sentence may seem to run on (A), this response is not relevant to the question of end stopping. This poem does not contain rhyming pairs of iambic pentameter lines (C). Petrarchan rhyme refers to a particular type of sonnet rhyme scheme (D). Juxtaposition (E) is the purposeful placement of one idea with another; this is not a relevant response to this question.

10. (E)

The poet's underlying meaning lies in the vessels that were created to serve a practical purpose and the humans who perform worthwhile labor—all else is meaningless. The other responses are, indeed, feelings of the narrator, but none of the other choices is as broad as choice (E), which BEST states the theme.

11. (D)

"Hopi vases that held corn, are put in museums/ but you know they were made to be used." The poet sees great irony in the fact that these items made for practical use are on display only to be looked at as treasures of antiquity.

12. (E)

The word *element*, line 5, is a reference to line 2, "jump into <u>work</u> headfirst."

13. (B)

Anaphora is the repetition of the same word or phrase at the beginning of successive phrases or clauses, as in the repetition of *who* in this stanza. Alliteration (A) is the repetition of initial consonant sounds. Apposition (C) is a renaming of a noun or pronoun, not a repetitive structure. Apostrophe (D) is an address to an inanimate object such as the wind or an ocean. Assonance (E) is the repetition of vowel sounds in a sequence of words with different endings such as "I will *sign* the papers, *wind* the clock, and *find* my way to bed."

Questions 14–23.

There is a canal two rods wide along the northerly and westerly sides of the pond, and wider still at the east end. A great field of ice has cracked off from the main body. I hear a song

(5) sparrow singing form the bushes on the shore. He too is helping to crack it. How handsome the great sweeping curves in the edge of the ice, answering somewhat to those of the shore, but more regular! It is unusually hard, owing to the recent severe but

(10) transient cold, and all watered or waved like a palace floor. But the wind slides eastward over its opaque surface in vain, till it reaches the living surface beyond. It is glorious to behold this ribbon of water sparkling in the sun, the bare face of the

(15) pond full of glee and youth, as if it spoke the joy of the fishes within it, and of the sands on its shore.

The change from storm and winter to serene and mild weather, from dark and sluggish hours

(20) to bright and elastic ones, is a memorable crisis which all things proclaim. It is seemingly instantaneous at last. Suddenly an influx of light filled my house, though the evening was at hand, and the clouds of winter still overhung it, and the eaves

(25) were dripping with sleety rain. I looked out the window, and lo! where yesterday was cold gray ice there lay the transparent pond already calm and full of hope as in a summer evening reflecting a summer evening sky in its bosom, though none

(30) was visible overhead. The pitch pines and shrub oaks about my house, which had so long drooped suddenly resumed their several characters, looked brighter, greener, and more erect and alive, as if effectually cleansed and restored by the rain. I

(35) know that it would not rain any more. You may tell by looking at any twig of the forest, aye, at your very woodpile, whether its winter is past or not. As it grew darker, I was startled by the honking of geese flying low over the woods, like weary

(40) travelers getting in late from southern lakes, and indulging at last in unrestrained complaint and mutual consolation. Standing at my door, I could hear the rush of their wings; when, driving toward my house, they suddenly spied my light, and with

(45) hushed clamor wheeled and settled in the pond.

In the morning I watched the geese from the door through the mist, sailing in the middle of the pond, fifty rods off, large and tumultuous. But when I stood on the shore they at once rose up

(50) with great flapping of wings at the signal of their commander, and when they had got into rank circled about over my head, twenty-nine of them, and then steered straight to Canada, with a regular honk from the leader at intervals. A plump of

(55) ducks rose at the same time and took the route to the north in the wake of their noisier cousins.

For a week I heard the circling groping clangor of some solitary goose in the foggy mornings, seeking its companion, and still peopling the

(60) woods with the sound of a larger life than they could sustain. In April the pigeons were seen again flying express in small flocks, and in due time I heard the martins twittering over my clearing, though it had not seemed that the township con-

(65) tained so many that it could afford me any, and I fancied that they were peculiarly of the ancient race that dwelt in hollow trees ere white men came. In almost all climes the tortoise and the frog are among the precursors and herald of this sea-

(70) son, and birds fly with song and glancing plumage, and plants spring and bloom, and winds blow to correct this slight oscillation of the poles and preserve the equilibrium of Nature.

As every season seems best to us in its turn, so

(75) the coming in of spring is like creation of Cosmos out of Chaos and the realization of the Golden Age.

14. (C)

This response must be inferred. The narrator says, lines 35–38, that looking at the woodpile can tell you winter is over—in other words, the wood supply is depleted. The geese returning (A) is an outright statement of fact, not an inference. Again, the melting (B) is a statement of fact, not an inference. (D) and (E) are also direct statements of fact within the passage.

15. (D)

The narrator is so excited, so taken by the changes he sees, he can only praise the coming of the spring. There is no proof for (A) and no basis for this judgment. (B) and (C) are too straightforward and are too specific to be correct; neither describes the passage's overall purpose. Although there is truth to (E), the melting pond is but one detail within the bigger picture.

16. (B)

Personification certainly prevails. For example, the geese are tired, squabbling travelers, seeking refuge for the night, wheeling around (as if in a car), falling into rank as ordered by their commander, etc. The description within this passage is anything but restrained (A). Bombast (C) has connotations of being affected. This narrator is not putting on any act within this writing. Although one may see the narrator's description as occasionally overdone, hyperbole (D) is not as predominant as personification. Rhetorical question (E), or a question meant to be answered by the writer, is not in evidence within this passage.

17. (E)

The narrator's clever use of figurative language, multiple levels of sensory images, and manipulation of sentence rhythms create a poetic tone to this passage. This passage uses too much figurative language to be just colloquial (A). Although the narrator shares information with the reader, (B) would not be the best description of the narrator's tone. Some may feel that the celebratory nature of this poem is out of control (C), but unrestrained is not the BEST response. Audacious, bold, and impudent (D), is not appropriate to describe the tone of this passage.

18. (E)

A mirror of the soul is not a comparison found in this passage. The other references can be found in the passage: (A), a canal two rods wide (line 1); (B), a ribbon (line 14); (C), a transparent pond (line 27); (D), a reflection of the sky (lines 28–29).

19. (E)

Lines 38–56 are loaded with sounds and visual images that bring the geese alive within this passage. Although the passage does contain both similes and metaphors (A), they do not dominate the description of the geese. Perhaps some might be amused by the narrator's descriptions (B), but comic descriptors is not the BEST description of the geese. The narrator does not reflect emotionally (C) in the description of the geese. The writer has tight control of the description; images are related (D).

20. (B)

Lines 68–70 state that in almost all regions, the tortoise and the frogs, not the geese, appear first in the spring. The simile of geese like weary travelers (A) can be found in lines 39–40. Lines 50–54 describe the regimental force of geese led by the honking commander (C). Lines 41–42 mentions the unrestrained complaint and mutual consolation (D) among the geese. Lines 54–56 talk about the ducks who are following their noisier cousins, the geese (E). Be on the lookout for questions using EXCEPT: You are being asked to identify that which is NOT present.

21. (B)

The innocence of mankind is NOT discussed within this passage. The passage itself reveals how very connected at least one person is to the world of nature (A). The narrator makes it clear that what is going on has happened before and will happen again (C). Obviously the narrator has been awaiting the passing of winter and has been looking forward to a new season (D). The geese and ducks' return, the tortoise, frogs, and other creatures are all announcing an imminent change (E).

22. (D)

Actually, there are very few simple sentences within this passage, making this the correct response. Some periodic sentences (A) are used in this passage, but so are many other sentence structures. Many prepositional phrases (B) are used in this passage. No rhetorical questions are evident within this passage (C). Although some parallelism exists in this piece, it is certainly not overused (E).

23. (D)

Plump in this case is most like the word *clutch*, which is a term meaning a brood of chicks. This is similar to other collective descriptors such as a *pride* of lions or a *pod* of whales.

Questions 24–33.

Ambush

Very gradually, in tiny slivers, day began to break through the fog, and from my position in the brush I could see ten or fifteen meters up the trail. The mosquitoes were fierce. I remember

(5) slapping at them…then looking up and seeing the young man come out of the fog. He wore black clothing and rubber sandals and a gray ammunition belt. His shoulders were slightly stooped, his head cocked to the side listening to something. He

(10) seemed at ease. He carried his weapon in one hand, muzzle down, moving without any hurry up the center of the trail. There was no sound at all— none that I can remember. In a way, it seemed, he was part of the morning fog, or my own imagina-

(15) tion, but there was also the reality of what was happening in my stomach. I had already pulled the pin on a grenade. I had come up to a crouch. It was entirely automatic. I did not hate the young man; I did not see him as the enemy; I did not

(20) ponder issues of morality or politics or military duty. I crouched and kept my head low. I tried to swallow whatever was rising from my stomach, which tasted like lemonade, something fruity and sour. I was terrified. There were no thoughts

(25) about killing. The grenade was to make him go away—just evaporate—and I leaned back and felt my mind go empty and then fill up again. I had already thrown the grenade before telling myself to throw it. The brush was thick and I had to lob

(30) it high, not aiming, and I remember the grenade seeming to freeze above me for an instant, as if a camera had clicked and I remember ducking down and holding my breath and seeing little wisps of fog rise from the earth. The grenade

(35) bounced once and rolled across the trail. I did not hear it, but there must've been a sound, because the young man dropped his weapon and began to run, just two or three quick steps, then he hesitat- ed, swiveling to his right, and he glanced down at

(40) the grenade and tried to cover his head but never did. It occurred to me then that he was about to die. I wanted to warn him. The grenade made a popping noise—not soft but not loud either—not what I'd expected—and there was a puff of dust

(45) and smoke—a small white puff—and the young man seemed to jerk upward as if pulled by invisi- ble wires. He fell on his back. His rubber sandals had been blown off. There was no wind. He lay at the center of the trail, his right leg bent beneath

(50) him, his one eye shut, his other eye a huge star- shaped blue.

All I could do was gape at the fact of the young man's body. Even now, I haven't finished sorting it out. Sometimes I forgive myself, other times I

(55) don't. In the ordinary hours of life I try not to dwell on it, but now and then, when I'm reading a newspaper or just sitting alone in a room, I'll look up and see the young man coming out of the morning fog. I'll watch him walk toward me, his

(60) shoulders slightly stooped, his head cocked to the side, and he'll pass within a few yards of me and suddenly smile at some secret thought and then continue up the trail to where it bends back into the fog.

24. (D)

The narrator responds to the enemy's presence by lobbing a grenade at him. The narrator is moved to action; he's not too scared to act (A). The passage ends as the narrator envisions the enemy continuing along the path without interruption, but this is a detail thrown in to confuse you; the narrator does not continue up the trail (B). The narrator does not shoot his rifle (C), and the passage gives no indication that the narrator makes much sound (E).

25. (C)

"I did not hate the young man; I did not see him as the enemy," lines 18–20, indicate that this is the correct response. The narrator does not feel anger towards the enemy. The narrator does say that "I wanted to warn him," line 42 (A). In lines 21–22, the narrator says that "I tried to swallow whatever was rising from my stomach" ((B) and (D)). The same reason that letter (C) is the correct answer makes (E) incorrect. The narrator feels no hatred towards his enemy.

26. (C)

Short, staccato sentences juxtaposed with longer ones builds tension within this paragraph. The variance may confuse some readers (A), but this is not the correct response. Sentence variation keeps the reader more, not less alert (B). (D) may be true, but the writer's sentence writing skill is not the BEST response to this question. We do not have the necessary information to determine the validity of (E).

27. (B)

In medias res is the correct response since the passage opens in the middle of the action, without any information building up to this scene. The opening may seem a bit mysterious, but there is no indication of a sinister mood (A). The passage is more matter-of-fact at the start than melodramatic (C). Although the narrator does not act until he sees the enemy, he is still actively attentive to his surroundings (D). There is no irony in the straightforward opening of this piece (E).

28. (B)

The narrator states that his mind went empty, and that he "had already thrown the grenade before telling [himself] to throw it," lines 28–29. These comments make the

response "arbitrary and random" the correct one. This difficult question is a good example of how process of elimination can get you to the right answer choice. In line 18 the narrator admits that his actions were "entirely automatic," ruling out (A). Although the narrator's actions are reactionary, one could not call them pragmatic (C); while they serve the purpose of eliminating an enemy, there isn't the forethought characteristic of a pragmatic act. Reflective and subjective (D) are not how the narrator reacts until later. The narrator's actions are too controversial to make heroic and laudable (E) appropriate adjectives to be the correct response to this question.

29. (B)

Regret and rationalization are the essence of the piece—this can be seen particularly in the last paragraph of the passage. The narrator admits fear, but he never talks about being angry (A). The narrator's humanity is mainly evidenced by his occasional regret at killing his "enemy"; while there is a hint of fraternity in the narrator's attitude toward his adversary, (C) is not the BEST choice. (D) and (E) are not found anywhere in this passage.

30. (C)

The passage contains no idiomatic expressions, that is, particular phrases or word combinations that are peculiar to a certain language or region of a country and that usually can't be translated literally, such as "It's raining cats and dogs." Onomatopoeia can be located in this passage in "there was a puff of dust and smoke" (lines 44–45), and in lines 42–43, "the grenade made a popping noise" (A). Foreshadowing (B) is present at the opening of the passage as soon as the narrator describes his hiding in the jungle and the appearance of the enemy with a gun. One of them is bound to be killed. Perhaps the most outstanding metaphor (D) can be found in the last sentence of the first paragraph in the "huge star-shaped blue" (lines 50–51) eye. The narrator refers to rationalizing—"sorting it out"; "sometimes I forgive myself" (lines 54–55)— in the last paragraph (E).

31. (C)

This is the best statement to summarize the theme of this particular passage. (A) needs to be read twice to see that it is incorrect. (B), (D), and (E) are trite responses that often describe the thematic undertones of war literature.

32. (D)

No simile is present in the last sentence of paragraph 1. Parallel structure (A) is found in the series of phrases describing the dead enemy (*his right leg bent, his one eye shut...*). Anaphora is present because phrases in the series repeat "his" (B). The eye as a star-shaped hole is certainly a vivid metaphor (C). The imagery of this sentence is vivid and disturbing (E).

33. (B)

Reminiscent of Marlow in Conrad's *Heart of Darkness,* it is the horror, the unbelievability of what is happening that the narrator is having difficulties with. The dash implies hesitation, speechlessness, as if the narrator cannot quite grasp that his survival instinct has caused this ghastly action and its result. The use of the dash does not generally qualify anyone as syntactically skillful (A). The conjunction and is used directly after the dashes (C). (D) is an opposite: The dashes are used for a specific effect in the piece. While the dashes do provide variety (E), the most likely reason for their use is to communicate the narrator's mood.

Questions 34–43.

"To-morrow at twelve o'clock I regain my freedom and the right to associate with other men,
but before I leave this room and see the sunshine,
I think it necessary to say a few words to you.
(5) With a clear conscience I tell you, as before God,
who beholds me, that I despise freedom and life
and health, and all that in your books is called the
good things of the world.

"For fifteen years I have been intently studying
(10) earthly life. It is true I have not seen the earth nor
men, but in your books I have drunk fragrant
wine, I have sung songs, I have hunted stags and
wild boars in the forests, have loved women. . . .
Beauties as ethereal as clouds, created by the
(15) magic of your poets and geniuses, have visited me
at night, and have whispered in my ears wonderful
tales that have set my brain in a whirl. In your
books I have climbed to the peaks of Elburz and
Mont Blanc, and from there I have seen the sun
(20) rise and have watched it at evening flood the sky,
the ocean, and the mountain-tops with gold and
crimson. I have watched from there the lightning
flashing over my head and cleaving the storm-
clouds. I have seen green forests, fields, rivers,
(25) lakes, towns. I have heard the singing of the sirens,
and the strains of the shepherds' pipes; I have
touched the wings of comely devils who flew
down to converse with me of God. . . . In your
books I have flung myself into the bottomless pit,
(30) performed miracles, slain, burned towns, preached
new religions, conquered whole kingdoms. . . .

"Your books have given me wisdom. All that the
unresting thought of man has created in the ages
is compressed into a small compass in my brain. I
(35) know that I am wiser than all of you.

"And I despise your books, I despise wisdom
and the blessings of this world. It is all worthless,
fleeting, illusory, and deceptive, like a mirage. You
may be proud, wise, and fine, but death will wipe
(40) you off the face of the earth as though you were
no more than mice burrowing under the floor,
and your posterity, your history, your immortal
geniuses will burn or freeze together with the
earthly globe.

(45) "You have lost your reason and taken the wrong
path. You have taken lies for truth, and hideousness for beauty. You would marvel if, owing to
strange events of some sorts, frogs and lizards
suddenly grew on apple and orange trees instead
(50) of fruit, or if roses began to smell like a sweating
horse; so I marvel at you who exchange heaven for
earth. I don't want to understand you.

"To prove to you in action how I despise all that
you live by, I renounce the two millions of which I
(55) once dreamed as of paradise and which now I
despise. To deprive myself of the right to the
money I shall go out from here five hours before
the time fixed, and so break the compact. . . ."

34. (E)

Paragraph I introduces the thematic idea of the passage; paragraph VI brings things around full circle by completing what is introduced in paragraph I. Looking at the other choices, paragraph I introduces the thematic idea of the passage, but II is just a background explanation (A). You can rule out (B): paragraph II offers background; IV is a continuation of III (B). Although paragraph I gives the thesis, IV is just a continuation (C). Paragraph III begins the narrator's lambaste of his fellow men; VI summarizes the main idea (D), but is best paired with paragraph I in this question.

35. (B)

The narrator never leaves until the end of the passage in which he indicates he will depart five hours short of the agreed upon time of his commitment. Paragraph II certainly supports (A); a list of adventures is given there. Philosophical turmoil (C) is certainly evident in paragraphs III, IV, and V. Lines 25–26 relate sounds he has "heard" within his reading (D). Taken in its true meaning, the narrator does not actually travel to heaven and hell, but his reading has enabled him to travel there virtually, not physically (E).

36. (A)

Paragraph IV is a vituperative condemnation of the narrator's audience—in this case, the actual people whom he is addressing as well as mankind in general. He is not happy with his fellow man, and contemptuous is the best descriptor of this tone. *Condescension* (B) is definitely present within the tone of this paragraph, but it is only a part of the bigger picture of pure contempt that the narrator presents. *Cantankerous* (C) means fussy and often hard to get along with. Although this speaker is disgusted, and unhappy with others, cantankerous does not describe such scathing dialog. A charismatic person is one who is so special that he or she seems to shine in contrast to others. It's as if a charismatic person projected an unusual aura when seen by others. This doesn't describe the narrator's tone; rule out (D). *Choleric* (E) refers to a temperament that is easily angered. Although there is anger underlying the narrator's tone, choleric is too mild a word to BEST describe the tone of this paragraph.

37. (C)

Offering the strong descriptors, *enmity* and *disgust*, (C) is the BEST response. Based on the above explanations, it should be clear that answer choices (A) and (B) are too positive to be the correct response. *Anger* and *resentment*, answer choice (E), do not have the impact nor strong enough connotations to be correct. Although it is true that the narrator is unhappy with mankind, (D) is not a strong enough description.

38. (C)

The narrator indicates no toleration within the invective presented in paragraph V; the tone is thoroughly disdainful (See line 52, "I don't want to understand you"). There is no indication of the imperative in this paragraph, ruling out (A). Although a sense of moralizing is present in this paragraph, didactic (B) is not the BEST response to this question; the narrator has no desire to instruct. The narrator is negative in this paragraph, but like response (B), derogatory is not the BEST choice. Determination (E) does not really relate to the tone of this paragraph.

39. (A)

The presentation of several independent clauses in lines 11–13 with absent intervening conjunctions and lacking proper punctuation is an example of asyndeton and anaphora. This syntax demonstrates both a repetition of the same clause structure, anaphora; but in some cases the clauses are missing the necessary coordinate conjunctions, demonstrating a form of asyndeton. Apostrophe is an address to an inanimate object, not the case in this essay, and assonance is the repetition of the same vowel sounds in words with different endings (B). Apposition is a renaming, not a repetition of syntactical structure; repetition is accurate but it cannot be the answer because it is paired with apposition (C). The only addition present is that of similar clauses; once again, assonance is the repetition of vowel sounds in words with different endings (D). Alliteration is the repetition of initial consonant sounds, and absolutism is a political term, not a literary term (E).

40. (B)

Antithesis is correct—one paragraph relates what the books have given him, and the next paragraph immediately rejects the first when he says he despises the books. Since these paragraphs do not reinforce each other, they are not complementary (A). Imbalance and parallelism cancel each other out (C). Paragraph III evinces some satisfaction on the narrator's part, but paragraph IV certainly does not. Neither insecurity nor diffidence (shyness) (E) is applicable to either of these paragraphs. Remember, in questions such as these, with two-part responses. BOTH parts must be correct for the response to be correct.

41. (C)

Apparently money was valuable to this narrator at one time since he had made a bargain for which he sacrificed his own freedom. This is not stated directly in the text, but must be inferred. It is clear that the narrator has been absent from the mainstream of life for a while, but nothing indicates that this was a sojourn to school (A). The only journey this narrator has been on has been in his mind (B). The narrator had only climbed mountains vicariously through his reading (D). The hardships (E) this narrator relates are those he has experienced within the pages of his books.

42. (B)

Certainly, this narrator has come to believe wholeheartedly that man is much too taken with himself and his own petty world of useless needs. Gambling will only lead to unhappiness (A) is just too trite a response to be the BEST answer. While the narrator does say, "I don't want to understand you!" (C), this is not his theme. Money surely is not everything (D), but this answer, like (A), is just too pat a response. The narrator sees things more in relation to mankind, and what it has evolved into. (E), money, is man's downfall, like (A) and (D), is too simplistic for this passage.

43. (E)

Despite all the "messages" delivered in each paragraph the narrator has written, the one that BEST shows his feelings towards others is paragraph V. In this paragraph he explains just how he thinks that mankind has lost touch with all that is truly worthwhile in this world.

Questions 44–58

Remembrance

Cold in the earth—and the deep snow piled above thee.
Far, far removed, cold in the dreary grave!
Have I forgot, my only Love, to love thee
Severed at last by Time's all-severing wave?

(5) Now, when alone, do my thoughts no longer hover
Over the mountains, on that northern shore,
Resting their wings where heath and fern leaves cover
Thy noble heart forever, ever more?

Cold in the earth—and fifteen wild Decembers,
(10) From those brown hills, have melted into spring;
Faithful indeed is the spirit that remembers
After such years of change and suffering!

Sweet Love of youth, forgive, if I forget thee,
While the world's tide is bearing me along;
(15) Other desires and other hopes beset me,
Hopes which obscure, but cannot do thee wrong!

No later light has lightened up my heaven,
No second morn has ever shone for me;
All my life's bliss from thee dear life has given,
(20) All my life's bliss is in the grave with thee.

But, when the days of golden dreams had perished,
And even Despair was powerless to destroy,
Then did I learn how existence could be cherished,
Strengthened, and fed without the aid of joy.

(25) Then did I check the tears of useless passion—
Weaned my young soul from yearning after thine;
Sternly denied its burning wish to hasten
Down to that tomb already more than mine.

And even yet, I dare not let it languish,
(30) Dare not indulge in memory's rapturous pain;
Once drinking deep of that divinest anguish,
How could I seek the empty world again?

44. (C)

This poem is an elegy, a lament over someone's death. Reject (A), ballad, based on the poem's meter and lack of refrain. An apostrophe (B) is an address to an inanimate object. While the poem has the intense emotion of a lyric (D), answer choice (C), elegy, fits the poem perfectly. The poem lacks the fourteen-line structure of a sonnet (E).

45. (E)

This poem alternates its rhyming lines within each four-line stanza, or quatrain. The incorrect rhyme scheme in (A) is designed to catch a careless test taker. Blank verse (B) consists of unrhymed lines in iambic pentameter. Free verse (C) is characterized by varying line lengths, lack of traditional meter, and nonrhyming lines. The rhyme scheme here is abab, eliminating (D).

46. (D)

All of stanza II concerns the narrator's thoughts. (A), (B), and (C) provide the background for the narrator's thoughts about her lover's gravesite, whereas (E) is a distractor: the narrator's thoughts, and not birds, hover.

47. (C)

Stanza V contains alliteration and assonance when it says "*later light* has *lightened…*" (line 17); anaphora is present in the "No" and "all my…" repetitions; consonance is present in line 17 as well ("*later light*").

48. (D)

The narrator makes it clear that she no longer weeps (A), that she has NOT found a new love, that her life may be cherished without joy (B), that she has trained herself not to yearn (C), and that she has, indeed, remained faithful to the departed (E). She does continue to remember her dead lover, however.

49. (E)

Look at the words *check, weaned, yearning, sternly denied, dare not indulge*, to see that the narrator has been working hard to keep her anguished soul from dwelling too long with rapturous but painful memories of the deceased.

50. (A)

Apology and clemency dominate these two stanzas. Although many of the other feelings are present throughout the poem and within these stanzas, the dominant tone is that of the narrator's sorrowful begging for forgiveness and exoneration from the departed spirit because she, the narrator, has picked up the pieces of her shattered life.

51. (D)

This response takes the reader back to stanza VII, line 26, where the narrator says "Weaned my young soul from yearning after thine." This "young soul" is the antecedent to the word *it* in line 29.

52. (A)

The narrator has stated her resolve to avoid the strong emotions of grief, and has decided to no longer suffer. Her present attitude can best be described as "wistful regret."

53. (D)

Although all of the sentiments offered in these responses may have a bit of credence, the BEST response for this poem is (D). Although someone has been departed for fifteen years, and life has had to continue for the living, thoughts of the departed are never far from the narrator's mind.

54. (B)

Some may think that these two stanzas hold the key to the poem's meaning (A), but the narrator's description of her life after her loss in the other stanzas is critical to the message of the poem. If the reader looks closely, he or she will find these stanzas have a redundancy about them which BEST suggests the cyclical or looping characteristic of the poem's structure.

55. (C)

The final stanza of Emily Brontë's poem has much to offer, including a rhetorical question. The middle two lines, which include "rapturous pain" and "divinest anguish" certainly offer two fine examples of oxymoron.

56. (D)

Stanza IV assures the reader that life continues, despite losses. No matter how much the loss is felt, life must go on; it is worth living.

57. (D)

Nowhere does it say that the narrator is actually incapable of living without the departed. Stanza III mentions fifteen Decembers which have subsequently melted into spring (A); stanza IV talks about other hopes, which beset the narrator (B); stanza II sets up the metaphor of thoughts as winged spirits (C). The final stanza mentions that the narrator fears for the soul that might linger in the memories of rapturous pain (E).

58. (E)

Although a reader might be tempted to choose several of these responses, the most accurate response, in light of the final stanza, is that the narrator must be careful NOT to let her soul linger too long in anguished memory, or the world and day-to-day life would seem "empty."

SECTION II: ESSAY QUESTIONS

Essay Question 1: Richard Wright's "Between the World and Me"

Prompt: Read the following poem carefully. Then, in a well-organized essay, analyze how the speaker uses the varied imagery of the poem to reveal his attitude toward what he has found and how it affects him, paying particular attention to the shifting point of view of the narrator.

Between the World and Me

And one morning while in the woods I stumbled suddenly upon the thing
Stumbled upon it in a grassy clearing guarded by scaly oaks and elms
And the sooty details of the scene rose, thrusting themselves between the world and me....

There was a design of white bones slumbering forgottenly upon a cushion of ashes.
(5) There was a charred stump of a sapling pointing a blunt finger accusingly at the sky.
There were torn tree limbs, tiny veins of burnt leaves, and a scorched coil of greasy hemp;
A vacant shoe, an empty tie, a ripped shirt, a lonely hat, and a pair of trousers stiff with black blood.
And upon the trampled grass were buttons, dead matches. Butt-ends of cigars and cigarettes, peanut
     shells, a drained gin-flask and a whore's lipstick;
(10) Scattered traces of tar, restless array of feathers, and the lingering smell of gasoline.
And through the morning air the sun poured yellow surprise into the eye sockets of the stony
     skull....

And while I stood my mind was frozen within cold pity for the life that was gone.
The ground gripped my feet and my heart was circled by icy walls of fear—
(15) The sun died in the sky; a night wind muttered in the grass and fumbled the leaves in the trees; the
     woods poured forth the hungry yelping of hounds; the darkness screamed with thirsty voices; and
        the witnesses rose and lived:
The dry bones stirred, rattled, lifted, melting themselves into my bones.
The grey ashes formed flesh firm and black, entering into my flesh.

(20) The gin-flask passed from mouth to mouth, cigars and cigarettes glowed, the whore smeared lipstick
     red upon her lips,
And a thousand faces swirled around me, clamoring that my life be burned.....
And then they had me, stripped me, battering my teeth into my throat till I swallowed my own
     blood.

(25) My voice was drowned in the roar of their voices, and my black wet body slipped and rolled in their
     hands as they bound me to the sapling.
And my skin clung to the bubbling hot tar, falling from me in limp patches.
And the down and quills of the white feathers sank into my raw flesh, and I moaned in my agony.
Then my blood was cooled mercifully, cooled by a baptism of gasoline.
(30) And in a blaze of red I leaped to the sky as pain rose like water, boiling my limbs
Panting, begging I clutched childlike, clutched to the hot sides of death.
Now I am dry bones and my face a stony skull staring in yellow surprise at the sun....

ANALYSIS OF ESSAY QUESTION 1

Although many of you may be familiar with the author, Richard Wright, not many people are familiar with this startling poem, "Between the World and Me." This powerful writing describes the discovery of what remains of the tar and feathering of a human being. What is particularly compelling is the narrator's almost cinematic shifting of the point of view. First the poem presents a panoramic shot; then, along with the narrator, the reader moves into the scene as the narrator experiences "cold pity for the life that was gone" (line 13). By the final stanza, the narrator (and thus the reader) becomes the victim, living the pain and horror of the atrocity that has taken place. The narrator concludes as "dry bones [and a] stony skull staring in yellow surprise at the sun…." (line 32).

The prompt directs you to analyze how the narrator uses *the varied imagery of the poem to reveal his attitude toward what he has found and how it affects him, paying particular attention to the shifting point of view of the narrator.* Do not be fooled by the seeming simplicity of this prompt. Imagery abounds in this poem and is therefore easily identified. You can readily note the imagery by rereading the piece, annotating as you go. The complication arises because you must use that imagery to analyze the narrator's attitude toward what he is experiencing. Close reading reveals that the narrator has moved from objectivity to empathy, and, finally, into total immersion. The poem can leave a reader wondering whether or not the narrator is having a vicarious or an actual experience. What drives the movement of the narrator into deeper and deeper involvement is this shifting point of view. It is not difficult for a reader to visualize a bystander who views from a distance, advances to take a better look, and, seemingly without volition, moves into the center of the drama.

A good approach to responding to a question such as this is first to decode the prompt thoroughly. Determine exactly what it is that you are being asked to do. Annotate the prompt itself to establish better what you are being asked. Reread the poem noting various things: analyze the dominant imagery the narrator chooses to describe and how it reveals his attitude; note how the impact of the observations affects the narrator; finally, be sure to observe closely the movement of the poem based on the narrator's shifting point of view. After you have reread the poem and before you begin to write, be sure to reread the prompt again.

It is always easy to present lists of what you find, hypothesize about the narrator's attitude, and even trace a changing point of view. The key to successful essay responses, however, is your ability to incorporate *all* of these into a significant whole. You can see by the following scoring guide that a response worthy of an upper half score shows that the perceptive student is able to analyze the poem, incorporate the directives of the prompt, and communicate successfully. These ideas must then be presented clearly with ample and worthwhile references to the poem itself. Integrate quotations and line references smoothly, making sure that you support each idea adequately. You must present your ideas immediately, being sure that a controlling idea or thesis is clearly evident. Spend a couple paragraphs developing and supporting your main points, and conclude strongly. A strong conclusion does not merely echo the opening lines of the essay. Instead it ties everything together, clearly indicating the student's successful analysis.

So just how does the narrator view the horror? How does he react? He first demonstrates mild curiosity, which quickly becomes horror. His final reaction is when he becomes the victim himself. When the narrator tells us that "The ground gripped my feet and my heart was circled by icy walls of fear—" in line 14, he himself becomes the victim of this horror. He becomes Everyman who has suffered all of mankind's atrocities.

SCORING GUIDE FOR QUESTION 1

9–8: Essays earning these scores demonstrate a successful writer who clearly recognizes Wright's masterful use of strong imagery. These essays display perceptive understanding of how the movement of the poem and its impact upon both the reader and the narrator is dependent upon the shifting point of view of the narrator. Well-developed and insightful, these essays are marked by a keen sense of understanding of imagery, and effect upon the reader. In addition, they indicate the students' sensitivity toward the subtle movement of the narrator from a casual observer to a highly empathetic witness, and, finally, to becoming one with the victim of the horror. In addition, they demonstrate, by means of quotation, how the language reveals the poet's shifting attitude. Although not without error, these essays indicate the students' ability to read poetry skillfully, to respond to the prompt accurately, and to write with clarity and skill.

6–7: These essays treat adequately most of the elements above but do so less thoroughly than the best papers. They will analyze imagery and point of view or narrator attitude less fully than 8–9 papers. They are well written, but use of evidence is less satisfactory. There may be occasional lapses in diction, syntax, or other writing skills, but these essays will demonstrate sufficient control to present the writers' ideas clearly.

5: These essays will be accurate and fairly well written, but they demonstrate some weaknesses. They may resort more to paraphrasing rather than using evidence as strong support. They may present many ideas without tying them together adequately. Or they may be strong in all but one or two aspects of analysis indicated by the prompt. These essays may reveal simplistic thinking and/or immature writing. The writing, however, is still sufficient to convey ideas convincingly.

4–3: These lower-half scores are for essays that inadequately respond to the task set out by the prompt. They may reflect an incomplete understanding of the poem. Often, they do not respond to part or parts of the question. Composition skills will be weak, often presenting many ideas but failing to tie things together. Often they demonstrate an incomplete or incorrect understanding of the poem.

2–1: These essays compound the weaknesses of the papers in the 4–3 range. They seriously misunderstand the prompt, the poem, or possibly both. Often poorly written, they may contain distracting grammar and usage errors. Although some attempt is made to answer the question, the writers' views are unclear, disorganized, incoherent, and/or lacking in supporting evidence. A score of 1 is usually given to those essays that may mention the poem or the prompt, but otherwise have no redeeming qualities.

STUDENT RESPONSES TO QUESTION 1

First response:

Wright's poem begins with what might be a pastoral tone when he mentions the "clearing guarded by scaly oaks and elms" but he undermines this tone immediately with the verb *stumbled* in both the first and second lines, and with the adjective *sooty* to describe the death scene. He is a passer-by who has happened upon something that draws his attention. By the end of the second stanza, however, his curious attitude soon changes.

Stanza 3 shows the narrator's objectivity change to one of empathy. The pile of human remains engages his emotions. He senses the dead victim's fear, his pain, and his degradation. By the end of stanza 3, the narrator moves from outside to inside the horror that he has stumbled upon. In lines 18–19, he says that the dry bones and burned flesh become his own bones and flesh. He says, "The dry bones stirred, rattled, lifted, melting themselves into my bones./The grey ashes formed flesh firm and black, entering into my flesh."

Stanza 4, only 2 lines, shows how the narrator's attitude has indeed altered. He "observes" what the tormenters were doing, not as another observer, but now as the victim. He visualizes the scene as it was, now saying that "faces swirled around [me], clamoring that my life be burned…."

The final stanza is the best (and the worst) of them all. The narrator—Wright or whoever—*is* the victim. He suffers; in pain, he wishes for death, and finally, at the end he receives the blessed relief he has longed for. He dies as the person whose remains he discovered in stanza one. It is his "face a stony skull staring in yellow surprise at the sun…."

Second response:

How many people innocently happen upon a curious scene, only to be engulfed in a more serious situation of horror, fear, and sometimes tragedy? Perhaps that is why we sometimes read or hear about someone who's been beaten or raped or even robbed while the rest of the world walks by, not wanting to "get involved." In this poem by Richard Wright, the bystander does not walk by, and what seems like nothing more than a peculiarity in the landscape becomes the narrator's own very personal tragedy.

The words *sooty* and *stumble* in the first stanza add a touch of foreboding, which intensifies in stanza two. Images of "white bones," "ashes" juxtaposed with "cushion," and death and sleep imagery when he describes the bones as "slumbering" all add to the narrator's apprehension. He further develops the imagery of death in the "charred stump…torn veins of burnt leaves, and a scorched coil…." His isolation is emphasized through the adjectives "vacant…empty…ripped…lonely…and trousers stiff with black blood." Might this be a type of genetic remembrance? Is he possibly reliving the terror of his own ancestors? The reader cannot avoid such thoughts while reading this powerful description. Lines 8–9 hammer this desolation home with trampled grass, dead matches, butt-ends and finally, "a drained gin flask and a whore's lipstick." He then strikes a further note of horror when he observes the tar, the feathers, and "the lingering smell of gasoline."

In the third stanza, the poet recalls the probable drama which produced all of this. He tells us his "mind was frozen within cold pity" and that he "was circled by icy walls of fear." Now the sun dies. Terror is enhanced with sound images of yelping hounds and screaming darkness. The "dry bones stirred, rattled, lifted, melting [into] the grey ashes which became his flesh."

Second Response (cont.)

Stanza four, although only two lines long, echoes the 2nd in its mention of gin flask, cigars and whore's lipstick. Now the narrator has shifted to present tense. He has moved everything into his own present time, now these images all clamor for his life to be burned.

Finally, they "stripped" him "battering" his teeth "till [he] swallowed [his] own blood." His "voice was drowned…" as they "bound" him. He feels the "bubbling hot tar" and the feathers "sank into raw flesh as he moaned in agony." Finally he "clutched the hot sides of death." In fact, he finds death a blessed release from his suffering. The gasoline cools his skin in its baptism of death. This poem offers no comfort to any of humanity—oppressor or oppressed. He becomes the Everyman of all who have suffered at the hands of other human beings' hatred.

When the poem is over, it is not over. There lingers a morbid aura of despair. The reader is reminded of the first half of the 20th century, when black men swung from trees, lynched, burned and mutilated. Meanwhile, their tormentors stagger to their long black sedans and weave their boozy way home, listening to Billy Holiday on the car radio. The curtain falls; the music still plays, and we sit in stunned silence in our seats. Will there never be a finale to such horror?

COMMENTARY ON STUDENT RESPONSES TO QUESTION 1

Both of these essays respond adequately to the prompt. Obviously, both writers have a clear understanding of Richard Wright's poem, and both have analyzed it successfully. In both responses you can see that the students address the narrator's attitude and how this attitude changes within the poem.

The first response demonstrates the student's understanding in this quite adequate essay. The essay would be enhanced had the writer used more support and explanation. The student successfully discusses the narrator's shifting attitude, but he or she reveals neither particularly outstanding insight nor profound treatment of Wright's message.

The second student essay is the stronger of the two. Not only has the writer understood the poem, he or she demonstrates an exceptional perception in the interpretation. This essay immediately engages the reader by opening with a common experience for most readers—that is, hearing or reading about the "I don't want to get involved" syndrome in action. In addition, seeing the victim as a 20th cen-

tury Everyman who represents others who have suffered at the hands of fellow humans clearly demonstrates this student's exceptional insight and maturity. The Billy Holiday comment (talented African American female singer from early in the last century) was an interesting touch. In addition, the stunned silence at the end is particularly insightful.

Both of these essays are upper-half responses. The first demonstrates lower upper-half success, somewhere in the 6 range. The second essay, though clearly not perfect, is a fine example of a very successful upper-half response, definitely an 8 response.

When you read the poem and the prompt, then read these student essays, you should be able to understand better the range of upper-half success. Poetry questions—both in the essay section and in the multiple-choice—can be difficult for some students. If you feel that you could never write anything like these essay responses, you should go to the chapter in this book on poetry. There you will find suggestions for reading poetry and tools you can use in analyzing the poems you will find in both the multiple-choice and essay portions of the AP English Literature and Composition Exam.

Essay Question 2: Lunch with Virginia Woolf

Prompt: In the following two passages, Virginia Woolf describes two different meals that she was served during a university visit. The first meal was served at the men's college, while the second meal was served at the women's college. Read the two passages carefully, then write a well-organized essay in which you explain how formal elements such as structure, syntax, diction, and imagery reveal not only the speaker's response to the two meals, but also discuss possible conclusions a reader might draw about the narrator's attitude, based upon these descriptions.

I. It is a curious fact that novelists have a way of making us believe that luncheon parties are invariably memorable for something very witty that was said, or for something very wise that was done. But
(5) they seldom spare a word for what was eaten. It is part of the novelist's convention not to mention soup and salmon and ducklings, as if soup and salmon and ducklings were of no importance whatsoever, as if nobody ever smoked a cigar or drank a
(10) glass of wine. Here, however, I shall take the liberty to defy that convention and to tell you that the lunch on this occasion began with soles, sunk in a deep dish, over which the college cook had spread a counterpane of the whitest cream, save that it was brand-
(15) ed here and there with brown spots like the spots on the flanks of a doe. After that came the partridges, but if this suggests a couple of bald, brown birds on a plate you are mistaken. The partridges, many and various, came with all their retinue of sauces and sal-
(20) ads, the sharp and sweet, each in its order, their potatoes, thin as coins but not so hard; their sprouts, foliated as rosebuds but more succulent. And no sooner had the roast and its retinue been done with than the silent serving man, the Beadle himself perhaps in a
(25) milder manifestation, set before us, wreathed in napkins, a confection which rose all sugar from the waves. To call it pudding and so relate it to rice and tapioca would be an insult. Meanwhile the wineglasses had flushed yellow and flushed crimson; had
(30) been emptied; had been filled. And thus by degrees was lit, halfway down the spine, which is the seat of the soul, not that hard little electric light which we call brilliance, as it pops in and out upon our lips, but the more profound, subtle and subterranean
(35) glow, which is the rich yellow flame of rational intercourse. No need to hurry. No need to sparkle. No

need to be anybody but oneself… How good life seemed, how sweet its rewards, how trivial this grudge or that grievance, how admirable friendship
(40) and the society of one's kind….

II. Everybody was assembled in the big dining-room. Dinner was ready. Here was the soup. It was a plain gravy soup. There was nothing to stir the fancy in that. One could have seen through the transpar-
(45) ent liquid any pattern that there might have been on the plate itself. But there was no pattern. The plate was plain. Next came beef with its attendant greens and potatoes—a homely trinity, suggesting the rumps of cattle in a muddy market, and sprouts
(50) curled and yellowed at the edge, and bargaining and cheapening, and women with string bags on Monday morning. There was no reason to complain of human nature's daily food, seeing that the supply was sufficient and coal miners doubtless were sitting
(55) down to less. Prunes and custard followed. And if any one complains that prunes, even when mitigated by custard, are an uncharitable vegetable (fruit they are not), stringy as a miser's heart and exuding a fluid such as might run in misers' veins who have
(60) denied themselves wine and warmth for eighty years and yet not given to the poor, he should reflect that there are people whose charity embraces even the prune. Biscuits and cheese came next, and here the water jug was liberally passed round, for it is the
(65) nature of biscuits to be dry, and these were biscuits to the core. That was all. The meal was over. Everybody scraped their chairs back; the swing-doors swung violently to and fro; soon the hall was emptied of every sign of food and made ready no
(70) doubt for breakfast the next morning.

ANALYSIS OF ESSAY QUESTION 2

Not all students will be familiar with the author Virginia Woolf. In fact, the designers of the AP English exams do not expect students to know any specific authors. They do expect, however, that students who have completed an Advanced Placement English Literature and Composition course will have developed their analytical and composition skills by studying novels, plays, and poems of literary merit. Therefore, the fact that Virginia Woolf was a British author who wrote in the early 20th century is not a fact that students necessarily need to know to respond to the prompt and the passages. Nevertheless, students who might know this author's work, and the era in which she wrote, could possibly find this information helpful in their analysis of Woolf's underlying intentions.

When two pieces of literature are to be compared and contrasted, students are often tempted to do just that: compare the passages without addressing the more general task(s) of the prompt. For instance, comparison and contrast is inevitable with this question. However, that is not the primary task required by the prompt. The prompt asks you to explain how elements such as structure, syntax, diction, and imagery reveal the narrator's attitude. Therefore, you must look for intimation of meaning not just in what she says, but also in what she does not say within these two revealing descriptions. If you explore implications and draw some sort of overall purpose or sense of the narrator's attitude, it will be much easier for you to write your essay without resorting to the back-and-forth discussion that often results when two passages are juxtaposed as they are in this question.

The most obvious difference in the two passages is their length. Within the longer passage you will soon discover that the sentences are also rather lengthy and filled with highly descriptive phrases and subordinate clauses. The syntax in the second passage, in contrast, has more short, simple sentences, or when sentences are longer, they still seem to be choppy due to the narrator's stringing together choppy phrases or abrupt clauses. For instance, blunt sentences are evident in lines 41–44, while lines 67–70 demonstrate a similar staccato rhythm.

The imagery in the two descriptions is superb. The meal in the men's dining room is sumptuous and elegant. Woolf

describes this opulence in such lines as 12–30, when cream becomes a white counterpane and partridges are presented as nobility accompanied by an entourage of suitable attendants. Wine flows throughout this meal, warming the soul accordingly. The leisurely, sumptuous, elegant meal is skillfully illustrated through Woolf's liberal use of superlatives. Unfortunately, the meal Woolf experiences in the women's college dining hall is not so enjoyable. The way the passage opens is the first hint that this is going to be a quite a different experience. There is no leisurely entré into this meal. The plain gravy soup is served immediately. It is so transparent that the bottom of the starkly plain, utilitarian bowl is visible. The main course, rather than accompanied by a royal entourage, is attended by a homely trinity of wilted vegetables, curled and yellowed at the edges. The supply of food is not scanty, and Woolf assures us that many poor people have even less. Nevertheless, that does nothing to lessen the impact of her comments on prunes, miser's hearts, dry biscuits, and cheese washed down by plain water, and finally (thankfully) a hasty dismissal.

You may be tempted to just say that the narrator liked and was impressed by the first meal and not so with the second. But what more is Woolf saying here? How well you can analyze the so-called *deeper meaning* of these two passages will make the difference in your score. What attitude can you infer from the description of these meals? Is Virginia Woolf just relaying two similar activities but very different experiences, or is she, perhaps, asking the reader to see further? Of course every reader will respond differently to passages such as these. Nevertheless, it is important to remember that the test development committee would be unlikely to choose two such passages for the AP English Literature and Composition Exam simply for your light-hearted amusement. Could you infer that she may be going so far as to comment on university education for men versus university education for women? Is she subtly telling society (and, of course, the reader) something about their own attitudes? Do you think she is so taken by the first meal that she will simply dismiss the paucity of extravagance in the second? These are the types of underlying possibilities you must consider when faced with a prompt such as this one. Seeing beyond the obvious is what separates good essays from those that are simply mediocre. Just as in the two meals—the first meal would garner an upper range score; the second meal, though substantial, is simply adequate.

SCORING GUIDE FOR QUESTION 2

9–8: Responses meriting these scores demonstrate an understanding of the differences between the two passages. They illustrate this understanding with a clear thesis and with persuasive references to the texts. Not only do these essays feature a strong inferential understanding of the content and tone of each passage, but they show that the writer perceives the narrator's attitudes as she describes similar activities but very different experiences. Well-conceived, well-developed, and well-organized, these essays provide frequent and adequate and accurate references to the Woolf passages, blending the comparison without setting up a volley between them. The writers of these essays comfortably explain Woolf's use of the formal elements and cleverly weave the significance of these elements into the response. Although these responses are not perfect, they clearly indicate the students' ability to read prose skillfully and respond to the prompt in mature composition style.

7–6: These essays feature solid understanding of the prompt and the two passages. Although essays in this range will not be as full nor as polished as the 9–8 responses, they are well written in an appropriate style, but often with less maturity than the top papers. They may be less fully developed, or they may demonstrate less insight. Nevertheless, the writing is sufficient to convey ideas, the presentation is sound, and it reflects the writers' ability to convey their points clearly.

5: Essays in this middle range are able to discuss how the two passages contrast, and what these differences might represent, but these responses are typically superficial or may be overly generalized. Often formal elements are identified, and possibly cited, but are poorly integrated into the response. Usually these responses demonstrate inconsistent control over the elements of composition and/or the student's analytical skills are erratic.

4–3: Responses earning these scores are likely to have one or more of these flaws: a simple recounting or restatement of the differences between the passages; imprecise or incomplete treatment of the formal elements within the two passages; little analysis; weak discussion about the author's attitudes within the two passages and what these differing attitudes may indicate; incomplete or sketchy support information. These responses often demonstrate a student's incomplete or incorrect understanding of either or both of the passages.

2–1: These essays unsuccessfully respond to the tasks of the prompt. They may misunderstand the prompt, the passages, or all of these. Although the student will make some attempt to answer, there is little clarity about the interpretation of the passages and only slight or misused evidence to develop this analysis. The writing often reveals consistent weaknesses in grammar or other basic composition skills such as organization, clarity, fluency, or development.

STUDENT RESPONSE TO QUESTION 2

Most of us get a pretty clear mental image when we think of school lunches, not always the most pleasant. Virginia Woolf offers us descriptions of two very different meals served in two very different university dining halls. In the first passage, she praises the meal, the ambience, and the leisurely pace of the luncheon. In contrast, the second describes a rather bland meal that sounds as if the only thing in its favor was quantity, certainly not quality. Why is there such discrepancy? The answer is simple—the first magnificent meal was in a *men's* dining hall. The other meal was in a *women's* dining hall. This, I believe is significant, not only to her attitude, but to the underlying purpose in her contrasting these—society's attitude toward the privileged young gentlemen of her time receiving their education, and the not so favorable response to women's education at that time.

The meal in the men's dining hall is fantastic! Virginia piles up the praise as she offers one extraordinary image after another. For instance, she refers to the fish appetizer as covered with a white cloth, and she assures us that the partridges that followed were hardly recognizable as the bald, brown birds they must have been under all the special sauces and creams and side dishes. Through her clever use of metaphor, she paints for the reader a picture of a royal bird accompanied by suitably noble vegetables, salads and other side dishes. The potatoes are thinly sliced, the sprouts look like flowers, and the service is quietly accomplished. Such a wonderful meal would not be complete without an appropriate desert, and this she also describes as a sweet creation made of sugar. Of course all of this is served with a variety of appropriate wines. Everyone is relaxed. Apparently no one has to go to class, because none seem to be in a hurry to leave.

The meal in the women's dining hall is quite another story. There is no introduction into the meal or why she is even interested in describing it. In the men's passage she works her way slowly into the meal by providing a brief introduction as to why she ought to be writing about it. In the women's dining hall, it sounds as if they no sooner sit down than the thinnest gravy soup in the world is put before them. Things go downhill from there. No fine ret-inue of royalty and retainers here. All they have is beef that she compares to a rump of cattle, and wilted vegetables that look like the leftovers a poor housewife might get at a bargain price "the day after." And, to make things even worse, they served prunes! The cheese and biscuits at the end can barely be swallowed. No wine here to wash it down—just plain water. It seems that she no sooner puts down her fork and people began to leave the hall. Who can blame them?

I believe that Virginia Woolf chose to present this contrast for a reason. She probably exaggerates both situations, but I have to wonder why. It was very uncommon for women to go to college, even up to World War II. It wasn't until the 50s and 60s that women started pursuing an education to prepare them for a career. Until then, a woman rarely studied beyond high school except maybe some sort of secretarial or similar training until she could find a husband and not have to worry about knowing anything besides being a wife and mother. I think that this really bothered Virginia Woolf. I believe that she herself was probably a woman before her time. She demonstrates how unfair she thought these biased attitudes were. Instead of giving a speech or producing a scathing letter, she let these two descriptions tell it for her. Young men were privileged, gentlemen who were to be pampered and cared for while they attained their higher education. Therefore, their meals (at least for the wealthier ones) might be like the first that Woolf described. Women, on the other hand, "had no business going to college anyway." People thought their place was in the home, caring for a family. This is demonstrated by Virginia's second description. There is no introduction— soup is served immediately. Everything is utilitarian. The women experience no frills, no special preparation. What are they doing there anyhow? They should be taking care of a husband and having babies.

I am not sure that dormitory food has improved since Virginia Woolf's time. I sure hope so. Nevertheless, what has improved is that women now, for the most part, share equal footing with men in the world of education and careers. I think Virginia Woolf would have been much happier living now than when she wrote these pieces.

COMMENTARY ON STUDENT RESPONSE TO QUESTION 2

This student essay opens with a rather provocative introduction. Most of us have not too pleasant memories of school lunchroom meals. Immediately this clever student manages to engage almost any reader by bringing to mind a common memory most of us have. From there the introduction goes on to talk about the two Virginia Woolf passages. The mention of when Woolf might have been writing (which was a fairly accurate guess) takes on more meaning as the student's essay evolves. Several errors in grammar and syntax are evident in this opening, but since no egregious error has been made, this essay gets off to a good start.

The discussion of the meal in the men's hall is the focus of the second paragraph. This description is aptly accomplished. Although this student has not given specific line numbers as support, nor has he or she used direct quotations, this description is easy to follow because specific things are mentioned. For example, the thin potatoes, noble pheasant, sugar confection dessert are referenced. The student has handled support references by mentioning specifics but at the same time avoiding the sometimes clumsy line-by-line references, or the often awkward direct quotations. The second paragraph does a nice job discussing the meal in the men's hall.

Paragraph 3 is dedicated to describing the contrasting meal in the women's dining hall. This description is also well handled. Although it is better not to use trite phrases such as "Things go downhill from there," this description is also successful. A bit of editorializing about prunes is not remiss here, albeit presented rather informally. However, the use of the exclamation point and the implication of what is not being said about prunes, makes this an appealing addition to this paragraph. Some may criticize the informal personalizing of the student's tone in this paragraph. By now, however, this response has established a relaxed, almost casual tone, so this paragraph also works very well in the essay.

This familiar tone continues into the fourth paragraph. It is here that the student shows that he or she has taken the obvious contrasts between these two passages and analyzes the reason why the author might have done such a thing. This paragraph in particular is what places this response firmly into the upper-half range. It is definitely a 7 response. More generous readers might even say the essay is deserving of an 8. Tying the two passages to the disparity of social attitudes about the higher education of young men and higher education for young women shows that this student has recognized the obvious differences in these passages. More importantly, however, the student senses that there is much to consider about why Virginia Woolf even bothered to write such description. The response infers that Virginia Woolf might just be making a social statement. Young men, especially in England, who attended university were truly of the privileged class. It was their right, their due, that they do so. It is no wonder, then, that their meals were an elaborate, even extravagant affair. This was synonymous with their privilege. Women, on the other hand, had no business attending university. If they took schooling beyond high school at all, it would be to train for some interim activity until the appropriate marriage could be made and they had a home and family to look after. If they were of privilege, they would have a household of staff to take care of everything while they carried out social duties expected of their class. Anything out of this norm would have been considered wrong. Women were to come out and "do their duty" in society. They had no business attending university. This essay response has managed to demonstrate a fine understanding of this societal injustice. Whether or not Virginia Woolf truly intended for such a message to be made is actually immaterial. The student who wrote this response was able to aptly support this interpretation.

Although the last very short paragraph is abrupt and somewhat trite, this is forgivable. It reminds us that the person writing this essay is still a student, not a social or literary critic. In addition, after the quite profound discussion of the previous paragraph, these last few lines remind us once again of the comfortable tone and engaging style with which the essay began.

Essay Question 3: Margaret Thatcher Quote

Prompt: Margaret Thatcher, former Prime Minister of Great Britain, once said, "In politics, if you want anything said, ask a man; if you want anything done, ask a woman."

Novels and plays often portray circumstances that reflect Margaret Thatcher's sentiment. Select a novel or play that includes a situation in which a woman is the strongest character, best able to carry out necessary action. In a well-written, focused essay, discuss how this idea contributes to the meaning as well as the outcome of the work as a whole. You may choose a work from the list below or another novel or play of literary merit.

ANALYSIS OF ESSAY QUESTION 3

The "open-ended" question on the AP English Literature and Composition exam is always a challenge for students. Now you must call upon an outside resource to create your response. You are asked to choose a novel or play of literary merit, to use as the basis of your response. Sometimes these questions are deceptive. This particular prompt is a case in point. It would be tempting for students to simply describe a book or a play wherein a strong female character directs the action, with much retelling of plot. Doubtlessly, such a response would garner a lower-half score.

This prompt, however, asks more from you. It asks you not only to discuss a literary work with a strong female character, but also it calls for you to discuss *how* the idea of a woman being more capable of executing necessary action contributes to the meaning of the piece. In addition, you must show how such action drives the plot and affects the outcome of the work. This prompt should certainly precipitate some thinking. Again, it is important to stress that a mere rehash of plot and action will not be enough.

Many literary works would be appropriate as a resource for your response. Nearly every high school student has read *Macbeth* and/or the *Scarlet Letter*. In addition, most students will be familiar with either or both *Antigone* or *Medea*. The resources are endless. Tony Morrison writes of strong and successful women, as does Louise Erdrich, Margaret Atwood, Amy Tan, and Henrick Ibsen. Usually a list of suggested works accompanies this open-ended prompt. It is not necessary for students to choose from the offered list. However, it is important that whatever literature you choose is "of literary merit." As much as you might like Stephen King's *Carrie*, she would not be an appropriate driving female character for you to write about.

The important thing to remember for this response is always to determine exactly what you are being asked to do with the piece of literature you choose. Of course it will be necessary to talk about the book or play you are using. Just be sure, however, that your references and story telling always have a purpose to them. Use these references wisely for support and explanation of the points you make.

SCORING GUIDE FOR QUESTION 3

9–8: Responses in this range select a work of literature where an exceptional female character either dominates the action of the work or at least is able to instigate action critical to the plot of the novel or play. These essays are well-conceived, well-developed and well-organized, and the student has been able to take their response a step further by making more insightful associations between the character's actions and the broader sense of the literary piece as a whole. These responses readily grasp the intent of the prompt, and they adeptly reveal how their choice of female character best lives up to the Margaret Thatcher quotation. They need not be without flaws; nevertheless, they demonstrate that the students have mastered not only the skill of analyzing a piece of literature appropriately, but also have mastered exceptional composition skills.

7–6: These essays treat satisfactorily most of the elements of the 9–8 papers, but they do so less thoroughly than the best papers. Their discussion of the significant female character is not as deft as that of the 9–8 responses. In addition, they tend to be less convincing than are the best responses. They adequately demonstrate how the chosen female character is a controlling force within the particular work, but they fail to go beyond the predictable. Although these writers do understand the tasks of the prompt, they do so with less maturity and control of writing skills than the top papers.

5: These essays are highly superficial. The analysis may be unconvincing, underdeveloped, or even somewhat inaccurate. The thinking demonstrated in these responses is less mature and less developed than the upper–half responses. Nevertheless, it is easy to recognize the intent of these responses, and they do not fall into the lower half range.

4–3: These lower-half essays may choose an acceptable work, but they fail to explain how the character fulfills the qualifications set up by the prompt. Their analysis is often trite and perfunctory. The writing usually conveys the writer's ideas, but it reveals weak control over such elements as diction, organization, syntax, or grammar. These essays may also demonstrate some misunderstanding of the prompt.

2–1: These essays compound the weaknesses of essays in the 4–3 range. They may misread the prompt, or choose a character inappropriate to the prompt. These essays are often quite brief, and they fail to give much support or development to any of the ideas they present. Although it is clear that these essays attempt to respond to the prompt, the ideas presented often display minimal clarity or coherence.

STUDENT RESPONSE TO OPEN-ENDED QUESTION 3

The Margaret Thatcher quotation is a provacative one. It seems to supplement the idea of action speaking louder than words. Many fine novels and plays have strong female characters whose actions dictate the movement of the story. In some cases there would be no story without them. One such character would be Lady Macbeth. Although Macbeth himself was certainly entranced by the predictions of the witches, I've always felt that he would not have done what he did without the urging of his extremely ambitious wife. By the time he returned home to tell her about the prediction, she was already thinking about being fitted for a crown!

By the time that King Duncan arrives for his visit, Lady Macbeth has her husband thoroughly psyched for action. She has some outstanding lines where she accuses her husband of weakness, of being "too full of human kindness" to act without her help. It was Lady Macbeth that gets the men guarding the visiting king drunk. She's the one who takes it upon herself to kill the king. But even she cannot go through with such an action. For some reason, the sleeping king looks like her father so she chickens out.

She returns to Macbeth. She still wants him to go through with their plans, but he's ready to back out of the entire thing. She keeps nagging him to kill the king, however. It is here that she goes on to say that she would have plucked her own child from her nursing breast and killed it if she had sworn to do so the way Macbeth had sworn to kill the king. She works on him long enough so that he finally goes in and does the bloody deed. He is so shook by what he has done that Lady Macbeth must go kill the guards for him and set them up to look like they killed the king. She thinks of everything.

Macbeth is soon made king. It seems that Lady Macbeth, the moving force in all of this has definitely succeeded where her husband probably would not have by himself. She had much to be smug about.

But this is a Shakespearean tragedy, and things never work out so easily. Eventually guilt over what they have done gets to both of them. Lady Macbeth, who was so strong in the beginning, eventually snaps under the pressure of her guilt. She actually goes crazy, and starts sleepwalking and trying to wash the blood off her hands Macbeth is not feeling too good about himself either, and without his strong wife to keep him propped up, things just fall apart for him. Of course he ends up dead at the end of the play and she commits suicide. So nothing came of all her efforts.

Although Macbeth and his wife lost everything they worked so hard to achieve, there is no doubt that without Lady Macbeth he wouldn't have gotten anywhere. Of course, if she was not the type of female that Margaret Thatcher's quote so readily applies to, neither of them would have been dead at the end of the play, either. Shakespeare's Lady Macbeth was truely a strong character. She was the one most responsible for what developed in the story. It was this strength that directed the action of the tragedy.

COMMENTARY ON STUDENT RESPONSE TO QUESTION 3

This student essay, although not brilliant, certainly is an adequate response to this particular prompt a 6 or most probably a 7. No doubt a prompt such as this one would elicit many essays citing Lady Macbeth as the mover and shaker of this play. There is nothing wrong with using the more obvious literature for such a response, but if you are comfortable in referencing a less typical literary choice, it might be to your benefit. The truth is, readers become very bored with the tedium of reading about the same play or novel again and again; therefore, a lesser known piece of literature is a welcome relief for them. Consequently, they may be inclined to have a more positive opinion of what you have written.

Nevertheless, this student essay is good. This student clearly has a fine handle on the story of *Macbeth*. The writer also feels confident that Lady Macbeth is the controlling character within the play. The response demonstrates no profound insight into the character's control and its effects, but it clearly shows that the student understands the prompt and its requirements. It begins with a very mundane opening. However, this ordinary introduction is not what earmarks this essay as simply adequate. The essay tells a lot of the *Macbeth* story, but it important for you to notice that the plot is not rehashed randomly. The incidents that are referenced are significant in responding to the prompt. This is important. This particular question, no matter what the prompt, requires you to talk about the plot of the piece of literature that you have chosen. But this retelling of plot must be limited to its use only as sup-

port for the points you are making. Be sure you do not become so carried away in the retelling of a story that you lose sight of the purpose of your reference. This student might easily have fallen into that trap by going on about Duncan's sons, Banquo, his ghost, McDuff and so on. Instead, this essay makes references to only those parts of the play that were relevant to the points the student was making.

Why then, you might wonder, would this response receive only a 7 if it seems to do everything it is supposed to? Look again at the scoring guide. Clearly the essays deserving an 8 or a 9 go beyond the very minimum of being an adequate response. These essays see more than what is the most obvious. These responses seem more able not only to make connections, but are also able to articulate these perceptions in a stylistically exceptional manner. AP reader jargon would say that an 8 response is quite successful, but a 9 response is one that shines. In contrast, this essay just plods along, making its points, but stirring no excitement with the points that it makes

This Lady Macbeth response is certainly upper-half. It might be what is often referred to as pedestrian, that is, somewhat predictable in what it reveals. There is nothing in it to stir the soul. Nevertheless, this student has a good command of composition skills, albeit a few errors are recognizable. The demands of the prompt are quite adequately satisfied. Though some may be tempted to say, "oh no, not another *Macbeth* response," this essay clearly and confidently demonstrates how this very persuasive lady was unmistakably the one in control of this well-known tragedy.

Practice Test Two Answer Sheet

1 Ⓐ Ⓑ Ⓒ Ⓓ Ⓔ
2 Ⓐ Ⓑ Ⓒ Ⓓ Ⓔ
3 Ⓐ Ⓑ Ⓒ Ⓓ Ⓔ
4 Ⓐ Ⓑ Ⓒ Ⓓ Ⓔ
5 Ⓐ Ⓑ Ⓒ Ⓓ Ⓔ
6 Ⓐ Ⓑ Ⓒ Ⓓ Ⓔ
7 Ⓐ Ⓑ Ⓒ Ⓓ Ⓔ
8 Ⓐ Ⓑ Ⓒ Ⓓ Ⓔ
9 Ⓐ Ⓑ Ⓒ Ⓓ Ⓔ
10 Ⓐ Ⓑ Ⓒ Ⓓ Ⓔ
11 Ⓐ Ⓑ Ⓒ Ⓓ Ⓔ
12 Ⓐ Ⓑ Ⓒ Ⓓ Ⓔ
13 Ⓐ Ⓑ Ⓒ Ⓓ Ⓔ
14 Ⓐ Ⓑ Ⓒ Ⓓ Ⓔ
15 Ⓐ Ⓑ Ⓒ Ⓓ Ⓔ
16 Ⓐ Ⓑ Ⓒ Ⓓ Ⓔ
17 Ⓐ Ⓑ Ⓒ Ⓓ Ⓔ
18 Ⓐ Ⓑ Ⓒ Ⓓ Ⓔ
19 Ⓐ Ⓑ Ⓒ Ⓓ Ⓔ
20 Ⓐ Ⓑ Ⓒ Ⓓ Ⓔ
21 Ⓐ Ⓑ Ⓒ Ⓓ Ⓔ

22 Ⓐ Ⓑ Ⓒ Ⓓ Ⓔ
23 Ⓐ Ⓑ Ⓒ Ⓓ Ⓔ
24 Ⓐ Ⓑ Ⓒ Ⓓ Ⓔ
25 Ⓐ Ⓑ Ⓒ Ⓓ Ⓔ
26 Ⓐ Ⓑ Ⓒ Ⓓ Ⓔ
27 Ⓐ Ⓑ Ⓒ Ⓓ Ⓔ
28 Ⓐ Ⓑ Ⓒ Ⓓ Ⓔ
29 Ⓐ Ⓑ Ⓒ Ⓓ Ⓔ
30 Ⓐ Ⓑ Ⓒ Ⓓ Ⓔ
31 Ⓐ Ⓑ Ⓒ Ⓓ Ⓔ
32 Ⓐ Ⓑ Ⓒ Ⓓ Ⓔ
33 Ⓐ Ⓑ Ⓒ Ⓓ Ⓔ
34 Ⓐ Ⓑ Ⓒ Ⓓ Ⓔ
35 Ⓐ Ⓑ Ⓒ Ⓓ Ⓔ
36 Ⓐ Ⓑ Ⓒ Ⓓ Ⓔ
37 Ⓐ Ⓑ Ⓒ Ⓓ Ⓔ
38 Ⓐ Ⓑ Ⓒ Ⓓ Ⓔ
39 Ⓐ Ⓑ Ⓒ Ⓓ Ⓔ
40 Ⓐ Ⓑ Ⓒ Ⓓ Ⓔ
41 Ⓐ Ⓑ Ⓒ Ⓓ Ⓔ
42 Ⓐ Ⓑ Ⓒ Ⓓ Ⓔ

43 Ⓐ Ⓑ Ⓒ Ⓓ Ⓔ
44 Ⓐ Ⓑ Ⓒ Ⓓ Ⓔ
45 Ⓐ Ⓑ Ⓒ Ⓓ Ⓔ
46 Ⓐ Ⓑ Ⓒ Ⓓ Ⓔ
47 Ⓐ Ⓑ Ⓒ Ⓓ Ⓔ
48 Ⓐ Ⓑ Ⓒ Ⓓ Ⓔ
49 Ⓐ Ⓑ Ⓒ Ⓓ Ⓔ
50 Ⓐ Ⓑ Ⓒ Ⓓ Ⓔ
51 Ⓐ Ⓑ Ⓒ Ⓓ Ⓔ
52 Ⓐ Ⓑ Ⓒ Ⓓ Ⓔ
53 Ⓐ Ⓑ Ⓒ Ⓓ Ⓔ
54 Ⓐ Ⓑ Ⓒ Ⓓ Ⓕ
55 Ⓐ Ⓑ Ⓒ Ⓓ Ⓔ
56 Ⓐ Ⓑ Ⓒ Ⓓ Ⓔ
57 Ⓐ Ⓑ Ⓒ Ⓓ Ⓔ
58 Ⓐ Ⓑ Ⓒ Ⓓ Ⓔ

Practice Test Two

Section I: Multiple-Choice Questions

Time: 1 hour
Number of questions: 54
Percent of total grade: 45

Directions: This section contains selections from literary works with questions on their content, style, form, and purpose. Read each selection, then choose the best answer from the five choices in each test item and fill in the corresponding oval on the answer sheet.

<u>**Note:**</u> Pay particular attention to the requirements of questions that contain the words **NOT, LEAST,** or **EXCEPT.**

<u>**Questions 1–13.**</u> Read the following essay carefully before you mark your answers.

The ant has no holidays, no eight-hour system, nor never strikes for higher wages. They are cheerful little toilers and have no malice nor back door to their hearts. There are no sedentary loafers
(5) among them and you never see one out of a job. They get up early, go to bed late, work all the time, and eat on the run.

You never see two ants arguing some foolish question that neither of them don't understand;
(10) they don't care whether the moon is inhabited or not; not whether a fish weighing two pounds put into a pail of water already full will make the pail slop over or weigh more. They ain't hunting after the philosopher's stone or getting crazy over the
(15) cause of the sudden earthquake. They don't care whether Jupiter is thirty or thirty-one millions of miles up in the air nor whether the earth bobs around on its axis or not, so long as it don't bob over their corncrib and spill their barley.

(20) They are simple, little, busy ants, full of faith, working hard, living prudently, praising God by minding their own business, and dying when their time comes, to make room for the next crop of ants. They are a reproach to the lazy, and encour-
(25) agement to the industrious, and a rebuke to the vicious.

Ants have bylaws and a constitution and they mean something. Their laws ain't like our laws, made with a hole in them so that a man can steal
(30) a horse and ride through them on a walk. They don't have any legislators that you can buy, nor any judges, lying around on the half-shell, ready to be swallowed.

I rather like the ants and think now I shall sell
(35) out my money and real estate and join them.

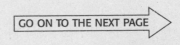

1. The phrase *back door to their hearts* in paragraph 1 is an example of a type of figurative language called

   (A) onomatopoeia

   (B) hyperbole

   (C) metaphor

   (D) alliteration

   (E) personification

2. The author is using the phrase *back door to their hearts* to

   (A) infer that ants, as with any other sentient creatures, can be won over by honest means

   (B) introduce the concept that people are far superior to ants because people can reason and make conscious decisions

   (C) conclude that ants are followers, not leaders

   (D) suggest that ants are straightforward and honest; they do not act in a hypocritical manner by saying one thing but meaning another

   (E) imply that ants cannot be trusted because they work by indirection

3. According to the first paragraph, ants do all of the following activities and have all the following traits EXCEPT

   (A) assail their enemies through devious means

   (B) labor in an honest fashion

   (C) deal openly and honestly with their fellow ants

   (D) rise early to get a head start on the day

   (E) work until the job is completed

4. The phrase *eat on the run* in paragraph 1 is a(n)

   (A) epigram

   (B) aphorism

   (C) idiom

   (D) hyperbole

   (E) paradox

5. From the diction and syntax in this passage, such as the substandard usage "ain't," you can conclude that

   (A) the author came from humble beginnings but he has worked hard to educate himself

   (B) the author is a misanthrope who believes that animals and insects are far superior to people

   (C) the author is using an earthy, vernacular English to appeal to his audience

   (D) the passage was written in the early seventeenth century

   (E) the selection is aimed primarily at farmers, laborers, and nonintellectuals

6. The repeated phrase *they don't care...* in the second paragraph is an example of a stylistic element called

   (A) parallel structure

   (B) dramatic irony

   (C) blank verse

   (D) figurative language

   (E) oxymoron

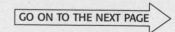

7. The author creates all the following effects through the use of the technique identified in question 6 EXCEPT

 (A) rhythm

 (B) irony

 (C) emphasis

 (D) balance

 (E) conciseness

8. What qualities of the ants, mentioned in paragraph 3, does the author imply could also characterize good human beings?

 (A) reverent, honest, and spontaneous

 (B) docile, circumspect, and devout

 (C) busy, little, and brilliant

 (D) faithful, hard-working, and virtuous

 (E) kindly, intelligent, submissive

9. The phrase *full of faith* (line 20) is an example of

 (A) assonance

 (B) an allusion

 (C) an anecdote

 (D) author's purpose

 (E) alliteration

10. The author of this passage is most likely a(n)

 (A) humorist or satirist

 (B) labor leader

 (C) naturalist

 (D) veterinarian

 (E) vegetarian

11. How are the ants' laws different from ours, according to the author?

 (A) the ants do not have laws; rather, they have unstated but understood regulations

 (B) the ants' laws have loopholes unlike our iron-clad laws

 (C) the ants' laws apply to horses and riding, unlike our own laws

 (D) the ants have a set of bylaws and a constitution, whereas we don't

 (E) the ants' laws have meaning and their law-givers cannot be corrupted

12. From the diction and syntax used in this passage, you can conclude that

 (A) the writer was poorly educated

 (B) the writer was trying to impress his readers by parading his learning

 (C) the passage was written by a contemporary author

 (D) the passage was written in the 16th century

 (E) the writer was using stylistic elements to defend common sense, fair play, and traditional values

13. The tone of this passage is best characterized as

 (A) bitter

 (B) satirical

 (C) serious

 (D) scathing

 (E) caustic

GO ON TO THE NEXT PAGE

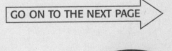

<u>Questions 14–29.</u> **Read the following poem carefully before you mark your answers.**

> Fair flower, that does so comely grow,
> Hid in this silent, dull retreat.
> Untouched thy honied blossoms blow,
> Unseen thy little branches greet:
> (5) No roving foot shall crush thee here,
> No busy hand provoke a tear.
>
> By Nature's self in white arrayed,
> She bade thee shun the vulgar eye,
> And planted here the guardian shade,
> (10) And sent soft waters murmuring by;
> Thus quietly thy summer goes,
> Thy days declining in repose.
>
> Smit with these charms, that must decay,
> I grieve to see your future doom;
> (15) They died—nor were those flowers more gay,
> The flowers that did in Eden bloom:
> Unpitying frosts, and Autumn's power
> Shall leave no vestige of this flower.
>
> From morning runs and evenings dews
> (20) At first thy little being came:
> If nothing once, you nothing lose,
> For when you die you are the same;
> The space between is but an hour,
> The frail duration of a flower.

14. According to the first stanza, the flower remains untouched because

    (A) it grows in out-of-the way places and so is overlooked nearly all the time

    (B) it has deliberately retreated from the world

    (C) it has been crushed by itinerants and uprooted by people passing by

    (D) it is an unattractive flower that looks like a shaggy comb

    (E) like a dull person, it is silent, pedestrian, and unobtrusive

15. In the first stanza, the poet uses a literary technique called an *apostrophe* when he

    (A) compares the flower to something else

    (B) directly addresses the flower

    (C) exaggerates the flower's good qualities

    (D) substitutes a part of something for the whole

    (E) states less than he indirectly suggests through understatement

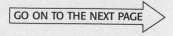
GO ON TO THE NEXT PAGE

16. The mood of the first stanza is BEST described as

    (A) bitter and resentful

    (B) somber and restrained

    (C) content and restful

    (D) elegiac and respectful

    (E) deferential and uneasy

17. According to stanza II, how has nature favored the wild honeysuckle?

    (A) Nature made the honeysuckle homely and dull so people would overlook it and it could then grow in peace.

    (B) Nature made the honeysuckle sweet so many insects would be attracted to it, resulting in the survival of the species.

    (C) Nature furnished the honeysuckle with tiny blossoms and branches, so it would not be seen easily. Then, it could grow in peace.

    (D) Nature bestowed poetic qualities on the honeysuckle so it could become a symbol of eternity.

    (E) Nature gave the honeysuckle a retreat in which to grow, planted trees to shade it, and provided a water source for it.

18. Which of the following literary techniques does the author use when he describes the soft waters as "murmuring by" in line 10?

    (A) personification and onomatopoeia

    (B) repetition and metonymy

    (C) hyperbole and alliteration

    (D) personification and synesthesia

    (E) ambiguity and personification

19. Based on context clues, which of the following choices is the best synonym for the word *smit* in line 13?

    (A) destroyed by

    (B) infatuated with

    (C) consumed by

    (D) rejected by

    (E) devastated by

20. Which of the statements below best describes the third stanza?

    (A) The stanza describes the flower's uncanny power over the speaker.

    (B) The stanza foreshadows the speaker's imminent death.

    (C) The stanza assumes a somber atmosphere that suggests the approach of death.

    (D) The stanza links the flower's survival to the passage of the seasons.

    (E) The stanza shifts to a happier tone as the speaker envisions a happy afterlife.

21. In the last stanza, the speaker adopts a thoughtful and reflective attitude because he

    (A) takes comfort in the thought that the plant came from nothing out of the cycle of nature and will complete its own cycle in returning to nature's province

    (B) understands the comfort that nature can bring to those seeking a path in life

    (C) realizes that he will live throughout eternity through his verse, as the flower will live through artistic representations of it

    (D) recognizes how similar he is to the flower and by extension, to nature's grandeur

    (E) comprehends that his inner qualities are far more valuable than any outward show

22. What literary technique is the author using in the last line when he refers to "The frail duration of a flower"?

    (A) personification

    (B) assonance

    (C) metaphor

    (D) alliteration

    (E) onomatopoeia

GO ON TO THE NEXT PAGE

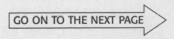

23. The poem's speaker is best described as

(A) the honeysuckle

(B) death

(C) Nature itself

(D) a naturalist

(E) someone walking through a field

24. The poem's rhyme pattern is

(A) *abbacc dedede ghghii jjkkii*

(B) *ababab dedede ghghgh jkjkjk*

(C) *ababcc dedeff ghghii jkjkii*

(D) *abbacc deedcc ghghcc jkjkcc*

(E) *abbacc dedecc ghghii jkjkii*

25. The poet's attitude in this poem moves from

(A) acrimony to acceptance as he realizes that beauty triumphs over mortality

(B) negative to positive as he links the flower's changes in nature to its demise and return to nature

(C) assured to pessimistic as he understands that nothing he can do will endure the long passage of time

(D) tranquillity to distress as he realizes that life is but a fleeting shadow

(E) bitterness to acceptance as he comes to rely on structure rather than emotion for comfort

26. You can infer that in this poem

(A) the speaker understands that human beings, like the honeysuckle, come into being from mysterious forces, endure for a long period, and effect great changes on their world

(B) the poet celebrates his awareness that human beings and flowers share a similar tenderness and brevity

(C) the poet wishes that he was a flower so he could be closer to nature

(D) the poet is using the flower's life cycle to metaphorically draw an analogy to human life and death

(E) the speaker sees death as a terrible tragedy

27. The best title for this poem is

(A) "Flower Power"

(B) "The Honeysuckle and Humankind"

(C) "The Wild Honeysuckle"

(D) "Life and Death"

(E) "Eternity"

28. Which generalization best states the theme of this poem?

(A) People, like flowers, are very fragile.

(B) Flowers are often great consolation to people, especially those who are suffering a personal loss.

(C) Poets experience emotion in a heightened way.

(D) Death is not a loss; rather, it is merely an inevitable return to a previous state.

(E) When we feel oppressed by life, we should seek solace in nature.

29. This poem reflects all the concepts of the Romantic era EXCEPT

(A) a deep belief in religion and the afterlife

(B) an awareness that the physical world is subject to decline and decay

(C) a belief in mutability, that everything changes and dies

(D) a belief that that the natural world provides the key to the human world

(E) a reliance on traditional forms and poetic conventions

GO ON TO THE NEXT PAGE

Questions 30–42. Read the following selection carefully before you mark your answers.

At the time the Lowell cotton mills were started, the factory girls were the lowest among women. In England, and in France particularly, great injustice had been done to her real character; she was repre-
(5) sented as subjected to influences that could not fail to destroy her purity and self-respect. In the eyes of her overseer she was but a brute, a slave, to be beaten, pinched, and pushed about. It was to overcome this prejudice that such high wages had been offered
(10) to women that they might be induced to become mill girls, in spite of the opprobrium that still clung to the "degrading occupation." At first only a few came; for, though tempted by the high wages to be regularly paid in "cash," there were many who still
(15) preferred to go on working at some more genteel employment at seventy-five cents a week and their board. But in a short time the prejudice against factory labor wore away, and the Lowell mills became filled with blooming and energetic New England
(20) women.

One of the first strikes of cotton-factory operatives that ever took place in this country was that in Lowell in October, 1836. When it was announced that the wages were to be cut down,
(25) great indignation was felt, and it was decided to strike, *en masse*. This was done. The mills were shut down, and the girls went in procession from their several corporations to the "grove" on Chapel Hill, and listened to "incendiary" speeches
(30) from early labor reformers.

One of the girls stood on a pump, and gave vent to the feelings of her companions in a neat speech, declaring that it was their duty to resist all attempts at cutting down the wages. This was the
(35) first time a woman had spoken in public in Lowell, and the event caused surprise and consternation among her audience.

Cutting down the wages was not their only grievance, nor the only cause of the strike.
(40) Hitherto the corporations had paid twenty-five cents a week towards the board of each operative, and now it was their purpose to have the girls pay the sum; and this, in addition to the cut in wages, would make a difference of at least one dollar a
(45) week. It was estimated that as many as twelve or

fifteen hundred girls turned out, and walked in procession through the streets. They had neither flags nor music, but sang songs…

My own recollection of this first strike (or "turn
(50) out" as it was called) is very vivid. I worked in a lower room, where I had heard the proposed strike fully, if not vehemently, discussed; I had been an ardent listener to what was said against this attempt at "oppression" on the part of the
(55) corporation, and naturally I took sides with the strikers. When the day came on which the girls were to turn out, those in the upper rooms started first, and so many of them left that our mill was at once shut down. Then, when the girls in my room
(60) stood irresolute, uncertain what to do, asking each other, "Would you?" or "Shall we turn out?" and not one of them having the courage to lead off, I, who began to think they would not go out, after all their talk, became impatient, and started on
(65) ahead, saying, with childish bravado, "I don't care what you do, *I* am going to turn out, whether anyone else does or not;" and I marched out, and was followed by the others.

As I looked back at the long line that followed me,
(70) I was more proud than I have ever been since at any success I may have achieved, and more proud than I shall ever be again until my own beloved State gives its women citizens the right of suffrage.

The agent of the corporation where I then
(75) worked took some small revenges on the supposed ringleaders; on the principle of sending the weaker to the wall, my mother was turned away from her boardinghouse, that functionary saying, "Mrs. Hanson, you could not prevent the older girls
(80) from turning out, but your daughter is a child, and *her* you could control."

It is hardly necessary to say that so far as results were concerned this strike did no good. The dissatisfaction of the operatives subsided, or burned itself
(85) out, and though the authorities did not accede to their demands, the majority returned to their work, and the corporation went on cutting down the wages.

GO ON TO THE NEXT PAGE

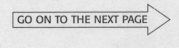

30. The selection opens with an historical overview of factory girls in order to

    (A) set the narrative that follows in context

    (B) establish the author's bias

    (C) argue that women have the right to equal pay for equal work

    (D) show that conditions have only slightly improved since the author's day

    (E) persuade readers to support the cause of female equality

31. Why did the author choose the word *overseer* (line 7) to describe the factory foreman?

    (A) The term suggests that the women were actually enslaved by law.

    (B) The word conveys the author's feeling that mill work, as with all manual labor, represents unfair subjugation of women.

    (C) The expression shows the author's loathing of authority.

    (D) The idiom foreshadows the author's fight for female suffrage.

    (E) The word connotes bondage, which reflects the author's view of the employer-employee relationship in the mills.

32. You can infer from context that *opprobrium* (line 11) means

    (A) esteem

    (B) respect

    (C) dirt

    (D) disgrace

    (E) praise

33. "Blooming and energetic New England women" (lines 19–20) eventually flocked to the mills because they

    (A) could not obtain more genteel work and so were forced to work in the mill

    (B) wanted to learn skills that would be necessary in the industrial age

    (C) received high wages paid in cash and factory work lost its negative overtones

    (D) were using the experience as fodder for their own writing

    (E) were won over by the author's persuasive prose

34. The phrase *en masse* (line 26) is in italics to indicate that

    (A) the author is using it sarcastically

    (B) the workers acted together, as one body

    (C) it is a foreign phrase

    (D) their group was unexpectedly large

    (E) the phrase is deliberately misspelled

35. According to the author, what caused the Lowell cotton factory strike?

    (A) a reduction in wages and a general sense of dissatisfaction

    (B) the girl who spoke from the pump

    (C) a cutback in wages and a plan to have the girls pay the board of each worker

    (D) cruel overseers who mistreated the female workers

    (E) a reduction in wages, a rabble-rousing speech, and the temper of the times

GO ON TO THE NEXT PAGE

36. Based on her voice in this selection and her description of her actions, the narrator can be characterized as

    (A) a fearless fighter for the underdog, but her strong personality unintentionally hurts those around her

    (B) a courageous leader who stands up for her beliefs and the rights of others

    (C) determined to get ahead, no matter what the cost

    (D) mature and composed, always thinking through her actions

    (E) smug about her hard-earned success

37. From which point of view is this selection narrated?

    (A) omniscient

    (B) second-person

    (C) third-person limited

    (D) first-person

    (E) all-knowing

38. Why is this point of view appropriate for this selection?

    (A) It gives the selection an immediacy and vividness that other points of view do not afford.

    (B) It allows the narrator to tell the story from different vantage points.

    (C) It permits the narrator to examine each character's motivation.

    (D) It allows the narrator to tell the story through the eyes of only a handful of characters.

    (E) It establishes the appropriate distance between the speaker and the audience.

39. You can infer that the narrator is NOT

    (A) a supporter of worker's rights

    (B) an elderly woman

    (C) against the speech at the pump

    (D) a participant

    (E) working on the lower level

40. This selection can BEST be categorized as

    (A) a novel

    (B) a fictional essay

    (C) a nonfiction essay

    (D) an excerpt from a short story

    (E) a prose poem

41. From the information in this selection, you can BEST conclude that

    (A) all women were united in the fight for equal rights in the late 19th century

    (B) women were powerless to improve their conditions in the late 19th century

    (C) the road to improvement of working conditions for women was long and arduous, with many setbacks

    (D) female mill workers had the most difficult time achieving pay parity because they were poorly educated

    (E) the author strongly supports factory walkouts and other job actions as the only way to achieve pay equality for women

42. The author's primary purpose in this selection is to

    (A) document a significant chapter in America's past

    (B) persuade readers that all women deserve equal rights

    (C) link pay issues to slavery and suffrage

    (D) argue that the mills must be shut down

    (E) allow some women access to equal education, social benefits, and jobs

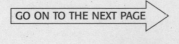

GO ON TO THE NEXT PAGE

KAPLAN
Test Prep and Admissions

Questions 43–54. Read the following poem carefully before you mark your answers.

Receive, dear friend, the truths I teach:
So shalt thou live beyond the reach
   Of adverse fortune's power;
Not always tempt the distant deep,
(5) Not always timorously creep
   Along the treacherous shore.

He that holds fast the golden mean,
And lives contentedly between
   The little and the great,
(10) Feels not the wants that pinch the poor,
Nor plagues that haunt the rich man's door,
   Embittering all his state.

The tallest pines feel the most power
Of winter blasts: the loftiest tower
(15)   Comes heaviest to the ground;
The bolts that spare the mountain's side,
His cloud-capped eminence divide,
   And spread the ruin around.

The well-informed philosopher
(20) Rejoices with a wholesome fear,
   And hopes, in spite of pain;
If winter bellow from the north,
Soon the sweet spring comes dancing forth,
   And nature laughs again.

(25) What if thine heaven be overcast?
The dark appearance will not last;
   Expect a brighter sky.
The God that strings the silver bow,
Awakes sometimes the Muses too,
(30)   And lays his arrows by.

If hindrances obstruct thy way,
Thy magnanimity display,
   And let thy strength be seen;
But Oh! if fortune fill thy sail,
(35) With more than a propitious gale,
   Take half thy canvas in.

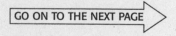

43. According to the first stanza, the author's purpose in this poem is to

    (A) entertain his readers

    (B) persuade his readers to let their reach exceed their grasp

    (C) teach his readers a painful but necessary lesson

    (D) advise his readers how to best live their lives

    (E) warn his readers about life's dangers

44. The poet presents his ideas in the first two stanzas with all of the following metaphors EXCEPT

    (A) the ocean's dangerous undersurface

    (B) people who creep between heaven and earth

    (C) the wants of the poor

    (D) the plagues that haunt the rich

    (E) the ocean's treacherous shore

45. The phrase *distant deep* (line 4) is an example of a literary technique called

    (A) end rhyme

    (B) antagonist

    (C) allusion

    (D) alliteration

    (E) apostrophe

46. What theme does the author state in the second stanza?

    (A) Do unto others as you would have them do unto you.

    (B) He who has the gold, rules.

    (C) Life is uncertain, so do not expect to succeed without great struggle.

    (D) The extremes of poverty and wealth are more similar than you think.

    (E) People will lead happier lives if they avoid extremes.

47. The conclusion the poet wants readers to draw from the description of tall trees and a lofty tower in lines 13–15 is that

    (A) The proudest and most powerful people can suffer the cruelest falls.

    (B) You never know how the future will turn out, so be prepared.

    (C) When great leaders fall, everyone suffers.

    (D) Winter destroys natural as well as man-made landmarks.

    (E) Save your money, because you will need it when tragedy strikes.

48. You can infer from context that the word *eminence* (line 17) means

    (A) a deeply religious person

    (B) insignificance

    (C) irrelevance

    (D) mountain peak

    (E) bottom

49. In the fourth stanza, what is the poet's main idea about the philosopher?

    (A) In bad times, he fears adversity will follow; in good times, he laughs.

    (B) The philosopher understands the natural rhythm of the seasons and adapts to it.

    (C) In good times, he rejoices only moderately; in bad times, he maintains hope for the future.

    (D) He keeps up with current events so he is well-prepared for any eventuality.

    (E) The philosopher is always fearful of the future, since he knows that decline and death are inevitable.

GO ON TO THE NEXT PAGE

50. Line 25, "thine heaven be overcast," can best be read

   (A) literally, referring to the havoc created by fierce storms

   (B) literally, referring to death

   (C) as a metaphor for illness

   (D) as a metaphor for general misfortune

   (E) as a symbol of bad luck

51. The tone of this poem is most accurately described as

   (A) somber and depressing

   (B) serious but uplifting

   (C) pessimistic

   (D) dismal

   (E) cynical

52. Line 28 is an allusion to the god Apollo, the patron of musicians and poets. The Greeks and Romans viewed Apollo as the embodiment of beauty and reasoning, but he could also be cruel and unforgiving. This allusion adds to the poem's meaning by

   (A) suggesting that beauty is fleeting and its loss is very cruel

   (B) hinting that the poet has experienced good and bad times in his own life

   (C) implying that life throws serious roadblocks in our way that no one can prevent

   (D) illustrating the speaker's point that life offers both affliction and good fortune

   (E) suggesting that an appreciation of the arts can give life meaning and help people overcome the difficult times

53. What does the poet mean in the last line when he advises readers to "Take half thy canvas in"?

   (A) Be careful when you sail, because careless sailors can cause serious accidents.

   (B) Don't sail when the weather is stormy.

   (C) Avoid extremes in happiness.

   (D) Only you can protect yourself against unexpected danger.

   (E) Good fortune, like adversity, strikes when we least expect it.

54. Which of the following titles best suits the poem's topic and theme?

   (A) "The Golden Mean"

   (B) "Sail at Your Own Peril"

   (C) "Life's Ups and Downs"

   (D) "Be Prepared"

   (E) "The Truth-Teller"

IF YOU FINISH BEFORE TIME IS CALLED, YOU MAY CHECK YOUR WORK ON THIS SECTION ONLY. DO NOT TURN TO ANY OTHER SECTION IN THE TEST. | STOP

Section II: Essay Questions

Time: 2 hour
Number of questions: 3
Percent of total grade: 55

Directions: This section contains three essay questions. Answer all three questions, budgeting your time carefully.

GO ON TO THE NEXT PAGE ▷

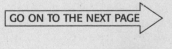

Question 1

<u>Suggested Time:</u> **40 minutes. Your response will count as one-third of your total score on the essay portion of the exam.**

1. Read these two poems—the first is by Horace, a Latin poet who lived from 65–8 B.C.E.; the second is by Robert Herrick, an English Cavalier poet who lived from 1591–1674.

    In a well-organized essay, consider how each poem utilizes poetic elements such as imagery, symbolism, and tone to express very similar ideas despite the centuries that separate the poets.

Carpe Diem
Horace

Strive not, Leuconoe,[1] to know what end
The gods above to me or thee will send;
Not with astrologers consult at all,
That thou mayest better know what can befall;
(5) Whether thou liv'st more winters, or thy last
Be this, which Tyrrhen waves[2] 'gainst rocks do cast
Be wise! Drink free, and in so short a space
Do not protracted hopes of life embrace.
Whilst we are talking, envious time doth slide
(10) This day's thine own; the next may be denied.

To Virgins, to Make Much of Time
Robert Herrick

Gather ye rosebuds while ye may,
Old Time is still a-flying;
And this same flower that smiles today,
To-morrow will be dying.
(5) The glorious lamp of heaven, the Sun,
The higher he's a-getting;
The sooner will his race be run,
And nearer he's to setting.
That age is best, which is the first,
(10) When youth and blood are warmer;
But being spent, the worse, and worst
Times still succeed the former.
Then be not coy, but use your time,
And while ye may, go marry;
(15) For having lost but once your prime,
You may for ever tarry.

[1] Leuconoe was the poet's friend.

[2] Tyrrhen waves is a reference to the Tyrrhenian Sea, part of the Mediterranean in southwest Italy.

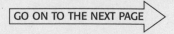

Write your essay here.

_____

_____

_____

_____

_____

_____

_____

_____

_____

_____

_____

_____

_____

_____

_____

_____

_____

_____

_____

GO ON TO THE NEXT PAGE

GO ON TO THE NEXT PAGE ⟩

_____

_____

_____

_____

_____

_____

_____

_____

_____

_____

_____

_____

_____

_____

_____

_____

_____

_____

_____

GO ON TO THE NEXT PAGE ▷

_____

_____

_____

_____

_____

_____

_____

_____

_____

_____

_____

_____

_____

_____

_____

_____

_____

_____

_____

_____

_____

_____

GO ON TO THE NEXT PAGE ⇒

Question 2

Suggested Time: 40 minutes. Your response will count for one-third of your total score on the essay portion of the exam.

2. This is a selection from the Preface of an early British novel. Read the passage carefully. In a well-organized essay discuss how the author's calculating style attempts to manipulate reader's curiosity in order to lure him or her into reading the book itself. Pay particular attention to such stylistic devices as diction, imagery, and inference.

The Author's Preface

The world is so taken up of late with novels and romances, that it will be hard for a private history to be taken for genuine, where the names and other circumstances of the person are concealed, and on
(5) this account we must be content to leave the reader to pass his own opinion upon the ensuing sheet, and take it just as he pleases.

The author is here supposed to be writing her own history, and in the very beginning of her
(10) account she gives the reasons why she thinks fit to conceal her true name, after which there is no occasion to say any more about that.

It is true that the original of this story is put into new words, and the style of the famous lady
(15) we here speak of is a little altered; particularly she is made to tell her own tale in modester words than she told it at first, the copy which came first to hand having been written in language more like one still in Newgate than one grown penitent and
(20) humble, as she afterwards pretends to be.

The pen employed in finishing her story, and making it what you now see it to be, has had no little difficulty to put it into a dress fit to be seen, and to make it speak language fit to be read. When a
(25) woman debauched from her youth, nay, even being the offspring of debauchery and vice, comes to give an account of all her vicious practices, and even to descend to the particular occasions and circumstances by which she ran through in threescore
(30) years, an author must be hard put to wrap it up so clean as not to give room, especially for vicious readers, to turn it to his disadvantage.

All possible care, however, has been taken to give no lewd ideas, no immodest turns in the new dress-
(35) ing up of this story; no, not to the worst parts of her expressions. To this purpose some of the vicious part of her life, which could not be modestly told, is quite left out, and several other parts are very much shortened. What is left 'tis hoped will

(40) not offend the chastest reader or the modest hearer; and as the best use is made even of the worst story, the moral 'tis hoped will keep the reader serious, even where the story might incline him to be otherwise. To give the history of a wicked life repented
(45) of, necessarily requires that the wicked part should be make as wicked as the real history of it will bear, to illustrate and give a beauty to the penitent part, which is certainly the best and brightest, if related with equal spirit and life.

(50) But as this work is chiefly recommended to those who know how to read it, and how to make the good uses of it which the story all along recommends to them, so it is to be hoped that such readers will be more pleased with the moral than
(55) the fable, with the application than with the relation, and with the end of the writer than with the life of the person written of.

There is in this story abundance of delightful incidents, and all of them usefully applied. There is
(60) an agreeable turn artfully given them in the relating, that naturally instructs the reader, either one way or other. The first part of her lewd life with the young gentleman at Colchester has so many happy turns given it to expose the crime, and warn all
(65) whose circumstances are adapted to it, of the ruinous end of such things, and the foolish, thoughtless, and abhorred conduct of both the parties, that it abundantly atones for all the lively description she gives of her folly and wickedness.

(70) Upon this foundation this book is recommended to the reader as a work from every part of which something may be learned, and some just and religious inference is drawn, by which the reader will have something of instruction, if he
(75) pleases to make use of it.

GO ON TO THE NEXT PAGE

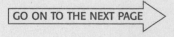

Write your essay here.

_____

_____

_____

_____

_____

_____

_____

_____

_____

_____

_____

_____

_____

_____

_____

_____

_____

_____

_____

GO ON TO THE NEXT PAGE ⟩

GO ON TO THE NEXT PAGE ➤

GO ON TO THE NEXT PAGE ⟩

GO ON TO THE NEXT PAGE ⟶

Question 3

<u>Suggested Time:</u> 40 minutes. Your response will count for one-third of your total score on the essay portion of the exam.

3. Often in literature, situations reach a "point of no return," a point after which the life of a character can never be the same. Choose a novel or play in which a character reaches this point and write an essay explaining the situation and its effect on the character, the other characters, and the theme. You may choose a work from the list below or another novel or full-length play of literary merit.

> *All My Sons*
> *As I Lay Dying*
> *Catch-22*
> *The Crucible*
> *David Copperfield*
> *Gulliver's Travels*
> *Hamlet*
> *The Iceman Cometh*
> *Jane Eyre*
> *Jude the Obscure*
> *King Lear*
> *Lord Jim*
> *Macbeth*
> *Moby-Dick*
> *1984*
> *The Oresteia*
> *Othello*
> *Saint Joan*
> *Sons and Lovers*
> *The Sound and the Fury*
> *The Turn of the Screw*
> *Waiting for Godot*
> *Wuthering Heights*

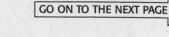 GO ON TO THE NEXT PAGE

Write your essay here.

_____

_____

_____

_____

_____

_____

_____

_____

_____

_____

_____

_____

_____

_____

_____

_____

_____

_____

_____

_____

_____

_____

_____

_____

_____

_____

_____

_____

_____

_____

_____

_____

_____

_____

_____

_____

_____

_____

_____

_____

_____

_____

_____

GO ON TO THE NEXT PAGE ⟹

GO ON TO THE NEXT PAGE ⟹

STOP

Practice Test Two: **Answer Key**

1.	C	19.	B	37.	D
2.	D	20.	C	38.	A
3.	A	21.	A	39.	C
4.	C	22.	D	40.	C
5.	C	23.	E	41.	C
6.	A	24.	C	42.	A
7.	B	25.	B	43.	D
8.	D	26.	D	44.	B
9.	E	27.	C	45.	D
10.	A	28.	D	46.	E
11.	E	29.	A	47.	A
12.	E	30.	A	48.	D
13.	B	31.	E	49.	C
14.	A	32.	D	50.	D
15.	B	33.	C	51.	B
16.	C	34.	C	52.	D
17.	E	35.	C	53.	C
18.	A	36.	B	54.	A

Answers and Explanations

SECTION I: MULTIPLE-CHOICE QUESTIONS

Questions 1–13.

The ant has no holidays, no eight-hour system, nor never strikes for higher wages. They are cheerful little toilers and have no malice nor back door to their hearts. There are no sedentary loafers
(5) among them and you never see one out of a job. They get up early, go to bed late, work all the time, and eat on the run.

You never see two ants arguing some foolish question that neither of them don't understand;
(10) they don't care whether the moon is inhabited or not; not whether a fish weighing two pounds put into a pail of water already full will make the pail slop over or weigh more. They ain't hunting after the philosopher's stone or getting crazy over the
(15) cause of the sudden earthquake. They don't care whether Jupiter is thirty or thirty-one millions of miles up in the air nor whether the earth bobs around on its axis or not, so long as it don't bob over their corncrib and spill their barley.

(20) They are simple, little, busy ants, full of faith, working hard, living prudently, praising God by minding their own business, and dying when their time comes, to make room for the next crop of ants. They are a reproach to the lazy, and encour-
(25) agement to the industrious, and a rebuke to the vicious.

Ants have bylaws and a constitution and they mean something. Their laws ain't like our laws, made with a hole in them so that a man can steal
(30) a horse and ride through them on a walk. They don't have any legislators that you can buy, nor any judges, lying around on the half-shell, ready to be swallowed.

I rather like the ants and think now I shall sell
(35) out my money and real estate and join them.

1. (C)

The phrase *back door to their hearts* in paragraph one is an example of a type of figurative language called metaphor. Remember that a metaphor is a direct comparison not using *like* or *as*. (A), onomatopoeia, is when a word sounds like what it is, such as "buzz of the bee." Hyperbole (B) is an exaggeration; (D), alliteration, is the repetition of initial consonant sounds, and (E), personification, is giving human characteristics to inanimate objects.

2. (D)

The author is using the phrase *back door to their hearts* to suggest that ants are straightforward and honest; they do not act in a hypocritical manner by saying one thing but meaning another. The overall message of the paragraph and the words *no malice* help to clarify letter (D) as the correct response. None of the other responses is appropriate to this question. In fact, the description of the ants in paragraph one is all positive: *The ant has no holidays, no eight-hour system, nor never strikes for higher wages. They are cheerful little toilers and have no malice nor back door to their hearts. There are no sedentary loafers among them and you never see one out of a job. They get up early, go to bed late, work all the time, and eat on the run.*

3. (A)

According to the first paragraph, ants do everything BUT assail their enemies through devious means. The first paragraph clearly describes the ants as hardworking and industrious creatures. Nowhere are negative or critical comments made.

4. (C)

The phrase *eat on the run* in paragraph one is an idiom. English has a number of expressions—idioms—that refer to an idea or concept not necessarily understood from strict meaning. For example, when someone says "I'm so hungry I could eat a horse," this expression is indicating a ravenous state, but does not mean, literally, that anyone plans to eat a horse. "Eating on the run" is certainly a characteristic most Americans are familiar with. An epigram (A) is a wise and witty, sometimes paradoxical, saying. An aphorism (B) is an adage or a terse statement of principle. Hyperbole (D) is an exaggeration, and paradox (E) is a seemingly contradictory statement.

5. (C)

From the diction and syntax in this passage, such as the substandard usage *ain't*, you can conclude that the author is using an earthy, vernacular English to appeal to his audience. Speaking in the vernacular means to speak in the language of the common folk. The expression *ain't* has always been considered informal and colloquial. The light but scholarly voice of the writer precludes (A) as a probable response. The author is probably not a misanthrope (one who despises humans) (B), even though he does seem to think that as a race we could learn much from the lowly ants. The language of this piece is not consistent with that from the early seventeenth century (D), and farmers, laborers and nonintellectuals (E) might be part of the reading audience, but certainly not all of it; the piece seems directed to more "sophisticated" folk who really need a lesson from the ants.

6. (A)

The repeated phrase *they don't care...* in the second paragraph can only be identified as parallel. One might even call such repetitive openings as exemplary of anaphora, repetition of introductory phrases or clauses. There's no unintentional meaning to this phrase, and thus no dramatic irony (B). Blank verse is poetry in iambic pentameter, not prose (C). The straightfoward phrase *they don't care* is not a metaphor, simile, or other figure, and an oxymoron (E) is two words with opposite meanings, like "jumbo shrimp."

7. (B)

The author creates all the effects of rhythm (A), emphasis (C), balance (D), and conciseness (E) through the use of parallel structure. However, the repetition of the "They don't care" structure contains no irony (B) whatsoever. Note: If you eliminated dramatic irony in question 6, you would have been able to do so here.

8. (D)

This question might have you confused. Remember, when more than one item is offered in response choices, all parts must be correct (or incorrect in a BUT question) for the response to be correct. The word *virtuous* makes (D) the best choice. The other qualities, faithful and hardworking, are easy to identify. The concept of "virtuous" is reinforced by the idea of prudence, "minding their own business" (line

22) and making room for others by dying when their time comes.

9. (E)

The phrase *full of faith* (line 20) is an example of alliteration. Repetition of initial consonant sounds is evident in the words *full* and *faith*. Assonance (A) is a repetition of vowel sounds. An allusion (B) is a reference, usually literary, to something outside the text. An anecdote (C) is a brief story, usually humorous. The author uses the depiction of the faith of the ants as part of his overall purpose (D), to illustrate the virtues he values and believes should be emulated by human beings. This is only a small part of the message, however.

10. (A)

The author of this passage is most likely a humorist or satirist. Although you might have been tempted to respond to this question with answer (C), naturalist, the passage is not technical nor clinical enough to justify this response. There is a feeling of tongue-in-cheek throughout the passage, which suggests a humorous tone to the piece.

11. (E)

The ants' laws have meaning and their lawgivers cannot be corrupted. The fifth paragraph of the passage assures the reader that ants don't have "any legislators that you can buy, nor any judges, lying around on the half-shell, ready to be swallowed" (lines 31–33). Ants do have laws, according to the author, ruling out (A). (B) is an opposite, designed to catch the hurried reader; (C) is an example of a distorted detail. (D) is an inference; nowhere is it stated that the "we" of the passage don't have a constitution.

12. (E)

The writer was using stylistic elements to defend common sense, fair play, and traditional values. Certainly the author has education (A), but there is no sense of the author trying to be particularly erudite (B). There is nothing to indicate that the author of this passage is either of Shakespeare's time (D) or the current time (C).

13. (B)

The tone of this passage is best characterized as satirical. As mentioned in the discussion of question 10, this author is writing with tongue-in-cheek, gently but successfully pointing out many flaws of mankind that ants seem to have avoided. Nevertheless, the writer is neither caustic (E) in his or her remarks nor particularly bitter (A) or scathing (D). Although the message is a moral one, the overall tone of the passage is far too lighthearted to be considered serious (C).

Questions 14–29.

Fair flower, that does so comely grow,
　Hid in this silent, dull retreat.
Untouched thy honied blossoms blow,
　Unseen thy little branches greet:
(5)　No roving foot shall crush thee here,
　No busy hand provoke a tear.

By Nature's self in white arrayed,
　She bade thee shun the vulgar eye,
And planted here the guardian shade,
(10)　And sent soft waters murmuring by;
　Thus quietly thy summer goes,
　Thy days declining in repose.

Smit with these charms, that must decay,
　I grieve to see your future doom;
(15) They died—nor were those flowers more gay,
　The flowers that did in Eden bloom:
　Unpitying frosts, and Autumn's power
　Shall leave no vestige of this flower.

From morning runs and evenings dews
(20)　At first thy little being came:
　If nothing once, you nothing lose,
　For when you die you are the same;
　The space between is but an hour,
　The frail duration of a flower.

14. (A)

The honeysuckle remains untouched because it grows in out-of-the way places and so is overlooked nearly all the time. Words in the first stanza such as *silent, dull retreat* (line 2) and *Unseen* (line 4) are testament for this response. (B) might be possible, but there's no evidence for this assumption in the first stanza. (C) is an opposite; the honeysuckle has not been crushed or uprooted because it is overlooked. The flower is "comely" (line 1), that is, quite attractive, eliminating (D). The retreat is "dull"; the "fair flower"(line 1) is not (E).

15. (B)

In the first stanza, the poet uses a literary technique called an *apostrophe* when he directly addresses the flower. Remember, an apostrophe is a direct address to an inanimate object, in this case the flower. Comparing the flower to something else (A) would be accomplished by metaphor or simile. Exaggerating the flower's good qualities (C) would be hyperbolic. The device of substituting a part for a whole (D) is synechdoche (for example, "a helping hand"). (E) describes the device called *litote*, as in the common "not bad!" to suggest something well done.

16. (C)

The mood of the first stanza is best described as content and restful. Scrutiny of stanza one reveals a positive tone—not bitter (A), somber (B), elegiac (mournful) (D), or uneasy (E). Remember, BOTH descriptors must be valid if the answer is to be valid.

17. (E)

Nature gave the honeysuckle a retreat in which to grow, planted trees to shade it, and provided a water source for it. Lines 9 and 10 give support to (E) as the correct response.

18. (A)

The author uses personification and onomatopoeia when he describes the soft waters as "murmuring by" in line 10. Remember, when choosing a response that has more than one element to it, all parts must be correct (or false if it is a BUT or EXCEPT question) in order for the answer to be correct. (A) is the only response which offers both parts as valid. Murmur is one of those words that sounds like what

it is, such as the *swish* of windshield wipers, making it an example of onomatopoeia. Murmuring is also a characteristic of humans, a whispered humming of voices, thereby making the phrase an example of personification as well. Metonomy (B), the figure of speech in which an attribute or associated feature is used to represent a thing (i.e., "the White House announced…) is incorrect. The line is not hyberbolic (C). In (D), personification is correct, but synesthesia, the subjective substitution of one sense for another (i.e., "blue music"), is not. The descriptive phrase is fairly unambiguous (E).

19. (B)

Perhaps you have run across the word *smitten,* which refers to a situation when one sex is bowled over by a member of the other sex. It means to be totally enraptured by. *Smit* is a derivation of smitten, and in the context, "Smit with these charms. . ." (line 13) means infatuated. The other choices have to do with the primary meaning of the word, *to have received a blow*.

20. (C)

The stanza assumes a somber atmosphere that suggests the approach of death. You should recognize that a shift in tone takes place in stanza three. Some of this can be inferred from the words *grieve* (line 14), *future doom* (line 14), *died* (line 15), *Unpitying frosts* (line 17), and *leave no vestige* (line 18), all words evoking negative connotation in contrast to the positive stanzas one and two. Although you might have been tempted by answer choice (D), the passage of the seasons, it is not the BEST response; note the words doom, died, and no vestige as death imagery. While you may surmise that the poem has an underlying connection to the poet's ultimate death, response (B), there is no connection made here with an imminent death.

21. (A)

The speaker takes comfort in the thought that the plant came from nothing out of the cycle of nature and will complete its own cycle in returning to nature's province. This response can be supported by line 20, "At first thy little being came:" and line 22, "For when you die you are the same." (D) is certainly tempting, as the poem does relate to human mortality, but nature's grandeur is not the topic here: a humble flower is. (B) is off the mark; the poem offers no guidance or "path" for life, but reflects on the cycle of nature. (C)

has no support in the last stanza—the flower was "nothing once" and will be "nothing" again, and (E) is also without any basis.

22. (D)

The author is using alliteration in the last line when he refers to "The frail duration of a flower." None of the other literary terms applies to this question. See the Key Terminology chapter for definitions of any of these you don't know cold.

23. (E)

Looking at the poem as a whole, no other response, but the idea of an idle observer who just happens upon the flowers makes sense as a response to this question. The narrator is definitely human (therefore eliminating answers (A), (B), and (C)). And the poem is certainly not the clinical product of a scientist (D).

24. (C)

The poem's rhyme pattern is *ababcc dedeff ghghii jkjkii.* An explanation of rhyme schemes can be found in the Key Terminology chapter.

25. (B)

The poet's attitude in this poem moves from negative to positive as he links the flower's changes in nature to its demise and return to nature. If you follow the progress of the poem, you will see that like many nature pieces, a cycle is described, and although death may take place, new life can grow from the old. Beauty doesn't survive (A)—not even Eden's flowers did. (C) and (D) miss the point: There is acceptance of nature's ways without pessimism or distress. The poet can not be said to have been bitter (E), and there's no shift from emotion to any particular "structure."

26. (D)

You can infer that in this poem the poet is using the flower's life cycle to metaphorically draw an analogy to human life and death. Rarely do poets speak of inanimate objects as just that. They are usually analogies for other things, often in reference to humans themselves. The final stanza gives the most credence to this response when it states, "For when you die you are the same;/The space between is but an hour,/The frail duration of a flower" (lines 22–24). Suddenly the reader/listener realizes that the "you" referred to here is more than just a dying honeysuckle.

27. (C)

The best title for this poem is "The Wild Honeysuckle." Although several layers of meaning might be uncovered within this poem, its focus is upon the flower, and that is the best source for its title. Remember, you are being asked to make the BEST selection, so you must be discerning as to all the nuances within the poem.

28. (D)

Death is not a loss; rather, it is merely an inevitable return to a previous state. The focus of this poem is on the cyclical qualities of nature and of mankind. This idea has been discussed in questions 25 and 26 as well.

29. (A)

This poem reflects all the concepts of the Romantic era EXCEPT a deep belief in religion and the afterlife. Notice this is an EXCEPT question. Remember that four of the responses will be true. Only one response (A) does not hold up to scrutiny. The other choices, which deal with the physical world (B), mutability (C), nature (D), and even the romantic poetic structure (E), are all correct descriptors of this poem.

At the time the Lowell cotton mills were started, the factory girls were the lowest among women. In England, and in France particularly, great injustice had been done to her real character; she was repre-
(5) sented as subjected to influences that could not fail to destroy her purity and self-respect. In the eyes of her overseer she was but a brute, a slave, to be beaten, pinched, and pushed about. It was to overcome this prejudice that such high wages had been offered
(10) to women that they might be induced to become mill girls, in spite of the opprobrium that still clung to the "degrading occupation." At first only a few came; for, though tempted by the high wages to be regularly paid in "cash," there were many who still
(15) preferred to go on working at some more genteel employment at seventy-five cents a week and their board. But in a short time the prejudice against factory labor wore away, and the Lowell mills became filled with blooming and energetic New England
(20) women.

One of the first strikes of cotton-factory operatives that ever took place in this country was that in Lowell in October, 1836. When it was announced that the wages were to be cut down,
(25) great indignation was felt, and it was decided to strike, *en masse*. This was done. The mills were shut down, and the girls went in procession from their several corporations to the "grove" on Chapel Hill, and listened to "incendiary" speeches
(30) from early labor reformers.

One of the girls stood on a pump, and gave vent to the feelings of her companions in a neat speech, declaring that it was their duty to resist all attempts at cutting down the wages. This was the
(35) first time a woman had spoken in public in Lowell, and the event caused surprise and consternation among her audience.

Cutting down the wages was not their only grievance, nor the only cause of the strike.
(40) Hitherto the corporations had paid twenty-five cents a week towards the board of each operative, and now it was their purpose to have the girls pay the sum; and this, in addition to the cut in wages, would make a difference of at least one dollar a
(45) week. It was estimated that as many as twelve or

fifteen hundred girls turned out, and walked in procession through the streets. They had neither flags nor music, but sang songs…

My own recollection of this first strike (or "turn
(50) out" as it was called) is very vivid. I worked in a lower room, where I had heard the proposed strike fully, if not vehemently, discussed; I had been an ardent listener to what was said against this attempt at "oppression" on the part of the
(55) corporation, and naturally I took sides with the strikers. When the day came on which the girls were to turn out, those in the upper rooms started first, and so many of them left that our mill was at once shut down. Then, when the girls in my room
(60) stood irresolute, uncertain what to do, asking each other, "Would you?" or "Shall we turn out?" and not one of them having the courage to lead off, I, who began to think they would not go out, after all their talk, became impatient, and started on
(65) ahead, saying, with childish bravado, "I don't care what you do, *I* am going to turn out, whether anyone else does or not;" and I marched out, and was followed by the others.

As I looked back at the long line that followed me,
(70) I was more proud than I have ever been since at any success I may have achieved, and more proud than I shall ever be again until my own beloved State gives its women citizens the right of suffrage.

The agent of the corporation where I then
(75) worked took some small revenges on the supposed ringleaders; on the principle of sending the weaker to the wall, my mother was turned away from her boardinghouse, that functionary saying, "Mrs. Hanson, you could not prevent the older girls
(80) from turning out, but your daughter is a child, and *her* you could control."

It is hardly necessary to say that so far as results were concerned this strike did no good. The dissatisfaction of the operatives subsided, or burned itself
(85) out, and though the authorities did not accede to their demands, the majority returned to their work, and the corporation went on cutting down the wages.

30. (A)

The selection opens with an historical overview of factory girls in order to set the narrative that follows in context. No bias (B) or argument ((C), (D), (E)) is established in the first paragraph. The opening overview acts as a preface to what follows.

31. (E)

The word *overseer* connotes bondage, which reflects the author's view of the employer-employee relationship in the mills. Although it may seem so in retrospect, *based on this passage*, there is no legal enslavement of the mill women (A). If you were tempted to choose (B), about subjugation, remember these women chose to defy the more conventional life of women at that time and actually liberated themselves by taking on factory jobs instead of more refined positions such as being a governess. In fact, they viewed their factory job as a liberation, not subjugation. There's no evidence the author loathes all authority (C). (D) is a far reach, and can't be supported by anything the author says about female suffrage in her state.

32. (D)

You can infer from context that *opprobrium* (line 11) means "disgrace." You should be able to infer that *opprobrium* is a negative word based on phrases such as *in spite of* (line 11) and *still clung to* (lines 11–12). Given only two negative words, the idea of disgrace (D) is far more appropriate when applied to a job than the word *dirt* (C). The other choices have positive connotations and therefore are not appropriate.

33. (C)

"Blooming and energetic New England women" (lines 19–20) eventually flocked to the mills because they received high wages paid in cash and factory work lost its negative overtones. The correct response is detailed in lines 12–20: "At first only a few came; for, though tempted by the high wages to be regularly paid in "cash," there were many who still preferred to go on working at some more genteel employment at seventy-five cents a week and their board. But in a short time the prejudice against factory labor wore away, and the Lowell mills became filled with blooming and energetic New England women." Note that "genteel" employment was available, ruling out (A). Cash was more

the incentive than learning skills (B). There's no evidence that many mill girls were budding authors (D), and the one mill girl turned author doesn't turn her talents to recruiting female factory hands (E).

34. (C)

The phrase *en masse* (line 26) is in italics to indicate that it is a foreign phrase. Whenever a foreign phrase (such as referring to someone's *carpe diem* behavior) is included in English, it should be italicized. That excludes those words such as restaurant, which have become a part of the English language. Quotation marks (A) are often used to signal sarcasm, but not italics. (B) is a correct definition, but not a correct answer: *en masse* means that the workers acted together, as one body, but that's not what the question is asking. Be careful to answer the question that is being asked.

35. (C)

A cutback in wages and a plan to have the girls pay the board of each worker caused the Lowell factory strike. You must ignore any prior knowledge you may have about these times in American history. You must rely solely upon the passage to answer the questions. Lines 38–45 give the essential information with which to answer this question.

36. (B)

Based on her voice in this selection and her description of her actions, the narrator can be characterized as a courageous leader who stands up for her beliefs and the rights of others. You might have been tempted to answer this question with (D). However mature and "together" this narrator seems, one could not rightly say that she thinks things through carefully. In fact she is described as reacting impetuously toward the strike. Response (A) is an example of overkill: although her mother is affected by her actions, this is only one instance, and we're not certain that the whole of the narrator's life is that of a fearless fighter for the underdog. (C) and (E) describe qualities/characteristics that are too negative for this particular narrator.

37. (D)

The narration is in the first person. It is not until paragraph five that we see that this is not an historical piece, but a passage written from the point of view of a participant in the action at the Lowell cotton mills. Line 49 begins with the phrase *My own recollection of this first strike....* It is at this point that the point of view is firmly established as first person.

38. (A)

The first-person point of view gives the selection an immediacy and vividness that other points of view do not afford. If you responded correctly to question 37, then you probably got this one right also. Always be aware that sometimes a correct response might give you clues to other correct answers about a passage. First-person narrators will always give the reader a more intimate look at the immediate story, although it usually limits our knowledge of what is going on with other characters.

39. (C)

You can infer that the narrator is NOT against the speech at the pump. The narrator calls the speech "neat" (line 32), a positive word then and now. This is one of those questions that offers you four correct responses and one that is incorrect. It is altogether possible that the narrator is an elderly woman, recounting an incident from her youth (B). (A), (D), (E) are all supported by the text.

40. (C)

This selection can BEST be categorized as a nonfiction essay. Unless the rest of the piece from which this passage is taken were to tell us differently, we can only surmise that this is a first-person, factual account. The only other option, not offered as a response, would be that this passage is from a piece of historical fiction. However, we are not given enough to justify choosing any response but (C).

41. (C)

From the information in this selection, you can BEST conclude that the road to improvement of working conditions for women was long and arduous, with many setbacks. Again, prior information may make you debate several of these responses as being the correct one. You are directed to choose the BEST conclusion, however, and that is response (C). Note the phrase in the prompt that directs you to consider only "the information in this selection."

42. (A)

The author's primary purpose in this selection is to document a significant chapter in America's past. Although you might think that the purpose of this selection is to argue for equal rights (B), based on the information we have been given, no obvious argument is being made. The passage is just a presentation of facts and events. The anecdote itself, however, might be used as an example in a larger argument for justice and equality for American women.

Questions 43–54.

Receive, dear friend, the truths I teach:
So shalt thou live beyond the reach
Of adverse fortune's power;
Not always tempt the distant deep,
(5) Not always timorously creep
Along the treacherous shore.

He that holds fast the golden mean,
And lives contentedly between
The little and the great,
(10) Feels not the wants that pinch the poor,
Nor plagues that haunt the rich man's door,
Embittering all his state.

The tallest pines feel the most power
Of winter blasts: the loftiest tower
(15) Comes heaviest to the ground;
The bolts that spare the mountain's side,
His cloud-capped eminence divide,
And spread the ruin around.

The well-informed philosopher
(20) Rejoices with a wholesome fear,
And hopes, in spite of pain;
If winter bellow from the north,
Soon the sweet spring comes dancing forth,
And nature laughs again.

(25) What if thine heaven be overcast?
The dark appearance will not last;
Expect a brighter sky.
The God that strings the silver bow,
Awakes sometimes the Muses too,
(30) And lays his arrows by.

If hindrances obstruct thy way,
Thy magnanimity display,
And let thy strength be seen;
But Oh! if fortune fill thy sail,
(35) With more than a propitious gale,
Take half thy canvas in.

43. (D)

According to the first stanza, the author's purpose in this poem is to advise his readers how to best live their lives. This response is best supported by the first two lines of the poem, "Receive, dear friend, the truths I teach:/So shalt thou live…." The use of the colon is also a clue telling the reader/listener that there will be several truths to pay note to.

44. (B)

The poet presents his ideas in the first two stanzas with all of the following metaphors EXCEPT "people who creep between heaven and earth." This is another one of those questions where you are given four correct answers, and you must find the fifth response that is incorrect. In fact, this phrase is not used in either of the first two stanzas, while the other four choices are all present within these stanzas.

45. (D)

The phrase *distant deep* (line 4) is an example of a literary technique called alliteration. Remember that alliteration is the repetition of initial consonant sounds. End rhyme (A) is poetry that rhymes at the end of each line; this poem rhymes, but the question is about "distant deep." (B), antagonist, is the main force opposing the protagonist in a play or novel; (C), allusion, is a reference to a literary or historical event, and (E), apostrophe, is a formal address to an inanimate object.

46. (E)

The theme of the second stanza, and of the poem as a whole, is the poet's belief that people will lead happier lives if they avoid extremes. Line 7, "He that holds fast the golden mean," is the key to this response, "mean" being the happy medium that the poet suggests we should all strive toward. (D) is tempting, related as it is to the stanza's lines about the rich and the poor, but is a partial answer; there's more to the stanza than this inference. Although you might find some truth in the other responses, none of them relates to the basic message of the second stanza.

47. (A)

The conclusion the poet wants readers to draw from the description of tall trees and a lofty tower in lines 13–15 is

that the proudest and most powerful people can suffer the cruelest falls. In lines 13–15, the poet tells us that "The tallest pines feel the most power/Of winter blasts: the loftiest tower/Comes heaviest to the ground." Choice (B) does not really relate to the message of the poet, that of following the mean. Choice (C) may be true, but the effect of the fall of the lofty on others is not discussed in the poem. (D) is a literal translation that you could make, but not the meaning the poet intends. (E) is a nice maxim to remember, but more than money is referenced in these lines.

48. (D)

You can infer that the word *eminence* (line 17) means "mountain peak." This somewhat outdated usage is like others you may encounter on the test, best figured out from context. Although some religious ranks are addressed as "your eminence" (A), in this poem's figure eminence refers to the contrast between the sides of the mountain and its top. Choices (B) and (C) could not be correct because they are negative words. (E), bottom, is an opposite.

49. (C)

In good times, the philosopher rejoices only moderately; in bad times, he maintains hope for the future. "The well informed philosopher/ Rejoices with a wholesome fear/And in spite of pain [he believes that in spring] nature laughs again" (lines 19–24). (A) is an opposite, contrary to the sense of the stanza. The seasons (B) are used figuratively, for good and bad times. (E) is an extreme, not suited to this poem about the "mean."

50. (D)

Line 25, "thine heaven be overcast," can best be read as a metaphor for general misfortune. (E) is close, but general misfortune is more inclusive than bad luck, and the figure is best seen as a metaphor.

51. (B)

The tone of this poem is most accurately described as serious but uplifting If you consider how the narrator is extolling us to expect bad times and learn to adjust, and not to have too many expectations either positive or negative, response (B) is the only one offered that indicates such a balance. The other responses either are too negative, and this poem consists of both negative and positives.

52. (D)

The allusion to Apollo adds to the poem's meaning by illustrating the speaker's point that life offers both affliction and good fortune. This question relates to number 51. The poem balances the good and the bad; it talks about the happy mean. Apollo, though he embodied beauty and reasoning, could be cruel and vengeful, further supporting this two-sided message. (E) is a stretch; the references to the Muses may have led you to think that there was a hidden message about the arts, but the main point is the balance between the good and bad in life.

53. (C)

The poet is cautioning the reader/listener to avoid extremes in happiness. Responses (A) and (B) are too literal. Responses (D) and (E) are not addressed by the poem.

54. (A)

Again we must go back to the underlying message of the poet—moderation, moderation, moderation. Do not become too upset; do not become too buoyed up—only moderation, sailing with an even keel, should be considered. You may not agree with this poet and the rather boring suggestions he makes, but you must rely only upon what is in the poem. Do not let your own reactions influence your responses to this passage. "Life's Ups and Downs" (C) may have tempted you, but the poem is about what to do about them—following "The Golden Mean."

SECTION II: ESSAY QUESTIONS

Essay Question 1: Carpe Diem **and** To Virgins, to Make Much of Time

Prompt: Read these two poems—the first is by Horace, a Latin poet who lived from 65–8 b.c.e.; the second is by Robert Herrick, an English Cavalier poet who lived from 1591–1674.

In a well-organized essay, consider how each poem utilizes poetic elements such as imagery, symbolism and tone to express very similar ideas despite the centuries that separate the poets.

Carpe Diem
Horace

Strive not, Leuconoe,[1] to know what end
The gods above to me or thee will send;
Not with astrologers consult at all,
That thou mayest better know what can befall;
(5) Whether thou liv'st more winters, or thy last
Be this, which Tyrrhen waves[2] 'gainst rocks do cast
Be wise! Drink free, and in so short a space
Do not protracted hopes of life embrace.
Whilst we are talking, envious time doth slide
(10) This day's thine own; the next may be denied.

To Virgins, to Make Much of Time
Robert Herrick

Gather ye rosebuds while ye may,
Old Time is still a-flying;
And this same flower that smiles today,
To-morrow will be dying.
(5) The glorious lamp of heaven, the Sun,
The higher he's a-getting;
The sooner will his race be run,
And nearer he's to setting.
That age is best, which is the first,
(10) When youth and blood are warmer;
But being spent, the worse, and worst
Times still succeed the former.
Then be not coy, but use your time,
And while ye may, go marry;
(15) For having lost but once your prime,
You may for ever tarry.

[1] Leuconoe was the poet's friend.

[2] Tyrrhen waves is a reference to the Tyrrhenian Sea, part of the Mediterranean in southwest Italy.

ANALYSIS OF ESSAY QUESTION 1

This is a challenging essay question. The Horace poem, of course, is a translation. In fact, some may question whether or not the original was even written in poetry format. Nevertheless, as the piece is presented here, you must consider it as a poem to be compared to the poem by Herrick.

Of course, the obvious contrast between the pieces is purely a physical one. The Horace piece is extremely brief—only ten lines of what seems to be iambic pentameter, though rather rough in places. This is not surprising, however, when a translation and a format has been altered as this has. In fact, the rhyme scheme should not even be considered since some translator has forced the original into rhymed English words. The Herrick poem is longer and alternates between iambic tetrameter and iambic trimeter with an extra unstressed syllable at every other line. Since the Herrick poem comes from the era of the Cavalier poets (1600s), one would expect such formality in structure. In fact, many of the Cavalier poets are known for their clever poetic structures.

None of these surface comparisons are very important, however, in answering the prompt for this question. The prompt directs you to consider how each poem utilizes poetic devices such as imagery, symbolism and tone to develop the underlying universal theme of *carpe diem,* "seize the day." Included in this prompt is the directive to consider how two such historically and culturally distant poets present such a similar philosophy.

The Horace poem seems more formal and serious. It is directed at a specific person, Leuconoe, who, according to the footnote was a friend of Horace's. In fact it is Horace who should be credited with the idea of *carpe diem,* although many will tell you that the philosophy was a product of the Cavaliers. Herrick's poem is flippant in tone, addressed to any comely virgin, urging her to take advantage of her attractions before they are gone due to old age.

Horace urges Leuconoe not to worry about what may happen. In lines 3–5 he admonishes him not to consult with astrologers, not to worry about how many winters are ahead. He says, line 7, to "Be wise! Drink free." One never knows whether today will be one day of many or the last of one's days. Herrick's approach is a bit different. He says to the Virgins to act quickly, use their charms while they have them. Time is marching on (in contrast to Horace, who says time may be at an end) and soon the Virgins will lose their prime. Tarry now, Herrick says, and you may tarry forever. Although the two poets present their ideas differently, they both have the same underlying message—act now; there may not be a tomorrow (or a marriage opportunity) if you don't enjoy life in the present.

In analyzing these poems, it would be important for you to stress that the action messages differ, but the meanings are much the same. Choose specific imagery and symbols to support what you say. Make references to lines and use short quotations where appropriate.

SCORING GUIDE FOR QUESTION 1

9–8: Responses meriting these scores demonstrate an understanding of the differences between the two poems. They illustrate this understanding with a clear thesis and with persuasive references to the poems. Not only do these essays feature a strong inferential understanding of the content and tone of each poem, but they show that the writers perceive the poets' attitudes as the two very different poets describe a similar thematic idea. Well-conceived, well-developed, and well-organized, these essays provide frequent and adequate and accurate references to the two poems, blending the comparison without setting up a volley between them. The writers of these essays comfortably explain each poet's use of poetic elements and cleverly weave the significance of these elements into the response. Although these responses are not perfect, they clearly indicate the students' ability to read poetry skillfully and respond to the prompt in mature composition style.

7–6: These essays feature solid understanding of the prompt and the two poems. Although essays in this range will not be as full nor as sophisticated as the 9–8 responses, they are well written in an appropriate style, but often with less maturity or polish than the top papers. They may be less fully developed, or they may demonstrate less insight. Nevertheless, the writing is sufficient to convey ideas, the presentation is sound, and it reflects the writers' ability to convey their points clearly.

5: Essays in this middle range are able to discuss how the two poems compare in their thematic message, and what the likenesses and differences might represent, but these responses are typically superficial or may be overly generalized. Often formal elements are identified, and possibly cited, but are poorly integrated into the response. Usually these responses demonstrate inconsistent control over the elements of composition and/or the students' analytical skills are erratic.

4–3: Responses earning these scores are likely to have one or more of these flaws: a simple recounting or restatement of the differences between the poems; imprecise or incomplete treatment of the formal elements within the two poems; little analysis; weak discussion about the authors' attitudes within the two poems and what these differing attitudes may indicate; incomplete or sketchy support information. These responses often demonstrate the students' incomplete or incorrect understanding of either or both of the passages.

2–1: These essays unsuccessfully respond to the tasks of the prompt. They may misunderstand the prompt, the passages, or all of these. Although the students will make some attempt to answer, there is little clarity about the interpretation of the poems and only slight or misused evidence to develop this analysis. The writings often reveal consistent weaknesses in grammar or other basic composition skills such as organization, clarity, fluency, or development.

STUDENT RESPONSE TO QUESTION 1

One thing that seems to be a quality of all worthwhile literature, that maintains its "staying power" is that it contains a universal message—a message that transcends all time and all languages. That is one of the reason, for instance, that Shakespeare has endured so well. No matter what language it is translated into, *Macbeth* continues to reach out to readers and viewers because they too can identify with ambition and the very human characteristic of wanting to succeed in life, to get ahead, even if it means cutting a few corners to get there. Many of today's politicians embrace this universal idea.

This is the case with these two poems, written by two very different authors from two very different centuries. The first poem, by Horace, is actually the source of the still-used expression that is also the title of the poem, *Carpe Diem*. Even before the birth of Christ this Roman poet/philosopher realized that we spend far too much time worrying about things that we cannot control. He urges his friend to take life as it is given to him, for there is no telling about any future, and we are unable to change what has already passed. In a similar manner, almost 1700 years later, Robert Herrick echoes these same sentiments. He urges the young women of his time to make the most of their youth and beauty before time passes and it is too late to enjoy life. I would venture to say, however, that Horace's advice is more solemn and almost philosophical in nature while Herrick sounds like he is trying to get some young lady to do something she has been reluctant to do.

Horace says that the gods cannot tell us; we can even consult the stars for insight into the future, but it won't help. All we can do, he assures his friend, is to enjoy the moment. "Be wise! Drink free, and in so short a space/Do not protracted hopes of life embrace." Although it sounds a bit like a contemporary beer advertisement, what Horace seems to be saying, very simply, is to live now: forget what's gone before, and do not worry about the future, for we cannot know weather we will live many winters or this will be our last. In fact, using personification he reminds

Leuconoe, his friend, that Time slides by while they stand around and talking. Take this day because you have it; you may not have any more.

Horace actually uses few poetic devices in this poem, but some of that may be the result of multiple translations. Nevertheless, Time becomes almost a tangible entity with a whimsical nature, and Horace's tone is urgent but serious as he delivers his message.

On the other hand, Herrick's tone seems far from serious. His attitude throughout the poem seems flippant and teasing. Even the very regular meter and rhyme scheme add to this sense of lightheartedness, while Horace's poem had no rhyme, and the meter is a bit muddled. This too could possibly a result of translations.

Herrick urges the young ladies of his time to loosen up while they have a chance to catch a man (or a rosebud). He says they must move while they are young, while "youth and blood are warmer." He then reminds them that once this bloom of youth is gone; "You [they] may for ever tarry."

Flowers and rosebuds, youth, blushing coy maidens, rising Sun (note personificated capitalization) are all part of the imagery of this poem. He seems less serious in his purpose than does Horace. Horace reminds his friend that we mortals fret and worry and cannot change what we cannot change. Herrick tells the girls that they'd better change (be less coy and more aggressive) while they can, for their "days in the sun" are limited. Although the poets' purposes may differ, their message is basically the same.

Both poets speak of living life to its fullest while you have it. Each expresses these sentiments with different purposes in mind. Nevertheless, the underlying message is the same. We cannot change what we cannot change. I may wish for a 9 on this essay, but if you, the reader, don't see it that way, there's nothing I can do to alter the score you mark down. All the fretting in the world will not change the ultimate outcome. Remember that, please.

COMMENTARY ON STUDENT RESPONSE TO QUESTION 1

This student has control of the language, demonstrates analytical competence, and exhibits composition skill. His or her approach is neither sophisticated nor very academic; nevertheless, this essay adequately responds to the prompt. In fact, based upon the preceding scoring guide, this student's response fulfills all the necessary qualities of at least a low-7 response.

Although the essay contains a few lapses in diction and grammar, these flaws don't seriously affect the overall impression the student has created. Had this student taken the time (or more likely had more time) to reread the essay more closely, these errors would likely to have been corrected. The student adequately addresses the prompt, but it could be enhanced by further exploration of the subject. Although the essay does make references to the specifics of both poems, other examples could have been included to support the points that are made. For instance, Horace is not dealt with in great depth, but one must commend the student for commenting on the poem's lack of "poetry" as probably being the result of multiple translations over the centuries. There is much truth to this. We probably would not even recognize this poem if we were to read it in its original, pre-Christian, Latin form.

Obviously the student is more comfortable with Robert Herrick's piece. This is probably the case for just about any reader of the two pieces. Herrick is fun; Horace is almost dour. The student successfully points out imagery and symbolism that are at the core of the Herrick poem. Also, the student infers much about the Herrick's attitude from the mere structure (rhyme and rhythm) of the poem; this is a good connection.

Perhaps the strongest point in this student's favor is his or her comments about the similarities of the underlying message despite the probable purpose or intended effects on the part of the authors. This insight would be one quality of this response that could arguably push it into the high 6, low 7 section of the scoring guide.

It is important for you to notice this student's final paragraph. In reality, the essay ends in the second to the last paragraph. The essential thoughts are brought to closure at that point. The final paragraph, somewhat of an addendum, would most likely be met with mixed responses from readers. Had the essay not been completed in the previous paragraph, this last paragraph would probably pull the score down. Since the essay has been completed, however, these last few comments from the student remind us that there certainly is a person penning this response. Perhaps not offering the sophisticated ending a reader would prefer, this student has, nevertheless, incorporated a very human element into this response by tying in the underlying philosophy of the poems to a very real-life situation.

Essay Question 2: The Author's Preface

Prompt: This is a selection from the Preface of an early British novel. Read the passage carefully. In a well-organized essay discuss how the author's calculating style attempts to manipulate reader's curiosity in order to lure him or her into reading the book itself. Pay particular attention to such stylistic devices as diction, imagery, and inference.

The Author's Preface

The world is so taken up of late with novels and romances, that it will be hard for a private history to be taken for genuine, where the names and other circumstances of the person are concealed, and on
(5) this account we must be content to leave the reader to pass his own opinion upon the ensuing sheet, and take it just as he pleases.

The author is here supposed to be writing her own history, and in the very beginning of her
(10) account she gives the reasons why she thinks fit to conceal her true name, after which there is no occasion to say any more about that.

It is true that the original of this story is put into new words, and the style of the famous lady
(15) we here speak of is a little altered; particularly she is made to tell her own tale in modester words than she told it at first, the copy which came first to hand having been written in language more like one still in Newgate than one grown penitent and
(20) humble, as she afterwards pretends to be.

The pen employed in finishing her story, and making it what you now see it to be, has had no little difficulty to put it into a dress fit to be seen, and to make it speak language fit to be read. When a
(25) woman debauched from her youth, nay, even being the offspring of debauchery and vice, comes to give an account of all her vicious practices, and even to descend to the particular occasions and circumstances by which she ran through in threescore
(30) years, an author must be hard put to wrap it up so clean as not to give room, especially for vicious readers, to turn it to his disadvantage.

All possible care, however, has been taken to give no lewd ideas, no immodest turns in the new dress-
(35) ing up of this story; no, not to the worst parts of her expressions. To this purpose some of the vicious part of her life, which could not be modestly told, is quite left out, and several other parts are very much shortened. What is left 'tis hoped will not offend

(40) the chastest reader or the modest hearer; and as the best use is made even of the worst story, the moral 'tis hoped will keep the reader serious, even where the story might incline him to be otherwise. To give the history of a wicked life repented of, necessarily
(45) requires that the wicked part should be make as wicked as the real history of it will bear, to illustrate and give a beauty to the penitent part, which is certainly the best and brightest, if related with equal spirit and life.

(50) But as this work is chiefly recommended to those who know how to read it, and how to make the good uses of it which the story all along recommends to them, so it is to be hoped that such readers will be more pleased with the moral than
(55) the fable, with the application than with the relation, and with the end of the writer than with the life of the person written of.

There is in this story abundance of delightful incidents, and all of them usefully applied. There is
(60) an agreeable turn artfully given them in the relating, that naturally instructs the reader, either one way or other. The first part of her lewd life with the young gentleman at Colchester has so many happy turns given it to expose the crime, and warn all
(65) whose circumstances are adapted to it, of the ruinous end of such things, and the foolish, thoughtless, and abhorred conduct of both the parties, that it abundantly atones for all the lively description she gives of her folly and wickedness.

(70) Upon this foundation this book is recommended to the reader as a work from every part of which something may be learned, and some just and religious inference is drawn, by which the reader will have something of instruction, if he
(75) pleases to make use of it.

ANALYSIS OF ESSAY QUESTION 2

Often referred to as the Father of the British Novel, Daniel Defoe's most famous literary success was *Robinson Crusoe*, sometimes considered the first novel ever written. Regardless of the truth of Defoe's role as father figure, this passage is taken from one of his later works, *The Fortunes and Misfortunes of the Famous Moll Flanders*. As an addendum to the book's title, the reader is also told:

> "Who was Born in Newgate, and during a Life of continu'd Variety for Threescore Years, besides her Childhood, was Twelve Year a Whore, five times a Wife (whereof once to her own Brother), Twelve Year a Thief, Eight Year a Transported Felon in Virginia, at last grew Rich, liv'd Honest, and dies a Penitent. Written from her own Memorandums."

The book then begins with a lengthy *Preface* from which the passage in question 2 was taken. No pun intended, novels were still a novelty in the early 1700s when Defoe produced a number of literary works rather late in his life. Because of this newness, the reading public was still somewhat dubious about reading anything that was purely a product of someone's imagination. It is for this reason, therefore, that tales such as those of Robinson Crusoe and Moll Flanders are presented as true and verifiable historical accounts. This perhaps assured readers that even if the main character's life and adventures was less than seemly, it was, after all, a true story.

With this is mind, it should be easier for you to better understand the cleverness of Daniel Defoe's *Preface* to *Moll Flanders*. He first mentions the main character as someone who must conceal her name from the public, and that the language has been cleaned up, since the original reflected the crude speech of an inmate of Newgate. In the fourth paragraph, Defoe employs the analogy of dress and fashion as he goes on to say that he must clothe the offspring of debauchery and vice in cleaner wrappings. He later hints that some of the more unseemly parts of the heroine's life even had to be omitted so as not to offend the reader. How clever he was to have titillated his readers, daring them to read more.

Defoe would probably find himself right at home as a writer for the *National Inquirer* or similar contemporary publication. Through his clever use of innuendo and his skillful manipulation of diction, Defoe grabs the reader's attention. What reader could resist turning to the next page of the book, at least to take "just a peek"? It is Defoe's cleverness that the prompt asks you to explore. You must consider the words he chooses to introduce the novel, the images he evokes in the reader's mind, and the inferences and innuendo he uses. You must not only discuss these stylistic devices, but also consider their intended (and probable) effect upon the curious reader. Perhaps the most telling word of the prompt is the verb *manipulate*. That should be the focus of your analysis.

SCORING GUIDE FOR QUESTION 2

9–8: Essays earning these scores demonstrate successful writers who clearly recognize Defoe's masterful use of strong imagery. These essays display perceptive understanding of how the manipulation of language impacts the reader and piques his or her intellectual curiosity. Well-developed and insightful, these essays are marked by a keen sense of understanding of diction, imagery, and inference and its effect upon the reader. They indicate the students' sensitivity toward the subtle maneuvering of the writer in this passage. In addition, they demonstrate by means of quotation how the language reveals the writer's cleverness. Although not without error, these essays indicate students' ability to read poetry skillfully, respond to the prompt accurately, and to write with clarity and skill.

7–6: These essays treat adequately most of the elements above but do so less thoroughly than the best papers. They will analyze diction, imagery, inference, and other literary devices less fully than 8–9 papers. They recognize Defoe's manipulative literary style, but are less successful in expressing its effectiveness. They are well written, but use of evidence is less satisfactory. There may be occasional lapses in diction, syntax, or other writing skills, but these essays will demonstrate sufficient control to present the writer's ideas clearly.

5: These essays will be accurate and fairly well written, but they demonstrate some weaknesses. They may resort more to paraphrasing rather than using evidence as strong support. They may present many ideas without tying them together adequately. Or they may be strong in all but one or two aspects of analysis indicated by the prompt. They may discuss style, but fail to talk about the effect of the style upon the reader. These essays may reveal simplistic thinking and/or immature writing. The writing, however, is still sufficient to convey ideas convincingly.

4–3: These lower-half scores are for essays that inadequately respond to the task set out by the prompt. They may reflect an incomplete understanding of the passage. Often, they do not respond to part or parts of the question. Composition skills will be weak, often presenting many ideas but failing to tie things together. Often they demonstrate an incomplete or incorrect understanding of the passage.

2–1: These essays compound the weaknesses of the papers in the 4–3 range. They seriously misunderstand the prompt, the passage, or possibly both. Often poorly written, they may contain distracting grammar and usage errors. Although some attempt is made to answer the question, the writer's views are unclear, disorganized, incoherent, and/or lacking in supporting evidence. A score of 1 should be given to those essays that may mention the poem or the prompt, but otherwise have no redeeming qualities.

STUDENT RESPONSE TO QUESTION 2

If I were a human relations director of a major publishing firm of contemporary literature, I would give this author a job in a nano second! What a tease he/she (although I am sure it is a he) is. Who could resist reading a book with such a preface? No one that I know could pass up such bait. This author truly displays a "calculating style" that manipulates the reader's curiosity with its innuendo, its word choice and its imagery. In fact, it is what the author does NOT say that makes this *Preface* so very successful.

The author assures the reader that this is a true story. Just as Holden Caulfield had to continually convince his "listener" that what he said was what <u>really</u> happened, this author uses a very similar ploy. He tells us that the author is "writing her own history," that she must "conceal her true name" (and we are all too familiar with the phrase that "names have been changed to protect the innocent," but he has had to tell her own tale "in modester words that she told it at first….[rather than in the language] like one still in Newgate." What a tease this author is from the very onset of his story.

This author chooses his words carefully. Words such as "conceal her true name," "language more like one still in Newgate," "a woman debauched from her youth," "off-spring of debauchery," "no lewd ideas" and "no immodest turns," "will not offend" are only a few choice phrases this author uses to lure the reader into reading his (or her, though I doubt it) book. Later in this passage the author assures us (the intrigued reader) that this book is "chiefly recommended to those who know how to read it," and that the story contains an "abundance of delightful incidents"—all of these phrases chosen specifically to assure the reader that he/she has made a good choice in pursuing the contents of this novel. If one were not to read his book then this would be a confession to the world that the reader does not "have what it takes" to take the challenge. It sort of reminds me of Regis and the Millionaire show!

Inference and innuendo control this *Preface*. It's as much what the author does not say, what he hints at but is too tasteful to verbalize that makes this passage so successful. Although some of the examples have already been used, I must again refer to the cleaned-up language of the Newgate prisoner, the debauchery and the child of debauchery (tsk, tsk, what might he be suggesting?), the suggestion that the author has taken great pains to "protect" even the "chastest" reader (protect this reader from what, may I ask?), and that despite its shortcomings, (and of course its these very "shortcomings" that the majority of the readers then and now would probably be most interested in) that something can be learned, even something of a religious nature if the reader is so inclined to need such assurance.

There is no doubt about it. This is an author who knows how to 'play' his reading audience. He knows how to tickle their fancy (and their most secret fantasy), and he does it with skill. Inference, imagery and diction all coordinate to lure the reader into turning the page and beginning chapter one of this tantalizing book.

COMMENTARY ON STUDENT RESPONSE TO QUESTION 2

This is a very successful student response, worthy of an upper-level score. The following is the description of an 8–9 essay, and it's easy to see that this particular response fulfills these requirements.

> "Essays earning these scores demonstrate successful writers who clearly recognize Defoe's masterful use of strong imagery. These essays display perceptive understanding of how the manipulation of language impacts the reader and piques his or her intellectual curiosity. Well-developed and insightful, these essays are marked by a keen sense of understanding of diction imagery, and inference and its affect upon the reader. In addition, they indicate the students' sensitivity toward the subtle maneuvering of the writer in this passage. In addition, they demonstrate by means of quotation, how the language reveals the writer's cleverness. Although not without error, these essays indicate students' ability to read poetry skillfully, respond to the prompt accurately, and to write with clarity and skill."

This student demonstrates a fine analytical understanding of the passage. The essay is written in a mature, though very personable style, with a strong student voice clearly evident. This essay has an interesting opening. The student interjects him or herself into the response by saying he or she would certainly be willing to hire a writer as skillful as Defoe. The rest of the response supports this statement while responding to the original prompt.

First the essay speaks about Defoe's appeal to veracity. Although you might find the reference to *Catcher in the Rye* a stretch as a comparison to Moll Flanders, in this case such a comparison works well. Then the student goes continues to outline the author's attempts at convincing the reader of the truth and authenticity of the book itself.

In the subsequent two paragraphs, the essay covers diction ("This author chooses his words carefully") and deduction ("Inference and innuendo control this *Preface*"). The task of the prompt is for students to *discuss how the author's calculating style attempts to manipulate the reader's curiosity in order to lure him or her into reading the book itself. Pay particular attention to such stylistic devices as diction, imagery, and inference.* This is precisely what this essay does. However, this student's own composition style is so strong that the structure of the response does not make the composition seem jerky or piecemeal. And, despite the traditional five-paragraph structure, the ideas flow smoothly into the whole. This student lets the rules of good composition work for him or her naturally, with no sense of a mechanical or technical paradigm underlying the structure.

All the rules have been followed: an interesting, though not lengthy introduction that establishes the thesis of the essay; body paragraphs that not only develop the points of the prompt, but also blend together smoothly and are well supported and developed; and, finally, a clever but succinct conclusion that ties everything together.

Without a doubt this essay would earn an 8 on this rubric scale. You may ask, if it's so good, why not a 9? It is a strong response; it is a very accurate response; it is well-written; but it does not shine or make one's toes curl. Some may say that it's at least a low 9 and they would not be amiss. To say this is but a high 7, however, would not be doing it justice. Precisely because it does fall between these parameters, it deserves an 8 score.

Essay Question 3: The Point of No Return

Prompt: Often in literature, situations reach a "point of no return," a point after which the life of a character can never be the same. Choose a novel or play in which a character reaches this point and write an essay explaining the situation and its effect on the character, the other characters, and the theme. You may choose a work from the list below or another novel or full-length play of literary merit.

ANALYSIS OF ESSAY QUESTION 3

In all the books and plays that you have read, you should find this prompt very approachable. Any good novel or play will have that "point of no return." Macbeth tells us if it is to be done, then better it be done quickly. From that point forward, there is no turning back for him. When King Lear banishes Cordelia, we know in our hearts that his life will never be the same. Huckleberry Finn worries about not turning Jim into the bounty hunters and decides that he will go to hell rather than turn on his friend; from there on his life is never be the same. Whether you choose to talk about Scout or Hester, Ralph or Santiago, each of their lives was affected by such a "point of no return."

SCORING GUIDE FOR QUESTION 3

9–8: Responses in this range carefully select a work of literature where a major character either makes a critical decision, or finds him or herself in a critical situation that affects his or her life so much that this character is never the same. These essays are well-conceived, well-developed and well-organized, and the student has been able to take the response a step further by making more insightful associations between the character's actions/decisions and the broader sense of the literary piece as a whole. These responses readily grasp the intent of the prompt, and they adeptly reveal how their choice of character best demonstrates the point of no return concept as introduced by the prompt. They need not be without flaws; nevertheless, they demonstrate that the student has mastered not only the skill of analyzing a piece of literature appropriately, but also has demonstrated exceptional composition skills.

7–6: These essays treat satisfactorily most of the elements of the 9–8 papers, but they do so less thoroughly than the best papers. Their discussion of the significant character and what has happened to change him or her, is not as deft as that of the 9–8 responses. In addition, they tend to be less convincing than are the best responses. They adequately demonstrate how the character is affected by this life-changing situation within the particular work, but they fail to go beyond the predictable. These essays are well written, but with less maturity and control of writing skills than the best responses. Although these writers do understand the task(s) of the prompt, they do so with less maturity and control than the top papers.

5: These essays are highly superficial. The analysis may be unconvincing, underdeveloped, or even somewhat inaccurate. The thinking demonstrated in these responses is less mature and less developed that the upper-half responses. Nevertheless, it is easy to recognize the intent of these responses, and they do not fall into the lower-half range.

4–3: These lower-half essays may choose an acceptable work, but they fail to explain how the character and or situation fulfills the qualifications set up by the prompt. Their analysis is often trite and perfunctory. The writing usually conveys the writer's ideas, but it reveals weak control over such elements as diction, organization, syntax, or grammar. These essays may also demonstrate some misunderstanding of the prompt.

2–1: These essays compound the weaknesses of essays in the 4–3 range. They may misread the prompt, or choose a character or situation inappropriate for the prompt. These essays are often quite brief, and they fail to give much support or development to any of the ideas they present. Although it is clear that these essays attempt to respond to the prompt, the ideas presented often display minimal clarity or coherence.

STUDENT RESPONSE TO QUESTION 3

King Lear was an old man who had lived for many years as the center of the universe which he ruled. He was used to being waited upon and being flattered and made to feel special. Generally, courtiers are no fools when it comes to knowing who it is to whom they must pay homage. With this in mind, King Lear, perhaps in a moment of boredom, perhaps at a moment in encroaching senility, decides he should settle his lands before he dies. Consequently, he sets up a sort of contest among his daughters, demanding that they tell their father just how very much they love him. This is Lear's folly, his point of no return. The first act of Shakespeare's play has barely begun when Lear makes a move that he will regret for the next four and a half acts of this play.

Of course his daughters tell him what he wants to hear—at least two of them do. When the third, youngest, and his favorite daughter, Cordelia, tells him in all honesty that she loves her father as a daughter ought, with no embellishments or falsehoods, Lear looses it. He banishes Cordelia from his sight (although he might have redeemed himself from the ridiculousness of the love-contest at this point) and divides the land between the two lying, conniving daughters who really don't love him at all.

It does not take Lear long to realize what a mistake he has made. First the daughters strip Lear of his retainers. This may not seem like much to us, but for a king at that time, his losing his men, his power, is the ultimate humiliation. Soon he is left with only one servant and a poor fool. This recently powerful king suddenly finds himself alone in a raging storm, ranting at everyone for what has happened. It takes awhile, however, before he realizes that the major

cause of all his loss is his very own self. Of course, it is this flaw that the play centers around. Until Lear can see himself for what he is and place the blame for his situation where it rightly belongs, the tragedy will continue.

Finally, near the end of the play, Lear does come to recognize the folly of his ways. He admits to all who are there to listen (not many listeners, by the way) that he never should have given up his lands; he never should have trusted his two bad daughters, Goneril and Regan; and most of all, he never, ever should have banished Cordelia, the only one who truly loved him. He recognizes what the reader/viewer has known for awhile, that Lear made a move that changed his life for ever after.

At the end of the play, Lear and Cordelia are reunited, and the audience/reader is hopeful that since the old foolish king has seen the error of his ways, things might get straightened out after all. However, we cannot forget that this is a Shakespearean tragedy, and as such, no happy endings are ever possible. Because he was stubborn and greedy to hear more and more praise, Lear set himself up for doom. Not only do things not get straightened out, but the only daughter who really loves him (as he now recognizes) is killed in prison, and the play ends with his weeping in despair over her dead body.

Just because an old man is foolish and perhaps a bit bored by the normal adulation of the crowd toward the king, Lear staged a silly contest. Of course he did not know that the contest was rigged from the start because two of the 3 participants were dishonest. Nevertheless, his life changed in a manner so terrible, that he lost everything that really mattered. Poor silly old man.

COMMENTARY ON STUDENT RESPONSE TO QUESTION 3

"Poor silly old man"—perceptive student or flippant, disrespectful teenager? In this case, "Poor silly old man," is a remark made by a discerning student who has chosen wisely to write about *King Lear* for question number 3. In *King Lear*, the point-of-no-return situation arrives early in the play and directs the entire outcome of the tragedy. This was a good play to write about for this prompt, and the essay demonstrates that this student has a good understanding of the play, the main character, and, consequently, he or she successfully fulfills the tasks of the prompt.

If you look at the scoring guide for this prompt, the only thing that this response falls short on is perhaps fulfilling the 9–8 characteristic that says "…able to take their response a step further by making more insightful associations…." This essay has some insight, but not enough to make it a 9 response. It is, however, a strong 7, probably a low 8 paper that is accurate, and one that demonstrates a strong student voice. This student has excellent composition skills, a strong vocabulary, and he or she makes his or her point quickly and develops it accordingly.

A sound understanding of Lear's personal shortcomings is evident. The essay discusses Lear's love for adulation, his egocentric setting up of the "love contest," and finally, the Old King's need to come to terms with who was really to blame for his tragic circumstances. This student has done

this well. Granted, he or she has indicated neither startlingly unusual analyses nor any particularly erudite insights. Nevertheless, this essay very successfully fulfills the tasks of the prompt, and demonstrates qualities of a very strong upper-half response.

No, the essay is not without a few flaws and shortcomings. A few usage errors are present, and more diverse sentence structures might have been used. Remember, however, readers know quite well the circumstances and incredible pressures that students are under when they write these essays. They realize that students like you have never seen these questions before. You've had no time to do brainstorming and initial planning. However, successful AP students the world over face these same constraints year after year, and like you, they worry, fret, and wonder how they will ever be able to perform well. Nonetheless, like you, they survive and they perform well, often exceptionally well.

Read the prompt again; look over the rubric and the short commentary about the prompt. Think about what is being asked. Consider the list of books that have been suggested. What other titles can you come up with that would also fulfill the needs of this particular essay? Outline some of your ideas; check with your AP English instructor to see what he or she thinks about your ideas. You will do fine. Be prepared; try to relax; concentrate and write like you've never written before. You can do it!

Practice Test Three Answer Sheet

1 Ⓐ Ⓑ Ⓒ Ⓓ Ⓔ   22 Ⓐ Ⓑ Ⓒ Ⓓ Ⓔ   43 Ⓐ Ⓑ Ⓒ Ⓓ Ⓔ

2 Ⓐ Ⓑ Ⓒ Ⓓ Ⓔ   23 Ⓐ Ⓑ Ⓒ Ⓓ Ⓔ   44 Ⓐ Ⓑ Ⓒ Ⓓ Ⓔ

3 Ⓐ Ⓑ Ⓒ Ⓓ Ⓔ   24 Ⓐ Ⓑ Ⓒ Ⓓ Ⓔ   45 Ⓐ Ⓑ Ⓒ Ⓓ Ⓔ

4 Ⓐ Ⓑ Ⓒ Ⓓ Ⓔ   25 Ⓐ Ⓑ Ⓒ Ⓓ Ⓔ   46 Ⓐ Ⓑ Ⓒ Ⓓ Ⓔ

5 Ⓐ Ⓑ Ⓒ Ⓓ Ⓔ   26 Ⓐ Ⓑ Ⓒ Ⓓ Ⓔ   47 Ⓐ Ⓑ Ⓒ Ⓓ Ⓔ

6 Ⓐ Ⓑ Ⓒ Ⓓ Ⓔ   27 Ⓐ Ⓑ Ⓒ Ⓓ Ⓔ   48 Ⓐ Ⓑ Ⓒ Ⓓ Ⓔ

7 Ⓐ Ⓑ Ⓒ Ⓓ Ⓔ   28 Ⓐ Ⓑ Ⓒ Ⓓ Ⓔ   49 Ⓐ Ⓑ Ⓒ Ⓓ Ⓔ

8 Ⓐ Ⓑ Ⓒ Ⓓ Ⓔ   29 Ⓐ Ⓑ Ⓒ Ⓓ Ⓔ   50 Ⓐ Ⓑ Ⓒ Ⓓ Ⓔ

9 Ⓐ Ⓑ Ⓒ Ⓓ Ⓔ   30 Ⓐ Ⓑ Ⓒ Ⓓ Ⓔ   51 Ⓐ Ⓑ Ⓒ Ⓓ Ⓔ

10 Ⓐ Ⓑ Ⓒ Ⓓ Ⓔ   31 Ⓐ Ⓑ Ⓒ Ⓓ Ⓔ   52 Ⓐ Ⓑ Ⓒ Ⓓ Ⓔ

11 Ⓐ Ⓑ Ⓒ Ⓓ Ⓔ   32 Ⓐ Ⓑ Ⓒ Ⓓ Ⓔ   53 Ⓐ Ⓑ Ⓒ Ⓓ Ⓔ

12 Ⓐ Ⓑ Ⓒ Ⓓ Ⓔ   33 Ⓐ Ⓑ Ⓒ Ⓓ Ⓔ   54 Ⓐ Ⓑ Ⓒ Ⓓ Ⓔ

13 Ⓐ Ⓑ Ⓒ Ⓓ Ⓔ   34 Ⓐ Ⓑ Ⓒ Ⓓ Ⓔ   55 Ⓐ Ⓑ Ⓒ Ⓓ Ⓔ

14 Ⓐ Ⓑ Ⓒ Ⓓ Ⓔ   35 Ⓐ Ⓑ Ⓒ Ⓓ Ⓔ   56 Ⓐ Ⓑ Ⓒ Ⓓ Ⓔ

15 Ⓐ Ⓑ Ⓒ Ⓓ Ⓔ   36 Ⓐ Ⓑ Ⓒ Ⓓ Ⓔ   57 Ⓐ Ⓑ Ⓒ Ⓓ Ⓔ

16 Ⓐ Ⓑ Ⓒ Ⓓ Ⓔ   37 Ⓐ Ⓑ Ⓒ Ⓓ Ⓔ   58 Ⓐ Ⓑ Ⓒ Ⓓ Ⓔ

17 Ⓐ Ⓑ Ⓒ Ⓓ Ⓔ   38 Ⓐ Ⓑ Ⓒ Ⓓ Ⓔ

18 Ⓐ Ⓑ Ⓒ Ⓓ Ⓔ   39 Ⓐ Ⓑ Ⓒ Ⓓ Ⓔ

19 Ⓐ Ⓑ Ⓒ Ⓓ Ⓔ   40 Ⓐ Ⓑ Ⓒ Ⓓ Ⓔ

20 Ⓐ Ⓑ Ⓒ Ⓓ Ⓔ   41 Ⓐ Ⓑ Ⓒ Ⓓ Ⓔ

21 Ⓐ Ⓑ Ⓒ Ⓓ Ⓔ   42 Ⓐ Ⓑ Ⓒ Ⓓ Ⓔ

Practice Test Three

Section I: Multiple-Choice Questions

Time: 1 hour
Number of questions: 54
Percent of total grade: 45

Directions: This section contains selections from literary works with questions on their content, style, form, and purpose. Read each selection, then choose the best answer from the five choices in each test item and fill in the corresponding oval on the answer sheet.

Note: Pay particular attention to the requirements of questions that contain the words **NOT, LEAST,** or **EXCEPT.**

Questions 1–13. Read the following essay carefully before you mark your answers.

Of these false Achitophel was first:
A name to all succeeding ages cursed.
For close designs, and crooked counsels fit;
Sagacious, bold, and turbulent of wit:
(5) Restless, unfixed in principles and place;
In power unpleased, impatient of disgrace.
A fiery soul, which worked out its way,
Fretted the pigmy body to decay:
And o'er informed the tenement of clay.
(10) A daring pilot in extremity;
Pleased with the danger, when the waves went high.
He sought the storms; but for a calm unfit,
Would steer too nigh the sands to boast his Wit.
Great wits are sure to madness near allied.
(15) And thin partitions do their bounds divide:
Else, why should he, with wealth and honor blessed,
Refuse his age the needful hours of rest?
Punish a body which he could not please;
Bankrupt of life, yet prodigal of ease?
(20) And all to leave, what with his toil he won,
To that unfeathered, two legged thing, a son…
Some of their chiefs were princes of the land:
In the first rank of these did Zimri stand:

A man so various that he seemed to be
(25) Not one, but all mankind's epitome.
Stiff in opinions, always in the wrong;
Was everything by starts, and nothing long:
But, in the course of one revolving moon,
Was chemist, fiddler, statesman, and buffoon:
(30) Then, all for women, painting, rhyming, drinking;
Besides ten thousands freaks that died in thinking.
Blest madman, who could every hour employ,
With something new to wish, or to enjoy!
Railing and praising were his usual themes;
(35) And both (to show his judgment) in extremes;
So over violent, or over civil,
That every man, with him, was God or Devil.
In squandering wealth was his peculiar art:
Nothing went unrewarded, but desert.[1]
(40) Beggared by fools, who still he found too late:
He had his jest, and they had his estate.
He laugh'd himself from court, then sought relief
By forming parties, but could ne'er be chief.

[1]*desert:* What a person deserves

GO ON TO THE NEXT PAGE

1. Which of the following literary techniques does the author use when he describes Achitophel as "A name to all succeeding ages cursed./For close designs, and crooked counsels fit" in lines 2–3?

   (A) alliteration

   (B) personification

   (C) onomatopoeia

   (D) metonymy

   (E) litote

2. The metaphor the poet uses in lines 10–12 to describe Achitophel's character is that Achitophel

   (A) represents the ocean's unpredictable changes

   (B) is compared to an unrestrained force of Nature

   (C) symbolizes the contradictory impulses in even the most restrained people

   (D) is compared to a pilot who saves the day when no one else can

   (E) is compared to a pilot who likes danger but is unfit for calm seas

3. Which of the following statements best paraphrases lines 14–15?

   (A) Humorists often insult their targets.

   (B) People who think they are funny are rarely as amusing as they think.

   (C) Only a thin line separates genius from madness.

   (D) Mad people must be locked away from the rest of society for their own safety.

   (E) Mad people often enjoy the company of humorists.

4. The poet describes Achitophel as all of the following EXCEPT

   (A) a name to be cursed through the ages

   (B) a fiery soul

   (C) a devil

   (D) a daring leader in tough times

   (E) false

5. The poet calls Zimri "so various, that he seemed to be/Not one, but all mankind's epitome"? (lines 24–25) because

   (A) His moods are so volatile that you can never depend on him.

   (B) His talents are so extensive that he symbolizes humanity's archetype.

   (C) His abilities suit him for just about any occupation, but tragically, he has chosen to fritter away his talents.

   (D) His personality is so variable and has so many facets to it that he seems to be more than one person.

   (E) His character is marked by such excessive energy that he seems to be in more than one place at a time.

6. The poet's purpose in describing Zimri in lines 24–25 was most likely intended to

   (A) proclaim high praise of him

   (B) insult him, even though the comment can be taken as praise in another context

   (C) suggest that Zimri is his role-model in life

   (D) glorify Zimri as the paragon of humankind

   (E) acclaim him, even though Zimri was insulted by it

GO ON TO THE NEXT PAGE

7. According to line 34, Zimri's usual themes are

   (A) helping other people to break physical and mental barriers

   (B) showing off his physical and mental abilities in front of others

   (C) bragging about himself and criticizing others

   (D) losing his temper and attacking others

   (E) insulting and complimenting other people

8. To what extent does Zimri employ the themes in question 7?

   (A) to extremes

   (B) rarely

   (C) occasionally

   (D) never

   (E) only when he feels over-mastered

9. At the end of the poem Zimri

   (A) became a court jester

   (B) was swindled out of his money because he was such a fool

   (C) enjoyed playing tricks on people, especially fools

   (D) became a beloved fixture at court

   (E) created many social and political groups and ruled them with much success

10. Based on context clues, the best synonym for the word *squandering* as it is used in line 38 is

   (A) saving

   (B) investing

   (C) wasting

   (D) misappropriating

   (E) acquiring

11. Given only these lines of the poem, the author most likely wrote this poem as a(n)

   (A) satire in which he criticizes the state of the monarchy

   (B) political tract to help rehabilitate the shattered reputations of government personalities

   (C) tribute designed to glorify the lives and careers of those in the court

   (D) thinly-disguised description of the two sides of his own character

   (E) bitter diatribe against two patrons who abandoned him

12. The form of this poem is

   (A) pairs of unrhymed lines in iambic pentameter

   (B) free verse

   (C) sonnet

   (D) villanelle

   (E) pairs of poetic lines in rhyming iambic pentameter

13. Based on the selection given, an appropriate satiric title for this lampoon of the monarchy of Dryden's era could be

   (A) "Revenge is Sweet"

   (B) "The Pen is Mightier than the Sword"

   (C) "Achitophel and Zimri the Not-So-Great"

   (D) "Zimri, Friend to Absalom and Achitophel"

   (E) "Absalom and Achitophel the Great"

GO ON TO THE NEXT PAGE

Questions 14–27. Read the following passage carefully before you mark your answers.

I received Everett's *Life of Washington* which you sent me, and enjoyed its perusal. How his spirit would be grieved could he see the wreck of his mighty labors! I will not, however, permit
(5) myself to believe, until all ground of hope is gone, that the fruit of his noble deeds will be destroyed, and that his precious advice and virtuous example will so soon be forgotten by his countrymen. As far as I can judge by the papers, we are between a
(10) state of anarchy and civil war. May God avert both of these evils from us! I see that four states had declared themselves out of the Union; four more will apparently follow their example. Then, if the border states are brought into the gulf of revolu-
(15) tion, one half of the country will be arrayed against the other. I must try and be patient and await the end, for I can do nothing to hasten or retard it.

The South, in my opinion, has been aggrieved
(20) by the acts of the North, as you say. I feel the aggression and am willing to take every proper step for redress. It is the principle I contend for, not individual or private benefit. As an American citizen, I take great pride in my country, her pros-
(25) perity and institutions, and would defend any state if her rights were invaded. But I can antici-pate no greater calamity for the country than a dissolution of the Union. It would be an accumu-lation of all the evils we complain of, and I am
(30) willing to sacrifice everything but honor for its preservation. I hope, therefore, that all constitu-tional means will be exhausted before there is a resort to force. Secession is nothing but revolu-tion. The framers of our Constitution never
(35) exhausted so much labor, wisdom, and forbear-ance in its formation, and surrounded it with so many guards and securities, for it was intended to be broken by every member of the Confederacy at will. It was intended for "perpetual union," so
(40) expressed in the preamble, and for the establish-ment of a government, not a compact, which can only be dissolved by revolution or the consent of all the people in convention assembled. It is idle to talk of secession. Anarchy would have been estab-
(45) lished, and not a government, by Washington,

Hamilton, Jefferson, Madison, and the other patri-ots of the Revolution…Still, a Union that can only be maintained by swords and bayonets, and in which strife and civil war are to take the place of
(50) brotherly love and kindness, has no charm for me. I shall mourn for my country and for the welfare and progress of mankind. If the Union is dis-solved, I shall return to my native state and share the miseries of my people; and, save in defense,
(55) will draw my sword on none.

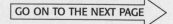
GO ON TO THE NEXT PAGE

14. As used in this context, *perusal* in the first sentence most nearly means

    (A) generosity

    (B) appearance

    (C) thoughtfulness

    (D) examination

    (E) arrival

15. The "he" the speaker refers to in the opening paragraph is

    (A) Everett, author of *Life of Washington*

    (B) George Washington

    (C) General Robert E. Lee

    (D) the president in office when the selection was written, Abraham Lincoln

    (E) the Supreme Deity

16. The narrator's attitude toward George Washington is that he

    (A) admires Washington for his personal traits but recognizes that his style of leadership is ill-suited to the present conflict

    (B) excoriates Washington for his unwillingness to take appropriate action

    (C) understands that Washington is aggrieved by the acts of the North

    (D) praises Washington as a man of great actions, fine advice, and unshakable ethics

    (E) believes that Washington has contributed to the present state of anarchy and civil war

17. Based on his description of George Washington, we can infer that the narrator/speaker

    (A) admires people of noble character and sought such greatness of spirit himself

    (B) is arrogant and egotistical

    (C) is intolerant of anyone who does not meet his exacting standards of behavior

    (D) is humble in the face of adversity but fully believes that he will be as famous as Washington one day

    (E) has great inner strength but shies away from physical confrontation

18. From his remarks, we can infer that the speaker

    (A) is a Northerner who strongly believes that the South has been wronged by the North in the present conflict

    (B) loves his country but not its leaders

    (C) is highly patriotic

    (D) is loyal but only to the point of actual war; then he will lay down his arms and be a martyr

    (E) believes that the dissolution of the Union would be a positive step because then a purer system of government can be created from the ashes

19. What conclusion can you draw about the speaker's character from the conclusion?

    (A) He is cowardly and faint-of-heart.

    (B) He is a natural leader who has much experience with public service.

    (C) He is judgmental and rigid.

    (D) He is belligerent and contemptuous of those who hesitate to take up arms for their country.

    (E) He is devoted to his state but abhors war.

20. The thesis or main idea of the passage is that

    (A) The Union is being tested by wrongs committed by both the North and the South.

    (B) The Union will always endure, no matter what happens.

    (C) Only the speaker is qualified to lead the Union in this time of terrible strife.

    (D) Anarchy is a healthy state because it leads to positive change.

    (E) People must take up arms in defense of their country; to do any less is cowardice.

GO ON TO THE NEXT PAGE

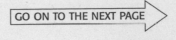

21. The three words *labor, wisdom,* and *forbearance* in the second paragraph are used to create a syntactical structure called

    (A) dramatic irony
    (B) parallelism
    (C) oxymoron
    (D) figurative language
    (E) blank verse

22. The author creates all the following effects through the use of the technique identified in the previous question EXCEPT

    (A) rhythm
    (B) emphasis
    (C) balance
    (D) juxtaposition
    (E) conciseness

23. Based on its point of view, tone, form, and content, this passage is most likely an excerpt from a

    (A) public speech
    (B) journal or diary entry
    (C) novel
    (D) short story
    (E) letter

24. The author's diction can best be characterized as

    (A) vernacular
    (B) informal and relaxed,
    (C) formal and precise
    (D) mediocre but educated
    (E) colloquial and informal

25. From the diction and syntax in this passage, you can conclude that

    (A) the selection is aimed primarily at Southerners who wanted to secede from the Union
    (B) the passage was written in the early seventeenth century
    (C) the author is highly educated
    (D) the author is a misanthrope who believes that people are incapable of governing themselves
    (E) the author came from humble beginnings but he has worked hard to educate himself

26. The author's style in this passage can BEST be characterized as

    (A) indirect and highly allusive
    (B) marked by elaborate conceits and other figures of speech
    (C) impersonal and detached; even cold
    (D) decorative
    (E) simple and direct

27. The tone of this passage can BEST be described as

    (A) highly emotional and fervent
    (B) deeply contemplative
    (C) caustic and regretful
    (D) melancholy
    (E) scathing

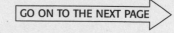
GO ON TO THE NEXT PAGE

Questions 28–41. Read the following poem carefully before you mark your answers.

My true love hath my heart and I have his,
By just exchange one for the other given:
I hold his dear, and mine he cannot miss,
There never was a bargain better driven.
(5) His heart in me keeps me and him in one;
My heart in him his thoughts and senses guides:
He loves my heart, for once it was his own;
I cherish his, because in me it bides.
His heart his wound received from my sight;
(10) My heart was wounded with his wounded heart;
For, as from me on him his hurt did light,
So still me-thought in me his hurt did smart:
Both equal hurt, in this change sought our bliss:
My true love hath my heart and I have his.

28. The first two lines serve to

   (A) establish the setting, the time and place of the action
   (B) help readers infer that the speaker is wise and worldly in the ways of love
   (C) present a vivid image of love
   (D) introduce the poem's central conflict: unrequited love
   (E) demonstrate the speaker's confusion over love

29. The central image that the poet creates with the phrases "just exchange" (line 2), "There never was a bargain better driven," (line 4), and "this change" (line 13) indicates love as

   (A) barter
   (B) steadfast
   (C) changeable
   (D) mere commerce
   (E) inherently unequal

30. The image in question 29 helps the poet convey his theme because the image

   (A) emphasizes how the lovers have carried out a trade
   (B) suggests that the speaker has been cheated
   (C) hints that the speaker has gotten the better end of the bargain
   (D) conveys the poet's conviction that love never lasts
   (E) alludes to the divinity of true love

31. What does the speaker mean in line 5 when he says: "His heart in me keeps me and him in one"?

   (A) The speaker would die if her lover deserted her.
   (B) The speaker and her lover go everywhere together and are accepted as a couple.
   (C) Because the speaker has already been disappointed in love, she will never relinquish her lover's heart.
   (D) Since the speaker holds her lover's heart in her heart, they are joined. They are as one person.
   (E) The speaker is astonished at the strength of their love, but it makes her feel stifled and trapped.

GO ON TO THE NEXT PAGE

Test Prep and Admissions

32. The word *bides* in line 8 most likely means

    (A) flourishes

    (B) grows

    (C) expires

    (D) dwells

    (E) regrows

33. The technique the poet uses in lines 9–10 to develop the poem's meaning is

    (A) onomatopoeia

    (B) understatement

    (C) repetition

    (D) litote

    (E) figurative language

34. This poem is constructed as a(n)

    (A) paradox

    (B) antithesis

    (C) conceit

    (D) logical argument

    (E) cause and effect

35. What does the speaker mean when she claims that both hearts are wounded?

    (A) The man is pretending to be wounded to show that his love is greater than the speaker's.

    (B) The man has suffered a heart attack and the woman feels sorrow at his precarious health.

    (C) The man's heart was pierced by Cupid's arrow when he saw the woman and her heart shares his pain.

    (D) Both the speaker and the man have survived previous relationships that caused them enduring pain.

    (E) The speaker knows that their love affair is coming to a close and the break-up will be agonizing for both of them.

36. The phrase that runs through the poem as a *motif* can BEST be identified as

    (A) true love

    (B) wounded heart

    (C) dear heart

    (D) heart for heart

    (E) blissful oneness

37. The tone of this poem is best characterized as

    (A) somber and restrained

    (B) bitter and resentful

    (C) elegiac and respectful

    (D) clever and witty

    (E) deferential and uneasy

38. The best synonym for *smart* as it is used in line 12 would be

    (A) sting

    (B) intelligent

    (C) bless

    (D) benefit

    (E) relieve

39. The poet achieves what effect by repeating the first line as the last line?

    (A) It underscores the similarity of all love affairs, no matter who is involved.

    (B) It ironically suggests the brief nature of love.

    (C) It reinforces the metaphor of the exchange of hearts.

    (D) It suggests that their love has grown in a surprisingly brief time span.

    (E) It concludes that love causes more pain than bliss.

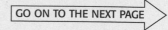

GO ON TO THE NEXT PAGE

40. The poem's rhythm and rhyme are BEST described as

    (A) blank verse with iambic pentameter

    (B) heroic couplets, rhyming pairs of lines in iambic pentameter

    (C) tercets, three-line stanzas of iambic pentameter

    (D) terza rima, three-line stanzas linked by rhyme to the next stanza (aba bcb cdc, etc.)

    (E) alternating rhyming lines of iambic pentameter and a final couplet

41. The form of this poem is best described as

    (A) an epic, with heroic couplets

    (B) a villanelle

    (C) a lyric

    (D) a sonnet

    (E) a narrative

GO ON TO THE NEXT PAGE

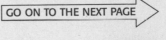

Questions 42–54. Read the following selection carefully before you mark your answers.

I love the land and the buffalo and will not part with it. I want you to understand well what I say. Write it down on paper...I hear a great deal of talk from the gentlemen whom the Great Father[1]
(5) sends us, but they never do what they say. I don't want any of the medicine lodges[2] within the country. I want the children raised as I was...

I have heard that you intend to settle us on a reservation near the mountains. I don't want to
(10) settle. I love to roam over the prairies. There I feel free and happy, but when we settle down, we grow pale and die. I have laid aside my lance, bow, and shield, and yet I feel safe in your presence. I have told you the truth. I have no little lies hid about
(15) me, but I don't know how it is with the commissioners. Are they as clear as I am? A long time ago this land belonged to our fathers; but when I go to the river, I see camps of soldiers on its banks. These soldiers cut down my timber; they kill my
(20) buffalo; and when I see that, my heart feels like bursting. I have spoken.

[1] *Great Father*: President Andrew Jackson
[2] *medicine lodges*: schools and churches

42. The probable reason why the passage opens with "I love the land and buffalo and will not part with it" is to

    (A) establish the speaker's purpose and bold tone immediately

    (B) refute charges that the speaker values possessions more than nature

    (C) coerce the speaker's audience into agreeing to his demands

    (D) set the narrative that follows in context

    (E) present a logical concession to this argument

43. One message the speaker in this passage makes clear is that he

    (A) embraces the notion of settling with his people on a reservation near the mountains

    (B) wants his children raised as he was

    (C) needs to feel safe in the presence of his audience

    (D) insists on being told the truth and not the usual pack of falsehoods

    (E) demands that the schools and churches of the white settlers allow his people access as well

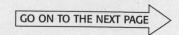
GO ON TO THE NEXT PAGE

44. The speaker does <u>not</u> want any of the following things EXCEPT

    (A) the white men to hunt buffalo any more

    (B) to negotiate with the commissioners who seem to have betrayed him in the past.

    (C) that the soldiers remain to help him protect his land

    (D) his people to be left alone to their own devices

    (E) the opportunities to share customs and culture of the white settlers

45. According to this passage, if the speaker's people are forced to relocate to a reservation, they will probably

    (A) adapt

    (B) perish

    (C) disappear

    (D) be resentful

    (E) lose their cultural identity

46. According to the speaker, what has happened to the forests and buffalo?

    (A) They have been used up by tribes of Native Americans.

    (B) They have been seized by the commissioners and allocated only sporadically to the tribes.

    (C) They have been forbidden to the Native Americans.

    (D) They have been destroyed by the soldiers.

    (E) They have been deeded to the speaker's father, but the treaties are ignored.

47. The speaker's ideals of good conduct encompass

    (A) sharing goods and services with everyone

    (B) roaming freely across the plains

    (C) keeping your word and not taking the property of other people

    (D) laying aside your weapons when you are negotiating

    (E) only taking that which you can use so the environment is preserved

48. From which point of view is this selection narrated?

    (A) omniscient

    (B) first-person

    (C) second-person

    (D) third-person limited

    (E) historical third-person

49. This point of view (question 48) is appropriate for this selection because it

    (A) allows the narrator to explain his feelings from different vantage points

    (B) establishes the appropriate distance between the speaker and the audience

    (C) enables the narrator to compare and contrast his behavior to the behavior of others

    (D) most effectively helps the speaker establish the tone and mood

    (E) gives the selection an immediacy and vividness that other points of view do not afford

GO ON TO THE NEXT PAGE

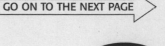

50. Based on the voice and attitude of the speaker in this passage, he can BEST be characterized as

   (A) a fearless combatant, ready to fight for what he sees as his due

   (B) determined to get his rights, no matter what the cost

   (C) a brave and honorable man.

   (D) smug about his way of life, which he believes is superior to the white man's conduct

   (E) naïve and unaware of the forces arrayed against him.

51. The speaker's tone in this selection is best described as

   (A) caustic and bitter

   (B) saddened and bold

   (C) serious but uplifting

   (D) cynical and suspicious

   (E) dismissive and ironic

52. The author's primary purpose in this selection is to evoke all of the following reactions from the government commissioners EXCEPT

   (A) empathy

   (B) violence

   (C) guilt

   (D) understanding

   (E) respect

53. This selection is MOST likely an excerpt from a (n)

   (A) essay

   (B) historical fiction

   (C) letter

   (D) speech

   (E) novel

54. The speaker ends the selection with the words *I have spoken*, a phrase that

   (A) illustrates the speaker's deep loathing of authority

   (B) foreshadows the speaker's determination to fight to the death

   (C) indicates the finality of the speaker's words and his assertions

   (D) shows that the speaker is unwilling to compromise

   (E) suggests that the speaker is offering a challenge

IF YOU FINISH BEFORE TIME IS CALLED, YOU MAY CHECK YOUR WORK ON THIS SECTION ONLY. DO NOT TURN TO ANY OTHER SECTION IN THE TEST.

STOP

Section II: Essay Questions

Time: 2 hour
Number of questions: 3
Percent of total grade: 55

<u>**Directions:**</u> This section contains three essay questions. Answer all three questions, budgeting your time carefully.

GO ON TO THE NEXT PAGE

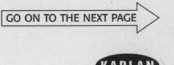

Question 1

<u>Suggested Time:</u> **40 minutes. Your response will count as one-third of your total score on the essay portion of the exam.**

1. The following passage is an excerpt from George Eliot's 1856 essay on Realism. Read the excerpt carefully. Then explain Eliot's attitude toward artists and their responsibility to "amplify our experiences and extend our contact with fellowman beyond the bounds of our personal lot." Pay particular attention to Eliot's use of tone, imagery, detail, and figurative language as you consider Eliot's attitudes towards artists and their responsibility to create Realism in their work.

The notion that peasants are joyous, that the typical moment to represent the man in the smock-frock is when he is cracking a joke and showing a round of sound teeth, that cottage
(5) matrons are usually buxom, and village children necessarily rosy and merry, are prejudices difficult to dislodge from the artistic mind, which looks for its subjects into literature instead of life...But no one who has seen much of actual plough-men
(10) thinks them jocund; no one who is well acquainted with English peasantry can pronounce them merry. The slow gaze, in which no sense of beauty beams, no humor twinkles, —the slow utterance, and the heavy slouching walk, reminds one rather
(15) of that melancholy animal the camel, than of the sturdy country-man, with his striped stockings, red waistcoat, and hat aside, who represents the traditional English peasant...

The greatest benefit we owe to the artist,
(20) whether painter, poet, or novelist, is the extension of our sympathies. Art is the nearest thing to life; it is the mode of amplifying experience and extending our contact with our fellowmen beyond the bounds of our personal lot. All the more sacred is
(25) the task of the artist when he undertakes to paint the life of the People. Falsification here is far more pernicious than in the more artificial aspects of life. It is not so very serious that we should have false ideas about evanescent fashions—about the
(30) manners and conversation of beaux and duchesses; but it *is* serious that our sympathy with the perennial joys and struggles, the toil, the tragedy, and the humor in life of our more heavily-laden fellow men should be perverted, and turned towards a
(35) false object instead of the true one. We want to be taught to feel, not for the heroic artisan or the sentimental peasant, but for the peasant in all his coarse apathy, and the artisan in all his suspicious selfishness.

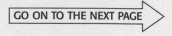

Write your essay here.

_____

_____

_____

_____

_____

_____

_____

_____

_____

_____

_____

_____

_____

_____

_____

_____

_____

_____

_____

GO ON TO THE NEXT PAGE ⟹

KAPLAN
Test Prep and Admissions

GO ON TO THE NEXT PAGE

GO ON TO THE NEXT PAGE

GO ON TO THE NEXT PAGE

Question 2

Suggested Time: 40 minutes. Your response will count for one-third of your total score on the essay portion of the exam.

2. Read the following poem by the American writer Herman Melville. In a well-organized essay, explain how Melville transforms a painful experience into something beautiful. In your analysis, consider such elements as imagery, tone, alliteration, symbolism, and end rhyme.

Shiloh

A Requiem
(April 1862)

Skimming lightly, wheeling still,
  The swallows fly low
Over the fields in clouded days,
  The forest-field of Shiloh—
(5) Over the field where April rain
Solaced the parched stretched in pain
Through the pause of night
That followed the Sunday fight
  Around the church of Shiloh—
(10) The church so lone, the log-built one,
That echoed to many a parting groan
  And natural prayer
  Of dying foemen mingled there—
Foemen at morn, but friends at eve—
(15)   Fame or country least their care:
(What like a bullet can undeceive!)
  But now they lie low,
While over them the swallows skim,
  And all is hushed at Shiloh.

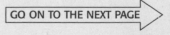

Write your essay here.

_____

_____

_____

_____

_____

_____

_____

_____

_____

_____

_____

_____

_____

_____

_____

_____

_____

_____

_____

_____

GO ON TO THE NEXT PAGE ▷

_____

_____

_____

_____

_____

_____

_____

_____

_____

_____

_____

_____

_____

_____

_____

_____

_____

_____

_____

_____

_____

_____

GO ON TO THE NEXT PAGE ⟹

_____

_____

_____

_____

_____

_____

_____

_____

_____

_____

_____

_____

_____

_____

_____

_____

_____

_____

_____

_____

_____

_____

GO ON TO THE NEXT PAGE ▷

_____

_____

_____

_____

_____

_____

_____

_____

_____

_____

_____

_____

_____

_____

_____

_____

_____

_____

_____

_____

GO ON TO THE NEXT PAGE

KAPLAN
Test Prep and Admissions

Question 3

<u>Suggested Time:</u> **40 minutes. Your response will count for one-third of your total score on the essay portion of the exam.**

3. Authors often create characters who refuse to compromise their principles. These characters may be heroic, tragic, or merely misguided. Choose a novel or full-length play in which a character declines to compromise a deeply-held belief. Identify the character, the principle in which the character believes, and show, by specific reference, the action the character took to uphold this principle and the outcome of that action. Finally, evaluate the character's decision to show if it is heroic, tragic, or misguided. You may choose a work from the list below or another novel or full-length play of literary merit.

All My Sons
As I Lay Dying
Catch-22
The Crucible
David Copperfield
A Doll's House
Gulliver's Travels
Hamlet
The Iceman Cometh
Jane Eyre
Jude the Obscure
King Lear
Lord Jim
Macbeth
Moby-Dick
1984
The Oresteia
Othello
Saint Joan
The Sound and the Fury
Sons and Lovers
The Turn of the Screw
Waiting for Godot
Wuthering Heights

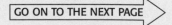
GO ON TO THE NEXT PAGE

Write your essay here.

_____

_____

_____

_____

_____

_____

_____

_____

_____

_____

_____

_____

_____

_____

_____

_____

_____

_____

_____

_____

_____

_____

_____

_____

_____

_____

_____

_____

_____

_____

_____

_____

_____

_____

_____

_____

_____

_____

_____

_____

_____

GO ON TO THE NEXT PAGE >

GO ON TO THE NEXT PAGE >

_____

_____

_____

_____

_____

_____

_____

_____

_____

_____

_____

_____

_____

_____

_____

_____

_____

_____

_____

STOP

Practice Test Three: **Answer Key**

1.	A	19.	E	37.	D
2.	E	20.	A	38.	A
3.	C	21.	B	39.	C
4.	C	22.	D	40.	E
5.	D	23.	E	41.	D
6.	B	24.	C	42.	A
7.	E	25.	C	43.	B
8.	A	26.	E	44.	D
9.	B	27.	B	45.	B
10.	C	28.	C	46.	D
11.	A	29.	A	47.	C
12.	E	30.	A	48.	B
13.	C	31.	D	49.	E
14.	D	32.	D	50.	C
15.	B	33.	C	51.	B
16.	D	34.	C	52.	B
17.	A	35.	C	53.	D
18.	C	36.	D	54.	C

Answers and Explanations

SECTION I: MULTIPLE-CHOICE QUESTIONS

Questions 1–13.

Of these false Achitophel was first:
A name to all succeeding ages cursed.
For close designs, and crooked counsels fit;
Sagacious, bold, and turbulent of wit:
(5) Restless, unfixed in principles and place;
In power unpleased, impatient of disgrace.
A fiery soul, which worked out its way,
Fretted the pigmy body to decay:
And o'er informed the tenement of clay.
(10) A daring pilot in extremity;
Pleased with the danger, when the waves went high.
He sought the storms; but for a calm unfit,
Would steer too nigh the sands to boast his Wit.
Great wits are sure to madness near allied.
(15) And thin partitions do their bounds divide:
Else, why should he, with wealth and honor blessed,
Refuse his age the needful hours of rest?
Punish a body which he could not please;
Bankrupt of life, yet prodigal of ease?
(20) And all to leave, what with his toil he won,
To that unfeathered, two legged thing, a son...
Some of their chiefs were princes of the land:
In the first rank of these did Zimri stand:

A man so various that he seemed to be
(25) Not one, but all mankind's epitome.
Stiff in opinions, always in the wrong;
Was everything by starts, and nothing long:
But, in the course of one revolving moon,
Was chemist, fiddler, statesman, and buffoon:
(30) Then, all for women, painting, rhyming, drinking;
Besides ten thousands freaks that died in thinking.
Blest madman, who could every hour employ,
With something new to wish, or to enjoy!
Railing and praising were his usual themes;
(35) And both (to show his judgment) in extremes;
So over violent, or over civil,
That every man, with him, was God or Devil.
In squandering wealth was his peculiar art:
Nothing went unrewarded, but desert.1
(40) Beggared by fools, who still he found too late:
He had his jest, and they had his estate.
He laugh'd himself from court, then sought relief
By forming parties, but could ne'er be chief.

[1]*desert:* What a person deserves

1. (A)

The repetition of the consonant hard "c" sound is evidence of alliteration as the correct response. Personification (B) requires an inanimate object to possess human characteristics. Onomatopoeia (C) captures or approximates the sound of what it describes in order to make a passage more effective for the reader or listener. Metonymy (D) requires that an attribute or commonly associated feature is used to name or designate something as in "All hands on deck." And finally, (E) litote is a figure of speech that emphasizes its subject by conscious understatement. For example, the understated "not bad" as a comment about something especially well done is a litote.

2. (E)

The metaphor the poet uses to describe Achitophel's character is that of a sea pilot who likes danger but is unfit for calm seas. Look at the diction in these lines for clues to this response. Words and phrases such as *daring pilot* and *extremity* (line 10) are clues. He is "pleased with the danger" caused by the high waves (line 11) and, finally, (line 12) this pilot seeks "storms" and is "unfit" for calm weather. All these portray Achitophel as one who does not shirk danger and is, in fact, not satisfied with calm waters.

3. (C)

The best paraphrase of these lines is that only a thin line separates genius from madness. "Great wits" are "to madness near allied" (line 14) and only "thin partitions" separate or "divide" one from the other (line 15). Choices (A), (B), and (E) are based on the homonym *wit* meaning humor, and (D) is a distortion based on the words *partitions* and *divide*. Although you might be tempted to agree with any one of the wrong responses, only (C) actually paraphrases the lines in question.

4. (C)

Nowhere is Achitophel described as a devil. This EXCEPT question gives you four correct responses and one incorrect response which you must find. Line 2 asserts response (A); line 7 begins with the phrase *A fiery soul* (B); line 10 refers to him as "a daring pilot in extremity" (D), and line 1 tells us he was "false" (E). Line 37 states that "every man, with him, was God or Devil," but the line is referring to Zimri, and does not say *he* was either God or Devil.

5. (D)

The poet calls Zimri "so various, that he seemed to be/Not one, but all mankinds epitome"? (lines 24–25) because Zimri's personality is so variable and has so many facets to it that he seems to be more than one person. *Epitome* refers to someone who is the embodiment of a certain characteristic or quality. In Zimri's case, he is apparently not one but *all* mankind's epitome. Choice (A) may be true, but does not apply to these lines. (B) is contradictory—if Zimri has multiple talents, he is probably not archetypal of humanity. And choices (C) and (E) are drawn from inferences about the rest of the poem, but do not hold up to scrutiny as the meaning of lines 24–25.

6. (B)

The poet's purpose in describing Zimri in lines 24–25 was most likely intended to insult Zimri, even though the comment can be taken as praise in another context. Look at lines 24–25 again, and then look at lines 26–27. To be an epitome might be construed as a good thing, but there is evidence that Zimri is inconstant, opinionated, and extreme. Lines 26–27 state that he presents himself as many state different things, can be stubborn in his errors, and never stays with one thing for any length of time. All of this clarifies the poet's true intention in lines 24–25. The other choices are too positive for the scathing send-up of Zimri by the poet.

7. (E)

According to line 34, Zimri's usual themes are insulting and complimenting other people. *Railing* means to abuse or even condemn another person. (D) is a partial response that doesn't include the flip side of railing, praising.

8. (A)

Zimri rails and praises to extremes. We can verify this response by looking at several lines from the poem. Line 35 refers to both judgments and his use of them "in extremes." In addition, line 36 tells us he is either "over violent" or "over civil." Finally, line 37 reiterates the point when it tells us that for Zimri, men were either "God or Devil."

9. (B)

At the end of the poem Zimri was swindled out of his money because he was such a fool. Perhaps many looked at Zimri as a court jester (A), but that is not what happened to him. He is the one who is used as a fool (C). He was not beloved at court (D); he became such a laughing stock. (E) is incorrect because of the last line of the poem that tells us that he did form parties but never became their ruler "chief" (line 43).

10. (C)

Based on context clues, the best synonym for the word *squandering* as it is used in line 38 is wasting. This response is supported by the last lines of the poem that tell us that fools stole his estate while he became the source for much amusement for his ineptness in court. Misappropriating (D) would imply the misuse of official funds; Zimri squanders his own.

11. (A)

Given only these lines of the poem, the best view of this poem is as a satire in which the author criticizes the state of the monarchy. "Absalom and Achitophel," by John Dryden, is often referred to as one of the finest poetic political satires of all time. It is an allegory in which the "real" story revolves around the successor of Charles II to the throne of England. Although he had no legitimate heirs, several "natural" sons aspired to succeed him. It is interesting to understand the history of the English monarchy at that time as well as the Story of David from the Old Testament, where Dryden found the names for this clever political satire. Zimri actually represents the Duke of Buckingham, and both Absalom and Achitophel are illegitimate sons of Charles II.

Given the other responses, and not necessarily having the background needed for full understanding of the poem, you must infer that much of what is said is not to be taken seriously. In addition, the mention of the court, wielding power,

"princes of the land" (line 22) etc. are all clues that this is most likely a political satire. The poet's desire is much too arch to harbor a wish to rehabilitate anyone (B), and this clearly is not a tribute; eliminate (C). Finally, there is no basis for thinking that the poet wrote this as a reflection of anything in his own life or career (D) and (E).

12. (E)

The form of this poem is pairs of poetic lines in rhyming iambic pentameter. Remember, iambic pentameter is five stressed syllables per lines, with the stresses on the second syllable of each word in the line. Rhyme is evident with each pair, negating choice (A). Free verse (B) is characterized by varying line lengths, lack of traditional meter, and nonrhyming lines. Choices (C) and (D) cannot be accurate because they are names of specific rhyme and meter structures (see the Key Terminology chapter for definitions), which have no relevance to Dryden's poem.

13. (C)

Based on the text given, an appropriate satiric title for this lampoon of the monarchy of Dryden's era would be "Achitophel and Zimri the Not-So-Great." The two "great men" presented are definitely "not-so-great." Achitophel is "false" and "cursed." Buffoon, jester, spendthrift, weak leader, dilettante—Dryden convinces us that Zimri is a failure at everything he does. Although the actual title of Dryden's satiric poem is "Absalom and Achitophel" (E), the selection presented here is not enough to deduce that the satire is more against them (representing two "natural" sons of Charles II) than their laughable friend Zimri. Half the text is about Achitophel, so (D) isn't the best choice. As a satiric title, then, "Achitophel and Zimri the Not-So-Great" is the most appropriate response.

Questions 14–27.

I received Everett's *Life of Washington* which you sent me, and enjoyed its perusal. How his spirit would be grieved could he see the wreck of his mighty labors! I will not, however, permit
(5) myself to believe, until all ground of hope is gone, that the fruit of his noble deeds will be destroyed, and that his precious advice and virtuous example will so soon be forgotten by his countrymen. As far as I can judge by the papers, we are between a
(10) state of anarchy and civil war. May God avert both of these evils from us! I see that four states had declared themselves out of the Union; four more will apparently follow their example. Then, if the border states are brought into the gulf of revolu-
(15) tion, one half of the country will be arrayed against the other. I must try and be patient and await the end, for I can do nothing to hasten or retard it.

The South, in my opinion, has been aggrieved
(20) by the acts of the North, as you say. I feel the aggression and am willing to take every proper step for redress. It is the principle I contend for, not individual or private benefit. As an American citizen, I take great pride in my country, her pros-
(25) perity and institutions, and would defend any state if her rights were invaded. But I can antici- pate no greater calamity for the country than a dissolution of the Union. It would be an accumu- lation of all the evils we complain of, and I am
(30) willing to sacrifice everything but honor for its preservation. I hope, therefore, that all constitu- tional means will be exhausted before there is a resort to force. Secession is nothing but revolu- tion. The framers of our Constitution never
(35) exhausted so much labor, wisdom, and forbear- ance in its formation, and surrounded it with so many guards and securities, for it was intended to be broken by every member of the Confederacy at will. It was intended for "perpetual union," so
(40) expressed in the preamble, and for the establish- ment of a government, not a compact, which can only be dissolved by revolution or the consent of all the people in convention assembled. It is idle to talk of secession. Anarchy would have been estab-
(45) lished, and not a government, by Washington,

Hamilton, Jefferson, Madison, and the other patri- ots of the Revolution…Still, a Union that can only be maintained by swords and bayonets, and in which strife and civil war are to take the place of
(50) brotherly love and kindness, has no charm for me. I shall mourn for my country and for the welfare and progress of mankind. If the Union is dis- solved, I shall return to my native state and share the miseries of my people; and, save in defense,
(55) will draw my sword on none.

14. (D)

As used in this context, *perusal* in the first sentence most nearly means examination. To *peruse* means to examine, to scrutinize, to look over, to inspect. The other choice that might have tempted you is (B) appearance. "Examination" is a closer synonym for this vocabulary word. You might be able to create a scenario for choice (E), that the book has recently arrived. However, upon reading the next couple of sentences, we understand that the narrator is actually referring to the reading of the book, not just its arrival. Neither (A) nor (C) would be appropriate synonyms for perusal as it is used in the first sentence of the passage.

15. (B)

The "he" the speaker refers to in the opening paragraph is George Washington. In this paragraph, "he" and "his" refer to the antecedent George Washington, as implied by the title of the book to which the narrator refers. The "wreck of *his* mighty labors" does not refer to the Everett's labors (the author) (A), but to the efforts of our Founding Father to establish the Union. Similar reference is found in the phrase "*his* (Washington's) noble deeds will be destroyed" (lines 6–7) and that the nation will soon forget all that *he* worked so hard to establish.

16. (D)

The narrator praises Washington as a man of great actions, fine advice and unshakable ethics. The narrator's attitude toward Washington is clearly expressed in the first paragraph. He refers to Washington's "noble deeds," his precious advice" and his "virtuous example" (lines 6, 7, 8). The only other response you might be tempted to choose would be choice (A). However, the narrator believes that Washington's example and advice are relevant to his day (lines 4–9). It would be inappropriate for the narrator to "excoriate" Washington (B) for his inaction since he is no longer alive at the beginning of the Civil War. That is also the argument against choice (C). Far from believing that Washington has contributed to anarchy, (E), he praises him for encouraging unity (line 40).

17. (A)

Based on his description of George Washington, we can infer that the narrator/speaker admires people of noble character and sought such greatness of spirit himself. In the first paragraph it is easy to recognize the admiration

the narrator holds for George Washington. He goes on to talk about how the country's disunity and movement toward anarchy grieves him. Then, in lines 30–31, he states that he is "willing to sacrifice *everything* but honor for its [the Union's] preservation." Nowhere does the passage imply that the speaker is (B) arrogant or egotistical, or (C) intolerant of those less ethical than he. Nowhere in the passage can you find justification for response (D), and though you may have been tempted to choose response (E), the narrator informs us that though he will not act offensively, he will not hesitate to be defensive in the upcoming conflict.

18. (C)

Not knowing the biographical details of this passage and the narrator, it is unclear whether he is from the North (A) or from the South. Since he chastises the North for "aggrieving" the South, chances are he is a Southerner. As for (B), he commends past leaders and seems to have little to say about the present day leaders. He will not be a martyr (D), for he says he will take up arms in his own defense, and he is totally against the dissolution of the Union (E) for any reason. This leads us to the conclusion that (C) he is a patriot who sincerely wishes that the country not become embroiled in any action or attitude that might undermine the intentions of the Constitution.

19. (E)

The speaker is devoted to his state but abhors war. Nothing suggests that the speaker is cowardly or faint-of-heart (A), nor does the passage mention anything about any special leadership abilities (B). Although it is clear he does not want to see any dissolution of the "perpetual Union" (line 40) there is no indication of his being judgmental and rigid (C), nor belligerent and contemptuous of others (D). He will wait to see what happens to the Union. He has no desire to see a Union that can be held together only through swords and bayonets. Strife and lack of brotherly love have "no charm" (line 51) for him. If the Union is dissolved he will return to his "native state" and share the "miseries of [his] people" (line 54–55). Obviously this man does not want to see the Union dissolved, but more importantly, he does not want to see war. He would rather suffer at home and separated from the Union than live in a state of strife and civil war.

20. (A)

The main idea of this passage is that the Union is being tested by wrongs committed by both the North and the South. It is the very fact that the Union may not endure (B) that has prompted the speaker/narrator to express himself. Again, nowhere does the passage refer to any great leadership prowess (C) on the part of the narrator. He makes it clear that anarchy (D) is not an acceptable situation, and he himself prefers to take up arms only in his own defense (E).

21. (B)

The three nouns *labor, wisdom,* and *forbearance* in the second paragraph are used to create a syntactical structure called parallelism. Dramatic irony (A) has nothing to do with sentence structure. Oxymoron (C) is a figure of speech that combines two apparently contradictory elements, as in "wise fool" or "jumbo shrimp." (D) Figurative language is not a structural (syntactical) concept. Finally, (E) blank verse is poetry written in unrhymed lines of iambic pentameter.

22. (D)

Look again at the sentence in question. "The framers of our Constitution never exhausted so much labor, wisdom, and forbearance in its formation, and surrounded it with so many guards and securities…." If you say the sentence aloud a couple times (or, in a testing situation, aloud inside your head), you will be able to detect the (A) rhythm of the words and the emphasis (B) and balance (C) the narrator develops with this sequence. The series is tight, it creates unity and conciseness (E) within the sentence. The words are not in juxtaposition (D), that is, the location of one thing as being adjacent or juxtaposed with another. This placing of two items side by side creates a certain effect, reveals an attitude, or accomplishes some purpose of the writer. These words create harmony, not contrast.

23. (E)

You must "listen" to the voice of this passage to determine the best response to this question. In particular, the references to "you" sending a book to "me" suggests a communication of some sort. There is a personal and a bit philosophical nature to the passage that indicates the speaker/writer has a relationship of some sort with his audience. The use of phrases such as "in my opinion," and

"I hope, therefore" also imply a close communication. Since we must also consider the setting for this passage—the time leading up to the Civil War—the only logical conclusion is that this is a letter that is being written. Although you may have considered this a journal or diary entry (B), that would not account for the "you" sending the book.

24. (C)

The author's diction can best be characterized as formal and precise. Take a look at the sentence in questions 21 and 22 for just one example of the author's carefully crafted word choice. Vernacular (A) is the language of the common people, also known as colloquial or informal speech (E). The author's word choice is better than mediocre (D), and it is hardly relaxed or informal (B).

25. (C)

From the diction and syntax in this passage, you can conclude that the author is highly educated. There is no indication as to whether the intended audience (specifically or generally) was either Northern or Southern (A). We know from the context that the passage was most likely written prior to the Civil War, which would have been in the 19th century (B). The author is upset with men who wish to wage war, but he could hardly be characterized as a misanthrope (D), and we have no indication of the author's early life, though he might indeed have started in humble beginnings (E).

26. (E)

The author's style in this passage is simple and direct. The author does not use allusion (A), which is a reference to a literary, religious, or historical event or figure, in this passage. Nor does the author use conceits (extended metaphors) or other figurative language (simile, metaphor, personification, etc.) (B) to make his point. He is very personal in his expression, not detached (C) at all, and his delivery, as mentioned in question 24, is straightforward and precise, thus making (D) incorrect and (E) the best choice.

27. (B)

The tone of this passage can BEST be described as deeply contemplative. Some knowledge of tone vocabulary words is helpful in selecting the correct response to this question. It is obvious that the speaker has much feeling for what he is saying, but he could not rightly be called highly emotional in his tone (A). Although he is certainly regretful, he is not caustic (C). Remember when a response has more than one part, both parts must be correct for the answer to be correct. The speaker feels regret for what is happening, but he is not melancholy (D), and despite his feelings of anger towards those who wish to ruin the Union, his tone is not scathing (E).

Questions 28–41.

My true love hath my heart and I have his,
By just exchange one for the other given:
I hold his dear, and mine he cannot miss,
There never was a bargain better driven.
(5) His heart in me keeps me and him in one;
My heart in him his thoughts and senses guides:
He loves my heart, for once it was his own;
I cherish his, because in me it bides.
His heart his wound received from my sight;
(10) My heart was wounded with his wounded heart;
For, as from me on him his hurt did light,
So still me-thought in me his hurt did smart:
Both equal hurt, in this change sought our bliss:
My true love hath my heart and I have his.

28. (C)

The first two lines of this Sydney poem present a vivid image of love. The "exchange" of hearts and the words *true love* should give you a clue as to the answer here. The first two lines do not establish the time or place or mood of the poem (A), and they tell us nothing about the speaker (B) other than the fact that she has a true love that has her heart, and vice versa. If the exchange indeed has taken place, then there is no suggestion of unrequited love (D), and at this point we cannot tell if the speaker is experiencing any confusion (E).

29. (A)

The central image that the poet creates with the phrases *just exchange* (line 2), *There never was a bargain better driven*, (line 4), and *this change* (line 13) indicates love as barter. Words such as *exchange* and *change* and *bargain* all refer to some aspect of trade, or barter. The phrases do not indicate whether or not the love will be steadfast (B) or changeable (C). You might have been tempted to choose answer (D), mere commerce, but the connotation of the word *mere* is not indicated by these phrases, and there is not indication of "inequality" (E).

30. (A)

The image in question 29 emphasizes how the lovers have carried out a trade. Referring to some sort of trade or barter, the image does not indicate any idea of anyone

being cheated (B) or nor does it hint at inequity (C). The image doesn't convey anything about the longevity (D) or the divinity (E) of love.

31. (D)

Since the speaker holds her lover's heart in her heart, they are joined. They are as one person. The phrase *me and him in one* (line 5) is the clue here. You could infer that the speaker would die if anything happened to her figurative heart transplant (A), but that's not the sense of the line, which proclaims the lovers' union. Choice (B) may very well be true; however, it is not indicated specifically by this line. There's nothing to suggest the speaker has been disappointed in love (C). Choice (E) cannot be justified at all by this line.

32. (D)

If you thought about the word *abode*, meaning dwelling, you also might have figured out the word *bides*, even if it was unfamiliar to you. Choices (A), flourishes, and (B), grows, might have looked attractive as the correct response, but neither is a synonym for bides. Choice (C) is too negative to be correct, and (E) is a bit too clinical to be appropriate.

33. (C)

The technique the poet uses in lines 9–10 to develop the poem's meaning is repetition. The juxtaposition of lines 9 and 10, "His heart his wound received from my sight;/My heart was wounded with his wounded heart" demonstrates a clever repetition of the words *wound* and *wounded*. Onomatopoeia (A), remember, is a word that sounds similar to what it is, such as the *buzz* of the bee. Understatement (B) and litote (D) are similar, and are not appropriate responses. Figurative language (E) is too general a term to be the best choice.

34. (C)

If you recall, a conceit is an extended (sometimes witty or clever) metaphor. The entire idea of exchanging hearts and heart wounds in this Sydney poem makes this the appropriate response. It is not a seeming contradiction, or paradox (A), nor is it antithesis (B) (opposite ideas in juxtaposition with each other). It contains no argumentative (D) characteristics, nor is it constructed in a cause and effect manner (E).

35. (C)

The man's heart was pierced by Cupid's arrow when he saw the woman, and her heart shares his pain. If you reread lines 9–14, you can eliminate the other responses.

36. (D)

The phrase that runs through the poem as a *motif* can BEST be identified as "heart for heart." The key to this response is to recall the meaning of *motif* as a recurrent device, formula, or situation that deliberately connects elements of an artistic work. Although all of the phrases certainly relate in some manner to this poem, the only truly recurrent idea offered is that of the exchange of hearts.

37. (D)

The tone of this poem is best characterized as clever and witty. There is nothing somber or restrained (A) about this poem. It contains no bitterness (B) nor uneasiness (E). Remember, an elegy is a poem having to do with death, so choice (C) cannot be correct.

38. (A)

The best synonym for *smart* as it is used in line 12 would be *sting*. If you burn your fingers, you might say that they

smart, meaning that they sting or hurt. Line 12 tells us that "So still me-thought in me his hurt did smart" as a rejoinder to line 11, "For, as from me on him his hurt did light." In other words, she "hurt" him when her love "struck" him as his love had "hurt" her when she was likewise "struck."

39. (C)

The poet reinforces the metaphor of the exchange of hearts by repeating the first line at the end of his poem. By reiterating the line "My true love hath my heart, and I have his," the poet has brought the entire poem full circle. In fact, considering the repetition and development of motif and conceit in this poem, it is a most appropriate way to bring closure to the entire creation. The poet announces that an exchange of hearts has taken place. He tells us how this all happened, and concludes by restating the opening pronouncement.

40. (E)

The poem's rhythm and rhyme are BEST described as alternating rhyming lines of iambic pentameter and a final couplet. This poem is most definitely iambic pentameter, that is a combination unstressed-stressed syllables in sets of 5-˘ / ˘ / ˘ / ˘ / ˘ /. The rhymes alternate, *abab cdcd efef*, and they conclude with a couplet, or two lines of rhymed iambic pentameter. Although the iambic pentameter part of (A), (B), and (C) is correct, only choice (E) is totally correct for this particular poem. (D) is incorrect in stanza and rhyme scheme. For further explanation of rhyme and meter, see the section on Key Terminology of this book.

41. D.

The poem is a sonnet. If you got question 40, you should have been able to note the 14 line structure and nail this question too. Process of elimination could help you here if you had any doubts. The poem lacks epic characters—our lovers are pretty ordinary (A). A villanelle consists of nineteen lines divided into six stanzas—five tercets (three-line stanzas) and one quatrain (four-line stanza). The poem lacks the emotion of a lyric (C), and there isn't any narration (E).

Questions 42–54.

I love the land and the buffalo and will not part with it. I want you to understand well what I say. Write it down on paper…I hear a great deal of talk from the gentlemen whom the Great Father[1]
(5) sends us, but they never do what they say. I don't want any of the medicine lodges[2] within the country. I want the children raised as I was…

I have heard that you intend to settle us on a reservation near the mountains. I don't want to
(10) settle. I love to roam over the prairies. There I feel free and happy, but when we settle down, we grow pale and die. I have laid aside my lance, bow, and shield, and yet I feel safe in your presence. I have told you the truth. I have no little lies hid about
(15) me, but I don't know how it is with the commissioners. Are they as clear as I am? A long time ago this land belonged to our fathers; but when I go to the river, I see camps of soldiers on its banks. These soldiers cut down my timber; they kill my
(20) buffalo; and when I see that, my heart feels like bursting. I have spoken.

---

[1] *Great Father*: President Andrew Jackson
[2] *medicine lodges*: schools and churches

42. (A)

The passage opens with a discussion of the land and the buffalo to establish the speaker's purpose and bold tone immediately. This speaker has a very definite point to make, and he is not going to make the telling a soft one. He wants to be heard, and he jumps right in with his strong tone and states his purpose. There really is no argument, so he is not refuting charges (B), nor is he offering any concession (E). He is not coercing anyone (C); he simply tells how he feels and hopes the right people are listening. These opening lines about the buffalo and land relate to the succeeding narrative (D), but don't provide a context or setting for it; the speaker has a purpose, and these opening lines declare his intentions from the very start.

43. (B)

This passage makes clear that the speaker wants his children raised as he was. The last sentence of the first paragraph states this message: "I want the children raised as I was…." Right after that he says "I don't want to settle" (lines 9–10) (A). The speaker says he feels safe with his audience, but this is more a declaration of his courage than a need to be protected (C). He says "I have told you the truth…[but] I don't know how it is with the commissioners" (lines 13–16), which suggests he may not have been told the truth, but this is not strong enough to sup-

port choice (D) an a response, because it uses the more fervent phrase, *usual pack of falsehoods*; nor is the speaker "insisting" on the honesty of his hearers. Finally, he makes no mention of Indians being allowed access to schools and churches of the white settlers (E).

44. (D)

The speaker wants his people to be left alone to their own devices. This is potentially a confusing question because it presents you with negatives (what he does *not* want) and the one thing he *does* want is what you must decide. If you read through the passage, you will see that he does *not* want white men to hunt his buffalo (A); he prefers *not* to negotiate with suspect commissioners (B); he does *not* want the soldiers on his land (C); and he does *not* want the white man's culture (E). The only thing he truly desires is that they just be left alone, making (D) the only possible response.

45. (B)

If the speaker's people are forced to relocate to a reservation, they will probably perish. The speaker is very clear about this. He tells his audience that he does not want to settle, but to be left to roam the prairies. He assures his listeners that "when we settle down, we grow pale and die" (lines 11–12). Despite any prior knowledge you may possess, you must look only to this passage to answer this question. The question reminds you that "According to this passage…" and that is all you must consider when you choose the correct response.

46. (D)

The forests and the buffalo have been destroyed by the soldiers. There is no indication that the land or the buffalo have been used up by Native American tribes (A). From what we read in this passage, we do not know if the Commissioner has allocated the lands or animals to anyone (B) or forbidden them to anyone (C). And, although treaties had most likely been broken (E), this is not part of this passage. The speaker says "I see camps of soldiers on its banks. These soldiers cut down my timber [forests]; they kill my buffalo; and when I see that, my heart feels like bursting" (lines 18–21).

47. (C)

The speaker's ideals of good conduct include keeping your word and not taking the property of other people. There is no indication that the speaker believes in sharing goods and services with everyone (A) in this passage, nor does he express any environmental philosophy (E). The speaker says, "I love to roam over the prairies" (line 10) (B), but that is what he desires to do, an activity not necessarily having to do with good conduct. (D) is a detail point; the speaker has laid aside his weapons, but whether this is his policy or not isn't stated. He does say, however, "I have told you the truth. I have no little lies hid about me, but I don't know how it is with the commissioners. Are they as clear as I am?" (lines 13–16). This clearly suggests letter **(C)** as the proper response to this question.

48. (B)

The use of the "I" pronoun clearly indicates a first-person narrator. This may seem like a too simple question for an AP exam, but notice that the next question builds upon your correct answer to this question. An omniscient (A) narrator is the all-knowing narrator. Second-person narration (C) is very rarely seen; it is usually limited to when the narrator addresses himself as "you." This passage could be written as a third-person limited (D), based only upon the speaker's (limited) point of view, but it is not. And, although the passage is historical (E), it is written in first, not third person.

49. (E)

The first-person point of view is *most* appropriate for this selection because it gives the selection an immediacy and vividness that other points of view do not. Of course the correct choice for this question depends upon your selecting the correct response to question 48. First person does not demonstrate different vantage points (A). First person draws the reader in rather than establishing any sort of appropriate distance (B). Because it is from his own perspective, the narrator does not have much leeway to compare and contrast his behavior with others (C); even though he does make a suggestion that perhaps the Commissioner is not as forthright as he, we don't get to see the actions of the commissioner as we might from an omniscient or third-person point of view. Finally, although it does help the speaker establish tone and mood (D), other points of view could be effective in this as well.

50. (C)

Based on the voice and attitude of the speaker in this passage, he can best be characterized as a brave and honorable man. The speaker is not interested in fighting (A) or ready to act regardless of consequences (B); he says "I have laid aside my lance, bow and shield" (lines 12–13). Although he obviously loves his own way of life, he does not imply it is superior to anyone else's (D). He is not naïve (E) at all. In fact, he seems to be quite savvy as to the potential wiliness of the white man.

51. (B)

The speaker's tone in this selection is best described as saddened and bold. Although the speaker is upset, caustic and bitter (A) have too strong a connotation to describe the tone of this short passage. He is serious (C), but not uplifting. Remember, both parts of a two-part description must be correct for an answer to be correct. This is also true of response (D). He is suspicious when he says "…but I don't know how it is with the commissioners" (line 15–16), but nowhere is his tone cynical. Although he might like to dismiss with the white man, he evinces no irony (E) within his message.

52. (B)

This is another question that actually provides you with four true responses and one false. You must choose the response that does not reflect the primary purpose of the passage as a whole. The speaker hopes to evoke in his listeners some sort of understanding or empathy (A). He even suggests that his listeners feel some guilt (C) for what they have caused him and his people to lose already. He asks for them to listen and comprehend what he says (D); he suggests that they "write it down on paper" (line 3). He asks that the listeners respect the ways of his people. (E). He assures his audience that he has laid down his weapons, and he is without guile, and protests the camps of soldiers. This makes it clear that violence (B) is not his intention.

53. (D)

This selection is most likely an excerpt from a speech. There is no doubt that this is an historical piece. It is an address to an audience, for the speaker uses the first person pronoun "I" and he often refers to "you" as if to an audience. It could an essay (A), but this is not the *most* likely response. It is historical, but probably not literature (B), which generally implies fiction. Possibly this could be a letter (C), but the tone is too immediate, and the missive for his audience to "Write it down on paper" implies that his audience is present and ought to be taking notes on what he is saying to them. Of course the passage could be excerpted from a novel, and be totally fiction (E), but this is not the most likely response.

54. (C)

"I have spoken" indicates the finality of the speaker's words and his assertions. The final words of this passage are reminiscent of the word *amen* at the end of a prayer. "So be it"—I have had my say and that's that. The ending does not imply any "deep loathing" (A). Nor does it foreshadow any plans he might have to become aggressive (B). This sentence suggests neither compromise (D) nor challenge (E). He has said what he wanted to say and that's all there is.

SECTION II: ESSAY QUESTIONS

Essay Question 1: George Eliot on Realism

Prompt: The following passage is an excerpt from George Eliot's 1856 essay on Realism. Read the excerpt carefully. Then explain Eliot's attitude toward artists and their responsibility to "amplify our experiences and extend our contact with fellowman beyond the bounds of our personal lot." Pay particular attention to Eliot's use of tone, imagery, detail, and figurative language as you consider Eliot's attitudes towards artists and their responsibility to create Realism in their work.

The notion that peasants are joyous, that the typical moment to represent the man in the smock-frock is when he is cracking a joke and showing a round of sound teeth, that cottage
(5) matrons are usually buxom, and village children necessarily rosy and merry, are prejudices difficult to dislodge from the artistic mind, which looks for its subjects into literature instead of life…But no one who has seen much of actual plough-men
(10) thinks them jocund; no one who is well acquainted with English peasantry can pronounce them merry. The slow gaze, in which no sense of beauty beams, no humor twinkles, —the slow utterance, and the heavy slouching walk, reminds one rather
(15) of that melancholy animal the camel, than of the sturdy country-man, with his striped stockings, red waistcoat, and hat aside, who represents the traditional English peasant…

The greatest benefit we owe to the artist,
(20) whether painter, poet, or novelist, is the extension of our sympathies. Art is the nearest thing to life; it is the mode of amplifying experience and extending our contact with our fellowmen beyond the bounds of our personal lot. All the more sacred is
(25) the task of the artist when he undertakes to paint the life of the People. Falsification here is far more pernicious than in the more artificial aspects of life. It is not so very serious that we should have false ideas about evanescent fashions—about the
(30) manners and conversation of beaux and duchesses; but it *is* serious that our sympathy with the perennial joys and struggles, the toil, the tragedy, and the humor in life of our more heavily-laden fellow men should be perverted, and turned towards a
(35) false object instead of the true one. We want to be taught to feel, not for the heroic artisan or the sentimental peasant, but for the peasant in all his coarse apathy, and the artisan in all his suspicious selfishness.

ANALYSIS OF ESSAY QUESTION 1

George Eliot presents artists with a challenging commission: to help us "feel, not for the heroic or the sentimental peasant, but for the peasant in all his coarse apathy and the artisan in all his suspicious selfishness" (lines 36–39).

To respond to this prompt successfully, you must avoid the trap of simply reiterating Eliot's fine words. Instead, look for words, images, and details that reveal her *attitudes* toward artists. She suggests that too often artists presents us rosy cheeks and flashing smiles when, instead we should be seeing gaunt, pinched faces and toothless grimaces.

Eliot believes that artists have a deeper obligation to recreate peasants accurately, without sentimentality. This is far more important than presenting us with the pomp and fluff of those from the higher strata of society. In addition, Eliot implores artists to portray the difficulty of peasant life and the toll it takes upon its victims, robbing them of the beauty and insight more Romantic artists ascribe to them. Art, Eliot reminds us, is central to life, and therefore, it must be honest in shaping reality. Eliot's tone is strong, didactic, and somewhat chastising. She implies that not all artists have held up to their responsibility. She subtly suggests that just because happy faces might sell more art or make people feel better, it is a pernicious disservice to the less fortunate, laboring class to present them less than realistically.

It is this message that you must focus upon as you formulate your response to this question. Pay attention to how she describes the less fortunate. She speaks of the rosy, buxom children of peasant pastorals as wrongfully prejudicial. It romanticizes the truth, and she feels that this is unfair—to the unfortunates in the pictures and to the audiences who view them. She says it is a depiction of a "false object" (line 35) to portray the "more heavily-laden" (lines 33–34) in such a manner.

SCORING GUIDE FOR QUESTION 1

9–8: Top-scoring essays thoroughly and gracefully summarize and analyze Eliot's assertion about the role of the artist in recreating life in literature. These writers display perceptive understanding of Eliot's belief that the artist has a deeper obligation to recreate peasants accurately, without sentimentality, than representing those in higher strata of society. In addition, these student writers understand Eliot's determination to portray the difficulty of peasant life and the toll it takes on its victims, robbing them of the beauty and insight Romantic artists mistakenly ascribe to them. These student writers also understand Eliot's belief in the centrality of art to life and its role in shaping reality. Indeed, to Eliot this task is holy ("sacred," line 24) when applied to the common humanity (the "People," line 26). The writer's ability to feel the peasants' pain and deadness is what creates true Art. Finally, these essays take a firm stand on this issue, explicating the students' feelings about the role of Art in life. While not error-free, these essays indicate students' ability to read prose closely, respond to the prompt precisely, and to write with clarity and style.

7–6: These essays treat adequately most of the elements above but do so less thoroughly than the best papers. They will analyze diction, imagery, inference, and other literary devices less fully than 8–9 papers. They recognize Eliot's literary style, but are less successful in expressing its effectiveness in expressing her attitudes. They are well written, but use of evidence is less satisfactory. There may be occasional lapses in diction, syntax, or other writing

skills, but these essays will demonstrate sufficient control to present the writer's ideas clearly.

5: These essays will be accurate and fairly well written, but they demonstrate some weaknesses. They may resort more to paraphrasing rather than using evidence as strong support. They may present many ideas without tying them together adequately. Or they may be strong in all but one or two aspects of analysis indicated by the prompt. They may discuss style, but fail to talk about the effect of the style upon the reader. These essays may reveal simplistic thinking and/or immature writing. The writing, however, is still sufficient to convey ideas convincingly.

4–3: These lower-half scores are for essays that inadequately respond to the task set out by the prompt. They may reflect an incomplete understanding of the passage. Often, they do not respond to part or parts of the question. Composition skills will be weak, often presenting many ideas but failing to tie things together. Often they demonstrate an incomplete or incorrect understanding of the passage.

2–1: These essays compound the weaknesses of the papers in the 4–3 range. They seriously misunderstand the prompt, the passage, or possibly both. Often poorly written, they may contain distracting grammar and usage errors. Although some attempt is made to answer the question, the writers' views are unclear, disorganized, incoherent, and/or lacking in supporting evidence. A score of 1 should be given to those essays that may mention the poem or the prompt, but otherwise have no redeeming qualities.

STUDENT RESPONSE TO QUESTION 1

You can bet that if you received a letter from this author, it would not have a smiley-face return address label on it. The label would be more likely to portray a face with wrinkles and moles than smooth and flawless. I doubt that she (I think I remember this George Eliot being a pen name for a woman) would ever have her senior pictures "touched up"—bad hair day or not. This lady believes that artists owe it to their subjects and to their audience to "tell it like it is."

Whether or not most of us agree with her, she does make a good case for her opinion. Her choice of details in describing the Romantic portrayal of peasant smiles and buxom, rosy-faced children is really true. She reminds us that "no one who has seen much of actual plough-men thinks them jocund," assuming jocund means happy. She refers to the reality of their "slow gaze" rather than unrealistic humorous twinkles. For what, in reality would this lower-class, over worked, often half-starved people have to feel humorous about?

Eliot's tone also indicates her attitude. This can be seen in the description of the people. Besides their "slow gaze," she refers to their "slouching walk," implying perhaps a sense of their downtrodden spirit. She continues her description with a rather unkind metaphor. She is reminded of a "melancholy animal the camel." Now that is a very revealing word choice. She might have referred to many other beasts of burden, some, like oxen or horses that work, but still maintain a sense of dignity. Camels, however, have nothing going for them other than they don't have to be watered often. From what little I've know about them, they are not considered smart, are always chewing a cud or something, and I believe they can be quite nasty and stubborn. Certainly a far cry from the "sturdy countryman, with his striped stockings, red waistcoat, and hat aside, who represents the traditional English peasant." No wonder Eliot is demanding Realism.

Eliot explains that if artists fail to be truthful in their depictions, then they are doing everyone a disservice—us, the audience, and the poor peasants as well. It is the responsibility of the artists to "extend our contact with our fellowmen beyond the bounds of our personal lot." If an artist fails to do that, in Eliot's opinion, "falsification" is wrong and downright harmful. It is actually a form of lying. It's as if the artists and we the audience owe these poor folks the right to their downtroddenness. She does not feel so strongly about us getting an incorrect impression of the wealthier classes; they don't seem to count as much in her book. But she has a fierce belief, demonstrated by a strong choice of words, that this is "serious." Her attitude is that we should gain a more accurate sense of the "struggles" and "toil" and "tragedy" of our "more heavily-laden fellow men."

Elliot's attitude is clear. Artists have a mission to tell it like it is. In today's society she would probably be a great investigative reporter. It is the artist's duty to do this. Anything less is cheating. Her attitude also extends to us, the audience. We must seek the truth. I think she is even suggesting to us, the potential audience, that we must be skeptical of art that is to "pretty," too Romantic in her opinion. Her attitude reminds me of something I read in the paper about PC. This woman was saying that at one time she was "poor" then she was "underprivileged" then she was "economically challenged" or something like that. It didn't really matter how she was labeled, her kids still did not have enough to eat!

It is no wonder that this woman chose to write under a man's name. Women in the mid 1800's were not supposed to have opinions, except maybe to echo the thoughts of their husbands. This lady has some strong opinions, and her attitude toward both the responsibility of artists to present truth and the disservice they can do to the subjects who are misrepresented, are clearly expressed through her tone, word choice and details.

COMMENTARY ON STUDENT RESPONSE TO QUESTION 1

This student, albeit not scholarly in his or her response, demonstrates a clear understanding of the prompt, a definite "feel" for Eliot's attitude, and an enjoyable, almost clever interpretation of the George Eliot passage.

Although the response is less than formal in tone and presentation, it is a very correct analysis of Eliot's passage and an adequate response to the tasks necessitated by the prompt. This is not an easy question. It requires the student to analyze Eliot's passage, but not in the same manner as some prose analysis questions. There is a definite edge of argumentation—both in Eliot's piece and within the requirements of the prompt. This student response has demonstrated that he or she recognizes this. The essay addresses some of the writing techniques that Eliot employs to express herself. It talks about the tone of Eliot's piece and, in particular, Eliot's use of details and imagery—especially of the camel. In addition, the student has explained the urgency and sincerity of Eliot's message to artists. Clearly this student recognizes the idea of artistic responsibility to be honest about the depiction of the subjects of the art—to express the subjects without prejudice so the audience receives a Realistic picture, not a Romanticized touch-up.

On the 9-point rubric, this response would easily garner the score of at least a 7. It is not without error or shortcomings, but it is truly an upper-half response. Albeit a bit casual in presentation, this student has successfully responded to the task he or she was given.

Essay Question 2: Herman Melville's "Shiloh"

Prompt: Read the following poem by the American writer Herman Melville. In a well-organized essay, explain how Melville transforms a painful experience into something beautiful. In your analysis, consider such elements as imagery, tone, alliteration, symbolism, and end rhyme.

Shiloh

A Requiem
(April 1862)

Skimming lightly, wheeling still,
    The swallows fly low
Over the fields in clouded days,
    The forest-field of Shiloh—
(5) Over the field where April rain
Solaced the parched stretched in pain
    Through the pause of night
    That followed the Sunday fight
    Around the church of Shiloh—
(10) The church so lone, the log-built one,
That echoed to many a parting groan
    And natural prayer
    Of dying foemen mingled there—
Foemen at morn, but friends at eve—
(15)   Fame or country least their care:
(What like a bullet can undeceive!)
    But now they lie low,
While over them the swallows skim,
    And all is hushed at Shiloh.

ANALYSIS OF ESSAY QUESTION 2

Most all Advanced Placement English Literature tests present poetry analysis as the first essay question. However, this is not a hard-and-fast rule, so do not ever assume there is no poetry on a particular essay test just because the poem does not appear in question 1. Successful responses to this question will demonstrate a writer who understands just how Melville uses literary techniques to transmute the pain of the battle into a song of peace and respect. By subtitling his poem "Requiem," Melville emphasizes the tragedy of war rather than glorifying pain and heroic death. This immediately pays homage to those who gave their lives in this battle. Melville uses images such as swallows, clouds, the forest-field, night, noon, and eve to create a peaceful tone. The April rain helps to alleviate human suffering, and the church, symbol of peace in death, becomes an appropriate resting place.

Melville uses the poetic technique of a refrain in lines 4, 9, and 19. Not only does this echo the musical nature of this poem, but the refrain also suggests the cyclical nature of this life and death scenario. In addition, the regularly irregular meter is soothing, lending a peaceful element to the tragedy of war. Finally, the poem contains an unusual amount of alliteration, much of it done with sibilants (*s* and *sh* sounds). This adds to the soothing, satisfying nature of this poem. It is a poem best read aloud.

As you prepare to take the AP English Literature exam, practice reading poetry aloud, listening to the sounds the various poems evoke. Then, transfer this reading to a silent reading while still hearing the words in your head. This will not only help with your understanding of a poem's style, but it will also aid in your appreciation of this artistic medium.

SCORING GUIDE FOR QUESTION 2

9–8: Essays earning this score demonstrate successful writers who understand how Melville uses literary techniques to transmute the pain of the battle into a song of peace and respect. Students are likely to begin by explaining that a "requiem" is a song, poem, or service that accompanies the laying to rest of the dead. By subtitling his poem a "requiem," Melville emphasizes the tragedy of war rather than glorifying a bloody battle. This immediately pays homage to those who gave their life for their country. Students will also cite specific lines from the poem to demonstrate how Melville uses such images as swallows, clouds, the forest-field, night, noon, and eve to create a peaceful tone. In addition, students should cite the symbolism of the rain (which shows how the gentleness of nature can help alleviate human suffering) and the church (a symbol of peace in death). Further, students who cite the strong end rhymes ("Shiloh," "fly low," "lie low") should note how these rhymes create a somber, respectful mood. Although not free from error, these essays indicate students' ability to read poetry skillfully, respond to the prompt accurately, and to write with clarity and style.

7–6. These essays treat adequately most of the elements above but do so less thoroughly than the best papers. They will analyze imagery and point of view or figurative transformation less fully than 8–9 papers. They are well written, but use of evidence is less satisfactory. There may be occasional lapses in diction, syntax or other writing skills, but these essays will demonstrate sufficient control to present the writers' ideas clearly.

5: These essays will be accurate and fairly well written, but they demonstrate some weaknesses. They may resort more to paraphrasing rather than using evidence as strong support. They may present many ideas without tying them together adequately. Or they may be strong in all but one or two aspects of analysis indicated by the prompt. These essays may reveal simplistic thinking and/or immature writing. The writing, however, is still sufficient to convey ideas convincingly.

4–3: These lower-half scores are for essays that inadequately respond to the task set out by the prompt. They may reflect an incomplete understanding of the poem. Often, they do not respond to part or parts of the question. Composition skills will be weaker, often presenting many ideas but failing to tie things together. Often they demonstrate an incomplete or incorrect understanding of the poem.

2–1: These essays compound the weaknesses of the papers in the 4–3 range. They seriously misunderstand the prompt, the poem, or possibly both. Often poorly written, they may contain distracting grammar and usage errors. Although some attempt is made to answer the question, the writers' views are unclear, disorganized, incoherent, and/or lacking in supporting evidence. A score of 1 should be given to those essays that may mention the poem or the prompt, but otherwise have no redeeming qualities.

STUDENT RESPONSE TO QUESTION 2

Swallows fly low, the land is hushed and the dead lie in the churchyard—not in earthen graves but above the ground with nothing but the sky to cover them. Shiloh was a devastating Civil War battle. So many young men, both blue and gray, lost their lives. In this "Requiem," Herman Melville honors those tragic young men.

No longer does it matter what color anyone's uniform was. He tells us these soldiers may have been "Foemen at morn," but now they share death, the great equalizer. They are now "friends at eve," and whatever side you might have been fighting for, means nothing now. They no longer care about "fame or country," for "like a bullet," partisanship has "la[id] them low"

Melville's tone is somber or—no pun intended—grave, but it projects a sense of peace rather than despair. The repetition of lines and phrases and his generous use of "s" and "sh" are like onomatopoeia, shushing the groans and anguished cries, reaching out and closing the eyes of the dead. Swallows skim (not lurking vultures or other carrion eaters) and as evening settles into night, so does death remove the pain and anguish from the battle's victims. There is no glory on this field, only the remnants of the battle. Rain washes the dead and dying, suggesting, perhaps, that these soldiers are being "cleansed" of their early pain and reborn (baptized?) into a (hopefully) better life.

Even the rhyme and rhythm of the poem is peaceful. This is neither patriotic marching song nor any call to battle. It is more like a lullaby, soothing the dying like a "natural prayer." For these men no longer need to worry about the color of their uniforms or keeping their muskets dry, for "fame or country [is the] least [of their] care." Through his use of sound, tone, imagery, and figurative language, Melville has managed to transform a "painful experience" into one that is not exactly "beautiful," but one that is "peaceful."

COMMENTARY ON STUDENT RESPONSE TO QUESTION 2

This student has written a very successful response to the poetry prompt. Not only does the student respond well to the tasks of the prompt, he or she demonstrates a fine understanding and seeming appreciation of the poem itself.

In a somewhat poetic style of its own, this essay incorporates key words and phrases from the poem in order to demonstrate how Melville has transformed the setting from the gory battlefield of night into the peaceful descent of evening, with only the sky to cover the dead and only swallows to watch with the dying. The battle cries of the day become the evensong of the night.

The essay addresses tone and sound within the poem, and these are the elements that dominate. The student recognizes that both the *s/sh* sounds and the rhyme and rhythm are critical elements of this poem. In addition, the student discusses imagery and is correct, albeit not positive about, (see parenthetical question regarding baptism) Melville's use of symbolism.

This essay hits upon the ultimate irony of any war literature—that it matters little who you were or what side you upheld—in death we are equal. The pain and anguish of the battlefield is a shared experience. It is this sharing that this student has particularly mentioned—the great equalizer cares little about the color of its victim's uniform.

Note how this student essay opens—it has a powerful, almost poetic introduction, one that cannot be ignored. The student develops ideas well, and offers adequate support to most statements. Finally, the student completes his or her response with a final informative paragraph that ends with a closure sentence.

Although this essay may not be long (developed) enough to elicit an 8 from most readers, it certainly would be awarded a 7 on the 9-point rubric. This is one of those essays that demonstrates strong writing skills and a sure style on the part of the student, but it still is not as developed as a very successful response should be.

Essay Question 3: "No Compromise" (Open-Ended Question)

Prompt: Authors often create characters who refuse to compromise their principles. These characters may be heroic, tragic, or merely misguided. Choose a novel or full-length play in which a character declines to compromise a deeply held belief. Identify the character, the principle in which the character believes, and show, by specific reference, the action the character took to uphold this principle and the outcome of that action. Finally, evaluate the character's decision to show if it is heroic, tragic, or misguided.

ANALYSIS OF ESSAY QUESTION 3

Essays earning upper-half scores for this question will reflect sophisticated writers who can use language to make a point. These essays should begin with a well-chosen character, clearly identified. The character's situation is fully explicated, especially the character's choice of a principle to uphold. It is important, however, that in responding to the prompt, writers stick to explication as it applies to the character and do not simply retell the plot of the chosen piece of literature.

Choices for this response are manifold. Ones that might be commonly used include *Romeo and Juliet, King Lear, Othello, St. Joan, Antigone,* and *The Adventures of Huckleberry Finn.* In addition, you might consider other works of merit such as *Cold Mountain, Poisonwood Bible, The Dollmaker, Chariots of Fire, Lord Jim, A Prayer for Owen Meany,* or *The Fountainhead.*

The focus of this essay should be on the uncompromising position of the character chosen. Stronger essays will most likely talk about stronger characters. Lear, for instance, in his stubborn determination to settle his lands (and the subsequent disowning of his youngest daughter), is actually a stronger candidate than Macbeth who must be wheedled and cajoled into action by his indomitable wife.

Regardless of whom you choose, you are likely to find at least one character from your years of English classes, or from reading on your own, that fits the needs of this particular prompt. Choose wisely; follow the tasks of the prompt; state your ideas clearly, and support them wherever possible. These are the best recommendations for your success in answering an open-ended question such as this one.

SCORING GUIDE FOR QUESTION 3

9–8: Responses in this range select a work of literature where an exceptional character declines to compromise a deeply held belief and the subsequent plot of the novel or play is affected by this character's convictions. These essays are well-conceived, well-developed and well-organized. These responses readily grasp the intent of the prompt, and they adeptly reveal how their choice of character best lives up to all the tasks of the prompt. Essays earning this score are the work of sophisticated writers who can use language to make a point. These essays begin with a well-chosen character, clearly identified. The character's situation is fully explicated, especially the character's choice of a principle to uphold. Then writers show through specific reference how the character upheld the principle and the result of his or her actions. The evaluation is perceptive, showing evidence of independent thought, as well as carefully reasoned and supported by specific textual and personal reference. Even though these essays may have minor errors, these errors do not intrude on the writers' points. In sum, these essays show the students' ability to read fiction or plays skillfully, respond to the prompt accurately, and to write with clarity and style.

7–6: These essays treat satisfactorily most of the elements of the 9–8 papers, but they do so less thoroughly than the best papers. Their discussion of the significant character is not as deft as that of the 9–8 responses. In addition, they tend to be less convincing than are the best responses. These

essays are well written, but with less maturity and control of writing skills than the best responses. Although these writers do understand the tasks of the prompt, their essays lack the clarity and style of the top papers.

5: These essays are highly superficial. Their analysis may be unconvincing, underdeveloped, or even somewhat inaccurate. Often these mid-range responses fail to address a major part of the prompt, but adequately respond to the remainder of the tasks it presents. The thinking demonstrated in these responses is less mature and less developed that the upper-half responses. Nevertheless, it is easy to recognize the intent of these responses, and they do not fall into the lower-half range.

4–3: These lower-half essays may choose an acceptable work, but they fail to explain how the character fulfills the qualifications set up by the prompt. Their analysis is often trite and perfunctory. The writing usually conveys the writer's ides, but it reveals weak control over such elements as diction, organization, syntax, or grammar. These essays may also demonstrate some misunderstanding of the prompt.

2–1: These essays compound the weaknesses of essays in the 4–3 range. They may misread the prompt, or choose a character inappropriate to the prompt. These essays are often quite brief, and they fail to give much support or development to any of the ideas they present. Although it is clear that these authors have attempted to respond to the prompt, the ideas presented often have minimal clarity or coherence.

STUDENT RESPONSE TO QUESTION 3:

In 1948, George Orwell wrote his infamous political novel, *1984.* Living through World War II and then its aftermath, Orwell viewed Communism as a viable threat to the physical and mental freedoms of man. More of a philosophical/psychological/political treatise than a novel, *1984* nevertheless has a specific plot, many conflicts and interesting characters. Winston Smith, whose desire to be an individual under the watchful eye of Big Brother, is so determined to maintain some semblance of freedom, that he becomes the Everyman of Orwell's infamous book.

The controlling force in *1984* is Big Brother. He is not a person but an omniscient government entity who rules the lives, minds and spirits of the people. The common folk, or Proles, do not count. They are dismissed as harmless drones who carry out the day-to-day grunt work of a society. The Inner Party are the mucky-mucks who run the country. We do not get to know too much about them other than the one who meets with and eventually is responsible for breaking, Winston Smith. It is the people of Winston's level, intelligent and important to the function of society, who must be controlled. Big Brother is always watching them. Winston, in his determination to be an individual, literally turns his back on Big Brother (not recommended with 2-way telescreens) and keeps a diary. He is like Everyman. Orwell uses Smith (what an Everyman name) to represent any one of us who values our personal freedoms.

Not only does Smith go to the black market in the Prole district to purchase a diary that he starts writing in regularly, he also begins an affair with another Party member—a rebellious act in Big Brother's book of rules. Smith is not stupid at all; in fact, it is his very intelligence that "does him in." He realizes that his job (to rewrite history) is only a propaganda tool of the State. He starts to recognize how much their minds are being manipulated by the propaganda gibberish of the government. He sees the reduction of the English language to be a terrible loss, not a great victory as his friend (comrade) seems to think. Finally, he cannot accept the idea of doublethink. He believes there is only one truth, and man cannot really hold two opposing beliefs simultaneously.

All of Winston's revelations are a result of his determination to be a free individual. And these discoveries are basically what run the action of the story. Finally he comes face-to-face with an Inner Party member. He attempts to explain himself, and he actually thinks he is "getting through" to this person with his logical reason. The reader realizes, however, that Winston is doomed.

It is this doom that leads to the climax of the story. This is then followed by a somewhat vague and depressing finale. Winston is broken by Big Brother. Even though we know that this will probably happen, we keep hoping that something will happen to "rescue" him and the terrible force of Big Brother will be overthrown. No such luck. By the end of the book, Winston readily agrees that 2 plus 2 can equal 4, and 2 plus 2 can equal 5—whatever Big Brother wants at the moment. Has his struggle been in vain? Perhaps it has in this particular piece of fiction, but if man ever loses this desire to be a free, individual, then we are all doomed. By reading about Winston, despite his "failure," perhaps others can take heart from his strong intentions.

The book closes on a very depressing note. Winston and his indomitable will drives the action of the story, but ultimately, everything ends as it began. Man must surrender to the stronger force. Freedom and individuality must be sacrificed to the power of the all-controlling Big Brother.

COMMENTARY ON STUDENT RESPONSE TO QUESTION 3

"They [the essays] need not be without flaws; nevertheless, they demonstrate that the student has mastered not only the skill of analyzing a piece of literature appropriately, but also has demonstrated exceptional composition skills." What a perfect description of this student's essay. He or she has grasped the purpose of the prompt: "identify the character, the principle in which the character believes, and show, by specific reference, the action the character took to uphold this principle and the outcome of that action." It is a very good essay—not without flaws, and though it does not go to any length in developing the last part of the prompt: "evaluate the character's decision to show if it is heroic, tragic, or misguided," it is a very good response.

This student has been particularly successful in limiting plot discussion just to how the character's beliefs drive the action of the story. He or she has drawn adequate support from the novel itself to provide only the necessary background and detail. The essay does not stray by adding extraneous information.

This student demonstrates a good understanding of *1984*. Although he or she seems to have forgotten the name of a minor character, and the essay is certainly not written without flaws, it represents an upper-half response to this challenging prompt. Most readers would undoubtedly place this within the 7–8 range of responses, with a definite leaning towards the 8.

This student has chosen book and character well. He or she understands the prompt. The essay's introduction is interesting; its body is well fed; and the conclusion, albeit not "optimistic," is strong. This student does not go into any detail as to his or her opinion as to "heroic" nature of Winston Smith's character. Nevertheless, through the use of the Everyman allusion, and the comment that Smith can be (hopefully) an inspiration to others, this task of the prompt is at least partially addressed. Overall, this essay deserves two thumbs up from its readers.

COMPUTE YOUR PRACTICE TEST SCORE

Multiple-Choice:

Number correct ☐ − (¼ × Number wrong*) = ☐ × 1.2417 = _____

Section I Multiple-Choice Score _____

*Do not include questions left blank.

Free-Response (Essay Questions):

Question 1: (out of 9) ☐ × 3.0351 = ☐ (do not round)

Question 2: (out of 9) ☐ × 3.0351 = ☐ (do not round)

Question 3: (out of 9) ☐ × 3.0351 = ☐ (do not round)

Total Questions 1, 2, and 3 = ☐

Section II Essay Questions Score _____ **(do not round)**

Composite Score

Section I Multiple-Choice Score ☐ + Section II Free Response Score ☐ =

Composite Score (round to the nearest whole number) _____

Conversion Chart**

Composite Score Range**	AP Grade
114–154	5
88–113	4
67–87	3
40–66	2
0–39	1

**For Practice Test III only. Students' scores on the AP Exam are weighted by formulas determined in advance each by the Development Committee to yield raw composite scores; the Chief Faculty Consultant is responsible for converting composite scores to the 5-point AP scale.

Need help preparing for the New SAT?
We've got some recommended reading.

Also Available

KAPLAN

Test Prep and Admissions

Published by Simon & Schuster

Ask for Kaplan wherever books are sold.